△ 1/24 HIS £6.50
(African)

D1179643

MARGERY PERHAM AND BRITISH RULE IN AFRICA

Margery Perham c. 1960

MARGERY PERHAM
AND
BRITISH RULE
IN AFRICA

Edited by

Alison Smith and Mary Bull

FRANK CASS

First published in 1991 in Great Britain by
FRANK CASS AND COMPANY LIMITED
Gainsborough House, 11 Gainsborough Road,
London E11 1RS

and in the United States of America by
FRANK CASS
c/o International Specialized Book Services, Inc.
5602 N.E. Hassalo Street
Portland, OR 927213–3640

British Library Cataloguing in Publication Data
Margery Perham and British rule in Africa.
I. Smith, Alison   II. Bull, Mary
967.0099

ISBN 0-7146-3451-4

Library of Congress Cataloging-in-Publication Data
Margery Perham and British rule in Africa / edited by Alison Smith and
Mary Bull.
    p. cm.
Includes bibliographical references and index.
ISBN 0-7146-3451-4 (HB) : $32.00
1. Perham, Margery Freda, Dame, 1895–   . 2. Colonial
administrators—Africa, Sub-Saharan—Biography. 3. Colonial
administrators—Great Britain—Biography. 4. Great Britain–
–Colonies—Africa—Administration. I. Smith, Alison. II. Bull,
Mary, 1930–
DT352.7.P476   1991
325.341'092—dc20   91-28215
[B]   CIP

This group of studies first appeared in a Special Issue on Margery Perham and
British Rule in Africa in The Journal of Imperial and Commonwealth History,
Vol. 19, No. 3, (October 1991) published by Frank Cass & Co. Ltd.

Printed in Great Britain by
Antony Rowe Ltd, Chippenham, Wiltshire

Contents

Acknowledgements

This book originated in a seminar made possible through the generosity of Rhodes House, the University of Texas, Queen Elizabeth House, Nuffield College and the Oxford University Committee for African Studies. The Rhodes Trust gave help towards the preparation for publication. We also give warm thanks to Alan Bell, the Librarian of Rhodes House Library, for his support throughout the project the staff of the Library, and the staff of the Queen Elizabeth House Library.

While we regret that it has not been possible to include more of the original papers presented at the seminar, those who attended will recognize how much the discussions have contributed to the chapters. The authors of these have responded patiently to many editorial importunities. Amongst those who have commented and criticized, we would like to thank Margery Mumford and Robert Rayne for information on the Perham family background; and Shirley Ardener, Helen Callaway, Dorothy Helly, Roger Highfield, Alaine Low, Frederick Madden, Isabel Roberts, David Throup and Marcia Wright. Our especial appreciation goes to Roger Louis for much advice and encouragement, as well as to Kenneth Robinson and Sally Chilver. Valerie Pakenham has generously shared information and reflections deriving from her own current work as Margery Perham's biographer. Finally, we owe a great debt to Patricia Pugh, who has put freely at our disposal both her time and her own unrivalled knowledge of Margery Perham and her papers.

For historical consistency, the names of countries and other places have been given in their contemporary form: such as Basutoland, Tanganyika, Bornu. In referring to Margery Perham, formal consistency was found to be unattainable. The only logical mode would have been to use 'Perham' throughout, but this seemed to obscure nuances of period and relationships which are essential to the composite quality of the emerging portrait. The authors, therefore, have used 'Margery Perham' in the major references, but elsewhere have followed their own individual practice.

Sadly, almost none of the Africans best known to Margery Perham is still alive. We are very conscious that without an African contribution the picture given here remains incomplete.

Introduction

Alison Smith and Mary Bull

Margery Perham was probably the best known figure in the study of British colonial administration in Africa from the 1930s until its ending in the 1960s. She died in 1982 at the age of 86, and her substantial collection of papers was left to Rhodes House Library, Oxford. In July 1989 a seminar was held at Rhodes House to celebrate the completion of the cataloguing of the seven hundred boxes of these papers by Patricia Pugh, and to assemble, as a help towards a biography, some of those who had known Margery Perham as colleagues, assistants and friends. This volume is based on a selection of the papers given at that seminar. The authors include those who, not having known Margery Perham, approached their topic simply as academic historians; those who mixed historical analysis with personal reminiscence; and those whose recollections have added material which would not be available elsewhere. The complete set of seminar papers, covering a larger variety of subjects, together with the taped record of the four sessions, and a summary of the discussions, have been deposited in Rhodes House Library.

These articles represent some preliminary probes into the resources of the newly available archive. Against the background of British colonial rule in Africa from the relative stability of the 1930s to the advent of independence in the 1950s and 1960s, they depict a personality of strong intellect and debating skills, huge industry, a consuming sense of moral purpose and compelling literary talent. To a remarkable degree she represented Britain's 'conscience' on Africa during this midcentury period of change and upheaval. She approached the problems of administration and politics in Africa with concepts that proved in the end inadequate to the dynamics of new growth, but within her own frame of reference she was perceptive and prescient, as well as generous in aspiration and passionately articulate – not least in setting African developments within the wider context of the continental and international scene. In these pages we see this 'imperial mind' in a very personal and human dimension, with enthusiasms, quirks and prejudices as well as the qualities which led to her being seen as the last in a chain of

1

personal contacts linking outstanding individuals who attempted to better the lives of Africans, stretching back through Frederick Lugard to John Kirk, David Livingstone and John Philip.[1]

Margery Perham came to the study of colonial administration from a background of historical studies. She was an undergraduate during the First World War, and later a Fellow, at St Hugh's College, Oxford – two periods interrupted by six years of teaching at Sheffield University. A childhood fascination with African exploration, developed by a visit in 1920–21 to her sister, married to a district commissioner in British Somaliland, directed her historical interests towards the administration and development of colonial territories. In the 1920s and 1930s, she was regarded as the independent, intellectual woman. She was tall, good-looking, athletic, riding motorcycles as well as horses, and was both researcher and protagonist for the causes she embraced. It was a characteristically bold step for her to resign from her regular teaching fellowship at St Hugh's in 1930 and live for five years on travel grants, journalism and her cashed-in superannuation until Oxford University created for her a lectureship in colonial administration. In 1939 she was appointed the first Official Fellow of the newly created Nuffield College – a college that for the remainder of her working life gave her not only an income but travel allowances, research and secretarial assistance, and office facilities. Nuffield was a graduate college, and Margery Perham's position there enabled her to remain on the margins of university life; she was not teaching undergraduates as she had been at St Hugh's, her lectures were directed to the special Colonial Service courses rather than to the requirements of university degrees, and her seminars and supervision were for the small number of graduate students, many from overseas, studying British imperial history. She was not much interested in the politics of the university, or even in those of her college; a parallel with the fact that in the years of decolonization she was as interested in constitutions and the training of an élite of administrators who could give good government, as in nationalist movements and the development of political parties which operated in an atmosphere of conflict and compromise. Oxford provided a base, one from which she could continue her contacts, official and unofficial, with policy-making individuals and groups in both London and Africa, and it gave her both the financial security and the academic status for research and writing on colonial administration. She was influenced by, and contributed to, the strong Oxford tradition of the study of Britain's imperial role as a moral responsibility. Her patriotism demanded that her country attain the highest standards in the government of colonial peoples, and she wanted the British public – or at least the policy-formulating elite amongst them to understand the nature and problems of colonial administration, and, after the Second World War, the demands for independence and the ending of colonial rule.

I

Men's lives, Margery Perham wrote of her work on the Lugard biography, were interesting only insofar as they reflected something of universal concern. Can we define such features in her own life and work? It is not easy to categorize her career. She was not a theorist whose ideas change our perception of a subject, and she was concerned primarily with the issues of her own day. The papers collected here offer a number of clues, ranging from her primary concern for British colonial administration, through her influence in broad policy matters, to her unique portrayal, in the biography of Lord Lugard, of the nature of imperial power and its limitations. But it may prove that her real significance lies in something more diffuse and difficult to analyse: the power to communicate and reflect on the issues of colonial rule and of decolonization, to both administrators and the wider British public, and to build into these reflections a sense of continuity and constructive opportunity for the African future. Yet she herself was often painfully aware of the way in which her life and achievements seemed fragmented and unsatisfying:

> What am I doing? I am in a sort of uneasy and outside position, balanced between sociology and history, between theory and practice. I am neither a scholar (though I bend myself painfully to what little scholarship I can attain), nor an administrator, though I flatter myself that I influence administrators on my tours and in my summer schools. My work, whatever it is, is extensive and superficial. It covers all aspects of half Africa. It is all at secondhand – picking other men's brains or reading their books.... More than ever – I know it now – I have neither the industry nor the method to master or even to keep pace at present standards.[2]

Or again, she wrote some years later: 'I accept that I have shot my bolt and missed my target which was only the poor one of reputation and influence in my generation. I see that these are worth little – even the best I could have achieved – but I have not replaced them by anything else' (28 Oct. 1945).

Many more such passages are to be found in the diaries in which she intermittently recorded her personal reflections on her life, its crises and its meaning, at least down to 1951. There are moments of excitement, commitment, fulfilment, and many fine descriptive passages: nevertheless as time goes on the predominant mood is sombre, often with the sense of missed potential, of self-criticism and sometimes despair. Yet it seems that she did envisage that the diary entries would one day be read; the writing is fluent and carefully drafted and amended. At all events, these diaries do demonstrate how often her outwardly ambitious and successful life was led against an inner sense of self-doubt and insecurity.

No such doubts about the significance of Margery Perham's life were felt by Roland Oliver, in his address opening the 1989 seminar. For him, her importance lay primarily not in research or in directly exercised political influence, but in her tireless work as a publicist and as an analyst of African affairs. For over forty years she wrote articles and letters, chiefly for *The Times*, at least every few months. More debatable may be his second main contention: that her career falls sharply into two periods and two approaches, divided by the cataclysm of the fall of Singapore in February 1942. This contention nevertheless provided a base for much of the discussion of the phasing of her life which emerges in this volume.

In the second essay, Cherry Gertzel traces how Margery Perham's image of Africa was shaped over the years not only by her own personality and social background, but also by the angle of her vision. At first it came mainly from Africa itself, later it was increasingly from Whitehall and her study in Oxford. Besides this there was the background of a fast-changing climate of imperial and international affairs. While some basic features of the image remain constant, it is striking that even in her sixties, although she largely failed to follow the contemporary modes of concern with economic development, she could respond to the new approaches which saw Africa's history in its own right and not merely as a product of European enterprise. Nevertheless, the dominant element in her perception was always of Africa and Africans as a field of government – at first through the British raj, eventually through the African élites which would replace it.

Gertzel rightly observes that in Margery Perham's view of African society, race largely obscured class. Certainly one of the most evident tensions in her outlook was between her passionate concern for progress towards equality and justice and her strong consciousness of race – its physical characteristics, its qualities, its possible limitations. This consciousness must in part have been linked to an early fascination with the literature of race and the 'race problem'; it was also one aspect of her intuitive reaction to Africa as artist and traveller. Readers may be startled in these pages by her candid descriptions: of 'reedy and potbellied' Hottentots, 'not a very attractive people'; or in Darfur, of the 'appearance and ... generally servile character' of negroes – 'not romantic'.[3] She was likewise prone to comment on the forms, colours and expressions of individuals, as here on the bearing of young black migrant mine workers on the Rand: 'It is hard to describe this beauty: it is partly in the carriage of the body, generally a fine body, and carried unselfconsciously, with the grace of an animal. ... There is the expression of the eyes which, whether defiant, sad or happy, seems to express a different system of thought from ours.'[4]

Although she advocated the training of anthropologists as an aid to administration, and although in the 1930s she even thought of herself studying a single 'tribe',[5] it is clear that in her early intellectual approach she had little in common with the generation of anthropologists being trained by Bronislaw Malinowski. She might welcome their commitment to the understanding and defence of indigenous communities, but from her own base in the administrative framework it was inconceivable for her to enter personally into the concept of participant and neutral observation. She had a more pragmatic belief than they did in the positive elevation of these communities in accordance with the precept of Article 22 of the League of Nations that disadvantaged peoples should be prepared to 'take their place in the strenuous conditions of the modern world'.[6]

For her the resolution of this discrepancy between the fact of 'backwardness' and the imperative of progress lay in the agency of a discreet, hardworking and incorruptible administrative service as a means towards justice and peaceful advance. As Oliver points out, she believed that the criteria of the qualities required for such a service were best met by the products of the English public schools and of Oxford and Cambridge universities; this gave her views a pronounced class bias – a bias which was shared to the full in senior Colonial Office circles.[7]

Her attitudes did mellow with the passage of time. She found it easier to work with anthropologists such as Daryll Forde and Meyer Fortes than with Malinowski. As the base of British university education, and her own inter-university experience, both broadened, her 'Oxbridge' bias was modified. And by the end of her university career, when she became the first president of the UK African Studies Association, she had moved far from the sharp racial reactions of her youth.

II

In 1920–21, when she was 25 years old, Margery Perham spent a year staying with her sister and brother-in-law at a remote post in British Somaliland. She always looked back on this visit as the real starting point of her career, and she wrote vividly of the Somali country in her first novel, *Major Dane's Garden*.[8] But from a second early and transparently autobiographical novel, it is clear that the sense of being destined to a life of achievement goes back to her childhood in a prosperous suburb of Harrogate in Yorkshire.[9] This conviction was given dramatic inspiration by a lecture from the historian Charles Grant Robertson early in her Oxford student life, a few weeks after the outbreak of war in 1914:

> I feel a new and exulting sense of my own importance as a member, and a thinking member, of a great empire ... I need no longer crush and kill my hopes and ambitions, for they are great, and if I can but carry on the degrading flesh with the inspiration of the spirit, I shall not have lived in vain.[10]

The detailed unfolding of such early ambitions must be a subject for her biographer. One major influence in her personal development is certain. In a large family mostly of boys, her closest relationships were with the youngest brother Edgar and her only sister Ethel. Edgar's death in action in 1916 was a shattering blow to her; Ethel remained a strong support almost throughout her life.

The young Miss Perham was to develop her ideas in the setting of British thought about the empire and Africa in the late 1920s and the 1930s – the period of the last peacetime manifestation of the 'imperial mind'. Deborah Lavin's article relates how she was fortunate to mature in association with a group of public figures who took Britain's African responsibilities very seriously. Partly through her friendship with Lugard, she was in touch with Hailey who undertook the *African Survey*, with educationalists such as Hanns Vischer, with the missionary spokesman Joseph Oldham, and with senior African administrators such as Donald Cameron, Philip Mitchell and Douglas Newbold. They not only treated her views with respect, they in some degree made her free of the privileged circle to which they belonged. By the time war broke out in 1939, her basic affinity with the establishment had become clear.

She was, it is true, also in dialogue with some of the left-wing critics of empire, such as Leonard Woolf and W.M. Macmillan, and in later years she liked to think of her own heroes, Lugard and Oldham, as defenders with them of African interests against more right-wing imperialists such as Lionel Curtis and Lord Lothian. Yet in the 1930s the lines were not so clearly drawn. Between the philanthropists and the 'ideological imperialists', as the more radical Macmillan acknowledged in retrospect, 'there seemed no such clearcut division of emphasis when one was dealing with the glimmerings of light which came from either of their fires'.[11] It was in fact with the help of Lothian, Curtis, and the Rhodes Trust that Margery had first been launched on her African journeyings; and it was in the Transkei that she had first gained practical experience of a form of indirect rule, which she was soon to be expounding as a remedy for the stagnation of the High Commission Territories. She had also welcomed Hertzog's policy of segregation, and initially had even envisaged something similar for East Africa. Lavin's foray into the Perham archive demonstrates this 'South African factor' in her early orientation.

Only after her research visit to West Africa, prompted and advised by Lugard, did she come to develop a wider view of indirect rule. Nigeria contained not only the great emirates of the north where Lugard and his successors had developed the practices of 'indirect rule', but also the southern cities with long contact with Europe, and with families who had had generations of western education. The problem of how to accommodate these within the framework of political advance through the development of traditional societies faced her here; as indeed it had on that first visit to South Africa, about whose educated detribalized Africans she had written with prescience to Lothian as early as 1930, 'We have lost the time when it lay with us to give, and reached that when it is for them to take.'[12]

The decade before the Second World War was also for Margery a time of inner conflict – another theme which is woven into Lavin's paper. She was in her late thirties, still strikingly attractive and fond of active sports, including swimming, riding and tennis. She rejoiced in being courted, and on her travels in Africa and elsewhere there was often the reflection that she might have settled for what one of her suitors described as her 'natural mission in life'. For her, opportunities for marriage posed an inexorable choice between dedicated ambition and emotional fulfilment. Sometimes she would try to define how her gender affected the relationship to Africa that she had chosen. Was it, as she held that one Colonial Office friend believed, that

> a woman, educated, emancipated, remains a housewife, eager to sweep and scrub and manage the world, instead of the lost house and depending family? Africa, then [he suggests], is my house, my husband and my children, and with my head bowed to the task I conscientiously wear myself out according to the ancient tradition of all serving women (27 Nov. 1938).[13]

No, she retorted, at this conceptual level the difference between him and herself was that whereas he was a career-bound administrator, divided between a professional and a philosophical plane, she was free to respond to Africa as an artist:

> I live on one plane – it is Africa always for me – I work, sleep, seek personal encounters, play games, enlarge my general knowledge,

> save my strength and money for Africa. Not – I do not pretend this – in some entire zeal for selfless service, but because I express myself in work for Africa (Ibid.).

But if she saw herself as an artist, it was as a woman artist. Some years later she lamented how that talent, as she had exercised it, could not be sustained indefinitely:

> ... as I get older I lose that grip, that glow, that degree of magnetism from the ardour of my interest, which enabled me to influence men and to gain their help and information. I have always played the woman, and do not know how to play the neuter. Also I think that ... my ardour was a sublimation of my sex, not the glow of my reason, and the one will die down with the other (18 Jan. 1941).

The tension between her sense of unrealized potential and her craving for fulfilment in close personal relationships was acute. Margery found it hard to envisage a life without the amenities of home, hospitality, and a sexually mixed society; a strong impulse in taking her to Africa had been the recoil from 'the chill corridors of a women's college' in Oxford.[14] In the event she was unashamedly dependent on others – her Colonial Service hosts, her research assistants, her college, and above all her sister – to supply these amenities. She herself was – notwithstanding her enormous personal kindness – inept at domestic roles, awkward with small children, impatient of any chores that interfered with her work. As she wryly observed in a letter to her friend Arthur Creech Jones, 'What a tragedy we did not live in the period of slavery – or even before 1914!'[15]

Her own work, as she saw it, demanded total dedication: it is tempting to connect her recurrent ill-health with the virtual denial to herself of any real relaxation. The dichotomy she saw between professional career and marriage was perhaps the main reason why her interpretation of the African scene involved only a very restricted view of the role of African women. Although she was persistent in pressing for the education of girls, it would seem that she had little idea of such education disturbing the accepted ordering of African society. It was primarily as educated wives and mothers that women would make their contribution to Africa's future; she thought them less likely than their menfolk to be carried away by heady gusts of nationalism.[16] The only African woman with whom she enjoyed a real personal friendship seems to have been the Ugandan student Florence Wamala.

It is interesting to find the anthropologist Audrey Richards chiding Margery Perham for fostering at Makerere College the kind of élitist Christianity that produced 'one or two Florence Wamalas' at the cost of the wider community.[17] Indeed, most of the distinguished British women

Africanists of the period certainly took a more inclusive view of African society, as well as a less rigid one of the rival claims of personal and professional life. A number of exceptionally able academic women were drawn to the African scene in the 1930s: among them Audrey Richards, Margaret Read, Lucy Mair, Margaret Green, Elspeth Huxley, Hilda Kuper, Monica Wilson. Most of these were concerned to study the lives of African women as well as men; several combined scholarship with marriage. None of them seems to have reflected as constantly as Margery did on the implications of her gender for the life and work on which she had embarked. It may be that her concern was one of a number of consequences of her viewing African problems as essentially problems of governance, to be studied primarily through the male administrative structure and those who operated it.

For Margery Perham's relationship with the British colonial adminis- trative service, as the main instrument of imperial control, became increasingly close during these formative inter-war years. In tracing this relationship, Anthony Kirk-Greene emphasizes the contrast between the respect accorded to her personal pre-eminence in the study of African administration on the one hand, and the emphatically male-ordered world which that study represented on the other. In doing so he perhaps identifies the paradox which particularly polarizes her choice between ambition and marriage. The world upon which she was directing her scholarship was one in which the role of women was one of recognized subordination – like that of the heroine Rhona in *Major Dane's Garden*. Kirk-Greene may be right – at least in the long view – in partially resolving the paradox by likening the role she eventually established to that of a godmother; thus in some measure making not Africa, but the colonial service as an institution, into 'the lost house and the depending family', which could reconcile her to such a renunciation.

Kirk-Greene limits himself here only to the beginning of the long story which links Margery Perham's career with the British Colonial Service, the phase in which she travelled widely in Africa to observe it. Future studies will follow up the sequel to the Oxford Summer Schools on colonial administration which she helped to inaugurate in 1937 and 1938, and will show how she used her many contacts to explore and discuss the problems of colonial rule. In particular, they will judge how far the restructuring of Colonial Service training that followed the Second World War, and in which she played a significant part, fully reflected the shift of emphasis towards preparation for self-government – a shift which radi- cally affected the role for which the administrator was being trained or re- trained.

Other questions need to be asked. The view of Africa through the medium of its colonial governance was limited in more ways than its male orientation. Gertzel has noted how Margery realized herself that it largely cut her off from the contact she would have liked with ordinary non-official Africans. This in turn probably impaired her capacity, even after she had accepted the pace of Africanization, to establish institutional as distinct from individual contacts with members of the African élites who would replace the colonial administrators – even more so to be in touch with the various popular nationalist movements. Again, her zeal for protecting the interests of administrators meant that she was sometimes manipulated by them – most conspicuously perhaps, in her advocacy of the Sudan Political Service in its closing months.[18]

Between the wars Margery Perham was not only a disciple of the leading figures in the field of African affairs, not only an enthusiastic supporter of colonial administrators and the 'indirect rule' by which they governed: she was also at first decidedly cool and distrustful towards the work of Christian missions, regarding them as a major disruptive influence in the indigenous African societies watched over by the administration. But her gradual move away from an unquestioning enthusiasm for indirect rule was accompanied, and in part caused, by a gradual shift in her attitude to missions and their work. This subject is opened up in the paper by Andrew Porter; he shows how the shift was partly prompted both by the achievements of J.H. Oldham in bringing the Christian missions to address themselves jointly to a more positive and creative interpretation of their task in Africa, and by the pragmatic need to rely heavily on missionary help in promoting educational development in East Africa. But this was also for Margery a time of deepening spiritual crisis; and it was no accident that the Second World War, which brought home to her the full menace of totalitarian threats to western culture, also brought her back decisively within the fold of Christian faith. She came to believe that Christian missionary activity might have a special role in the future precisely because it could remain free of compromising connection with the colonial government which she now perceived to be in swift decline. With the 'steel frame' of imperial control weakening, the civilizing effects of Christian culture, represented by both missionary work and the establishment of African universities, might help to check the forces of disintegration.

III

When war broke out in 1939 Margery Perham was 44 years old. The war years proved to be the watershed of her personal and professional life. Certainly this is the impression that emerges from the pages of her private diary, where these years are the most densely represented, and where they poignantly re-evoke her student experiences of the 1914–18 war.[19] She had become a founder-fellow of Nuffield College in Oxford and Reader in Colonial Administration, positions which her friends believed would enable her to have a real influence on colonial affairs.[20] But the unfolding drama of the war and the disruption of much routine activity, together with the cutting short of overseas travel, made her restless for action:

> Too great self-command is required for us to sit still or to work on in our appointed places. We need to find rest in action that is part of the great struggle we are watching … As others are called we dramatise ourselves as actors in the crisis and the wild hope springs up that in this or that act of the drama we might take the centre of the stage (18 Jan. 1941).

By contrast, her own life seemed to be slipping past without achievement. 'I see that the war has broken across the work I planned to do. The conviction comes to me as to many others that life has more than half passed and I have fulfilled neither my hopes nor my powers.' From this she went on to question the importance of her African work, and to consider alternatives. She thought about entering politics, teaching at African institutions, or – most compelling – about devoting herself to creative writing. This had been a constantly recurring aspiration:[21] 'that glorious hope of the artist is not wholly quenched … Art alone can ever justify a human life as I wish mine, middle-aged, unmated, to be justified for the long effort of its living' (18 Jan. 1941).

As in 1914–18, she was deeply absorbed by the course of the war itself, particularly in the twenty months from the defeat of France in 1940 to the fall of Singapore in 1942, as she directly experienced its crises – the retreat from Dunkirk, the battle of Britain, the bombing of London – and saw members of her sister's family exposed to its dangers. One of her nephews was killed and another posted missing for weeks before he was known to be a prisoner. Against this background she contemplated the implications of defeat for Britain and of the end of the world order as she had known it. 'I feel nearer despair than at any other time, not at the prospect of discomfort, danger or death, even of the collapse of another Empire, but of the collapse of human morality and culture.' (28 June 1940) Roland Oliver, in his introductory article, is right to stress as a key point in her life Margery's re-evaluation of Britain's colonial mission in her *Times* articles of March 1942 after the fall of Singapore, but this was the culmination of many months of heart-searching and continuing reappraisal.

These early war years were for Margery, as Porter shows, also a time of intense spiritual crisis. She acknowledged herself to have been 'formed by education as a religious woman' (5 Dec. 1938); yet for more than twenty years, from her brother Edgar's death in 1916, she claimed she had lived in near total agnosticism (12 Nov. 1941). But always with a sense of loss:

> As there is no love and no religion and no philosophy in my life, I have no reserves. I find I have no true courage and cannot even attain a bare façade of stoicism. As I get older and lose what personal attractions and physical delights I had of riding and swimming and the rest, the intermittent compensations of attracting interest and affection and attaining animal contentment are lost. I look into my own emptiness... (2 May 1940)

Even before the war, however, her practical attitude to Christianity in its African context had begun to become more positive, and in 1940 she had opened the first of her press cuttings files on Christian missions. She herself dated her 'reconversion' to hearing Dorothy Sayers' play *The Man Born to be King* broadcast in Holy Week 1943: but this seems more like the quickening of an already smouldering perception.

Porter describes how this spiritual rebirth radically affected her attitude to Christian missions in Africa. Hers became a militant Christianity, which readily warmed to the causes espoused by such radical priests as Michael Scott and Trevor Huddleston. It also evidently helped to rekindle the sense of purpose and commitment which she so restlessly sought. It was true that she would never again enjoy quite that intensive first-hand familiarity with Africa, and with the Colonial Service in the field, of her early travels. But by 1944 she was centrally involved in the great enterprise of developing African university education and in the major restructuring of the courses in colonial administration. Years of teaching, travelling, and campaigning lay ahead of her. The Lugard biography, which was to be her greatest single work, would be hailed by very diverse critics as a fine piece of the creative writing which she had often believed to be an impossible dream. It was not the end of her creative life and work; it was in the post-war years that she grew to her full stature.

Only two of the contributions included here are concerned specifically with those war years. Both are short and somewhat peripheral to the main concerns of her career. Yet both illustrate how the circumstances of the war pressed her into unfamiliar assignments which challenged and broadened her earlier approach to the subject of European rule in Africa.

The desire to be of use to her country during the war led her to undertake tasks that she might otherwise have refused. Michael Twaddle relates how in 1940 she agreed to a request from Oxford University Press to write a short book, in a series for African readers, which came to have the title *Africans and British Rule*. It was to be her last attempt to expound the doctrine of indirect rule in a way which, she hoped, would lead Africans with some secondary education to understand and accept it, as well as convincing them of the basic justice and good faith of British rule. The simple English which she was enjoined to adopt confronted her with some fundamental ambiguities in her own approach. How was she to reconcile her advocacy in principle of African political advancement against settler opposition with her deeply ingrained gradualist view of the African potential for that advancement? Predictably the modest little book was bitterly attacked both by defenders of African rights (such as the West Indian economist Arthur Lewis) and by settlers in Kenya. Such episodes as this were probably, as Twaddle suggests, among the factors leading to her major reappraisal in 1942 of the colonial scene.

The chief diversion, however, in Margery Perham's research and writing caused by the war resulted from a request from the Foreign Office to the Royal Institute of International Affairs for information on the government of Ethiopia. This was in the anticipation that the British government would be involved in administering that country after its liberation from Italian occupation. Margery had been fiercely concerned over the Italian invasion of Ethiopia before the war, and Patricia Pugh has contributed a brief note showing how she came to be drawn into the research project. But the Foreign Office did not share the high regard in which Miss Perham was held in the Colonial Office – this was to be demonstrated again over the Sudan – and collaboration broke down over access to the department's records; leaving Margery to complete, without adequate documentation and without the benefit of visiting the country, a work in a field outside her main interests. Edward Ullendorff's short reminiscence on the episode gives a sympathetic account of Margery's own response to the substantial deflection of her energies, and of her deep misgivings over this, her only publication on a country which she had never visited. Yet *The Government of Ethiopia* has proved a distinguished and enduring analysis.

IV

It was in 1945, as the war was ending, that Margery Perham embarked on what was to be her principal work of scholarship, the biography of Lord Lugard. First commissioned in the 1930s when Margery was the friend and disciple of Lugard, it was completed when Nigeria – the territory to which he had devoted his main administrative life – was on the brink of independence. It posed problems of ethical standards and personal involvement. Along with the broadly changing perceptions of empire and imperialism, there was the shift in her own evaluations with the process of time and with her growing familiarity with the main character of the story.

The work took fifteen years, and Mary Bull has demonstrated the tremendous demands it made on her physical and mental resources. Although she succeeded in shedding some teaching and administrative responsibilities – she resigned as University Reader and as Director of the Oxford Institute of Colonial Studies – most of her regular activities continued unabated. She continued to edit volumes in the Nuffield-sponsored Colonial Series and often to furnish them with introductions or forewords. This was the period when she was most heavily involved in official or semi-official committee work in London; in particular, as a member of the executive committee of the Inter-University Council for Higher Education in the Colonies. She visited Africa almost annually. In Oxford, there was the constant stream of visitors, including African students with many different interests. Meanwhile the files of correspondence and documentation on the Sudan, Kenya, Central Africa and other areas of crisis expanded and multiplied.

The biography was written in the hours and days between these activities. It was a distinguished historical work: yet she herself chafed at the delay it entailed in work on other books she had planned, on the Sudan and East Africa in particular. However, with the radically altered time-scale of change following the war, it may be questioned whether even by the late 1940s, studies of the kind she had envisaged were any longer feasible. More realistically, it might be suggested that her preoccupation with Lugard was one reason why she found it difficult to adjust to the political climate of African nationalism; she claimed as much in one of her letters to the Kenya nationalist politician Tom Mboya.[22] On the other hand, the long perspective afforded by the study of Lugard's career, beginning with the necessity of learning more about the pre-colonial Africa that he first entered, enhanced her ability to place current events in a historical setting. Also, his involvement in tropical Africa over sixty years, with his practice and his theories of administration, enabled her to survey the whole process of imperial domination and to develop an increasingly sophisticated view of the 'good government' that she hoped to inculcate in the new African administrations.

The year 1945, which saw the death of Lugard and the beginning of work on his biography, also brought the loss of Sir Douglas Newbold, the Civil Secretary of the Sudan, and one of Margery Perham's closest friends. From her first visit to the Sudan in 1936, largely through his support and guidance, she had been collecting material for a study on the lines of *Native Administration in Nigeria*. But in these post-war years – quite apart from her preoccupation with the biography – events in the Sudan moved too fast for a description of a functioning system, and between 1945 and 1955 the territory was precipitated into what Margery and many others regarded as premature independence. The Sudan was on the fringe of the African colonial world, and was subject to international pressures arising from the extreme delicacy of Britain's interests in the Middle East. This enabled Egypt to exercise strong political leverage through her share in the condominium; there was also the growing influence in the region of the United States.

In no other African territory had Margery Perham been so conscious of what she felt to be at once the glamour and the beneficence of empire. The Sudan Political Service of a few scores of picked officers was to her the quintessence of colonial administrative virtue. Moreover, it was in the Sudan that, following up her radical rethinking of Britain's colonial mission, she was already helping with steps to train young Sudanese officials – gradually – to take their places. Her anguish at witnessing the abrupt forced withdrawal of British administration is described by Roger Louis mainly through her diaries and exchanges with two or three of the senior British Sudan administrators. Her support for them did nothing to improve her relations with the Foreign Office, already strained over Ethiopia. After the Sudan's independence she seems to have made no attempt – as she did in other British African territories – to maintain contacts or to influence directly developments there, although she did what she could to publicize the troubles of the Christian south.

In the early 1950s it was apparent, to Margery Perham more clearly than to many others, that the forces of change precipitated in the Sudan were moving all over colonial Africa. As she declared in a broadcast in 1954, 'independence is something that cannot be given, but must be taken. And first it has to be demanded ... by more than the first handful of "nationalists" who have created a miniature copy of the Indian Congress.' This meant that they must first of all set about 'breaking the crust of habitual subservience to the colonial government.'[23] It was happening, in different ways, in the Gold Coast, in Nigeria, in Uganda and elsewhere; and in the early 1950s, most fiercely and incomprehensibly in Kenya, a land to which Margery was drawn by its natural beauties and its problems as well as by strong personal ties.[24] When in 1952 the Mau Mau uprising brought murder and intimidation to the Kenya Highlands, she was one of the comparatively few who recognized in it a core of genuine nationalism. It was in this context that she endeavoured to make friendly contact with African political aspirations in the person of the young Luo politician Tom Mboya, by inaugurating a correspondence with him destined – on the lines of her earlier controversies with Lionel Curtis and Elspeth Huxley[25] – for eventual publication. This is the subject of Alison Smith's article.

Although there was no overt break between them, the letters were never published. Partly this was because the gap between the two, in background and political outlook, was too great; for all her wish to communicate, Margery remained too deeply embedded in her own world of British liberal imperialism to enter into the discourse of African politics. But it was also because she was becoming less effective as a mediator, and one of her aims had been to build bridges between African nationalism and colonial authority. However, her own direct influence on British government, which in the 1940s had been considerable, was diminishing. Although she was still in touch with colonial secretaries and with some colonial governors, it seems that they had less time to listen to her. This became more evident with the major shift in Britain's African policy implicit in the 'wind of change' at the end of the decade; the age of administration had given way to that of political bargaining and dis-engagement.

Margery Perham had always seen her role as a student of British administration in Africa as directly bearing on how that administration could best be carried out. How was she regarded in the Colonial Office, the government department which bore the chief responsibility for ex-ecuting British policy in Africa? Kenneth Robinson, writing partly from personal recollection, seeks to distil something of the nature of the official and political contacts which are widely thought of as central to her influence, an influence that some have exaggerated. However, it is a question which would need to be pursued much further than has so far been possible: both in the Perham papers where, as the account of the archive makes clear, such evidence as there is is often fragmentary and elusive; and in many other collections, including for instance the papers of Sir Christopher Cox, Sir Douglas Newbold, and Sir James Robertson. It is a particular loss that she destroyed the letters written to her by Arthur Creech Jones.

By the 1950s Margery Perham's direct influence in government quarters may have been waning. But in some areas of policy determina-tion she was still a force to be reckoned with. Her practical experience, her academic standing, and her wide-ranging knowledge of African developments made her a leading figure on the executive committee of the Inter-University Council on overseas higher education; on one occasion she described the Council's work as 'perhaps the greatest contribution which this country has made to the colonies'.[26] Ever since the 1930s, moreover, she had been in particularly close touch with Makerere College in Uganda, and for seventeen years, from 1946 to 1963, she was on its Council. This involved frequent visits to East Africa, and gave special scope for her warm personal solicitude; with staff appointments and pastoral care as well as the problems of individual teachers and sometimes students.

She was also taking an increasing interest in the way that African university students would approach their countries' history – an interest stimulated by the explosive growth in the study of Africa's pre-European past. Official belief in such study as a constructive educational force for the future was demonstrated when in the 1950s the British government was persuaded to finance a three-volume history of East Africa beginning in the Stone Age. This was through the agency of the Colonial Social Science Research Council, the main other official body in which Margery Perham took part, thus keeping in touch with the widening field of social research in Africa.

She continued to write regularly for the press. Moreover, Prudence Smith, who was producer of many of her BBC talks, suggests that this was precisely the period when her public influence as a broadcaster reached its peak. In this view one of Margery Perham's greatest contributions was to enable her radio audiences to regard the imperial period as one in which they could have pride; and to recognize the opportunities and achievements, as well as the problems, in its ending. This was very much the theme of Margery Perham's series of Reith Lectures, which the BBC invited her to deliver in 1961 and which she subsequently published as *The Colonial Reckoning*.

One of Margery Perham's last major undertakings was to preside in 1961 over the launching of the Oxford Colonial Records Project, which during more than twenty years built up an unrivalled collection of personal papers relating to British administration in the late colonial period. This collection is preserved at Rhodes House, and constitutes not indeed her most important but one of her most tangible legacies. It is complemented by the wealth of papers in her own archive. It is right that Patricia Pugh, who arranged and catalogued her papers, should conclude this volume with an illuminating account of how the Perham archive grew and acquired the shape which her own skills have restored.

Margery Perham retired from Nuffield College and university teaching in 1963, and gradually the stream of visitors – African leaders and students, ex-colonial officials and other British experts on Africa – diminished. Indeed, although she remained busy in many fields, the 1960s were for her principally a time of retrospect and recollection, rather than of attempting to grapple with the issues and approaches of the unfamiliar world of African politics. One of the most remarkable fruits of this was the presidential address she delivered at the inaugural meeting of the African Studies Association of the UK in 1964. It reviewed her personal odyssey, not only as a participant in the changing political and constitutional thinking on Africa, but also as a student of the whole African historical and cultural background. In 1965 she was created a DCMG (Dame Commander of the Order of St Michael and St George) – a uniquely fitting tribute to her services to the colonial empire. She continued to pursue good causes, particularly in relation to missionary work, and she became more actively concerned with the welfare of animals, especially in protests against the cruelties involved in factory farming and the export of live cattle and horses. Yet one African crisis did draw her back into active involvement. In 1967–68 Dame Margery, now in her seventies, was deeply distressed at the slide into violence in Nigeria that led to the secession of Biafra and to civil war. Martin Dent in a short and partly reminiscent account describes the visit to Nigeria and its sequel which was her last active intervention on the African scene.

V

'Nothing is worse', Margery Perham once wrote, 'than a biography written in an attitude of piety.'[27] Readers of the papers in this volume may find themselves at the end of it still hard put to it to define fully the nature and the extent of her historical contribution. Despite her ambition and the achievements recorded in the chronology of her life, her career was not one of unalloyed success. The people in whom she invested the strongest emotional commitment – the colonial administrators – were by the end of her time outdated and largely dispersed; with the dismantling of British colonial rule her own influence at the centre of government was negligible. As in government, so in contemporary African studies, she had ceased to play a significant part. Her study shelves were filled with files of plans and laboriously collected research materials for books that had to be abandoned because they were no longer relevant. She had largely failed in her sincere efforts to understand and relate to the forces at work in the new African states. On the other hand, the bibliography of her writings, and above all the biography of Lugard, together with the Colonial Records collection, testify to her richly productive academic and public life. Perhaps its most consistent quality is that of reflective expression – the power to absorb and convey the character and preoccupations of the closing thirty years of colonial rule in Africa. In doing this she left her own personal imprint on the process of decolonization.

The articles published here make no claim to be more than a beginning of an evaluation of Margery Perham's place in the record of British colonial administration and the subsequent decolonization in Africa. Many other important topics in her life remain to be explored: her continuing relations with elements of the political left in Britain; the more thorough examination of her views on the practice of colonial administration; her involvement with southern African issues (among them the affairs of Bechuanaland), and with Central African ones, notably the Central African Federation; her concern with Uganda and with Makerere University College; and above all her contribution over twenty-five years to the process of universitybuilding in Africa. Virtually none of the articles represents an exhaustive study of the Perham Papers, and few have exploited archival sources elsewhere. On the other hand they have the asset of including a substantial element of reminiscence, a resource which is fast dwindling. Margery Perham herself would be the first to welcome the hard light of critical investigation and assessment which will come later; a major biographical study by Valerie Pakenham is already well advanced. Meanwhile we hope that these articles will raise some of the questions that will need to be answered.

NOTES

1. Anthony Low drew attention to this chain of personal friendships in a review article in *African Affairs*, 70 (1971), 172–5.
2. Private Diary 1932–51, 18 Jan. 1941, Perham Papers (hereafter PP), Rhodes House Library, Oxford, Box 33, file 4. Subsequent references to this diary will be made by date only in the text.
3. See Chapters 3 and 9 below.
4. Margery Perham, *African Apprenticeship* (London, 1974), p. 147.
5. See Chapter 3 below, p. 50. In 1931 she briefly studied anthropology under Malinowski at the London School of Economics.
6. See Chapter 3 below, p. 47.
7. See especially Sir Ralph Furse, *Aucuparius: recollections of a recruiting officer* (London, 1962).
8. See 'The Time of my Life', the *Listener*, 20 Jan. 1970, reprinted in *African Apprenticeship*, pp. 15–28; M.F. Perham, *Major Dane's Garden* (London, 1925).
9. M.F. Perham, *Josie Vine* (London, 1927). Patricia Pugh gives a fuller account of these early years in Chapter 14.
10. Private Diary 1914–1918, PP 33/2.
11. W.M. Macmillan, *My South African Years* (Cape Town, 1975), p.196, quoted in Chapter 3 below.
12. See Chapter 3 below, p. 59.
13 Account of a conversation with A.J. Dawe, then head of the Africa Department at the Colonial Office.
14. See Chapter 5 below, p. 87.
15. See Chapter 11 below, p. 190.

16. Evidence to de la Warr Commission, 8 Feb. 1937, PP 516/1 f.34. A few years later she was reflecting, in relation to Makerere, whether 'it is only ... perhaps in the third generation of education in which mothers have shared that people become able to learn by the activities of reasoning, by use of the printed and spoken word.' Perham to George Turner, 10 Aug. 1945, PP 515/1.
17. Richards to Perham, 7 Feb. 1950, 515/5.
18. See Chapter 9 below.
19. See Private Diary 1914–1918, PP 33/2.
20. See Chapter 3 below, p. 57.
21. See, for example, Diary entries 7 Jan. 1938, 27 Oct. 1940, PP 33/4.
22. See Chapter 10 below, p. 178.
23. See Chapter 1 below, p. 25.
24. Several members of her family were working there; there were also other close friends, including the Finance Minister Ernest Vasey.
25. Margery Perham and Lionel Curtis, *The Protectorates of South Africa* (London, 1935); Elspeth Huxley and Margery Perham, *Race and Politics in Kenya* (London, 1944).
26. Paper for the IUC Executive Council, Feb. 1957, PP 719/4 f.1.
27. Perham to Creech Jones, 2 Sept. 1945, PP 23/1.

Prologue: The Two Miss Perhams

Roland Oliver

I have been asking myself where, in the record of her many achievements, the essence of Margery Perham's historical significance is to be found. And I have no doubt that it is in the immense effort, maintained through forty years, to address the opinion-forming public in Britain, at monthly or sometimes even fortnightly intervals, on the aspect of public affairs which was also her academic speciality. This was not done for any significant financial reward, much of it not even in response to any positive invitation. Most of it was supplied quite free, in the correspondence columns of the *The Times*, seizing the opportunities offered by the news of the day, or the opinions of other correspondents. It was gruelling, always interrupting, work which brooked no delay, and usually allowed no time for second thoughts. Yet it was this work which, cumulatively, brought her the public respect which hardly any academic expert enjoys. It is one thing to gather golden reviews for the book which it has taken ten years to write, and quite another to be judged by the opinions hammered out at three in the morning and rushed to the post before breakfast.

Looking through these ephemeral writings, as she later presented them selectively in the two volumes of her *Colonial Sequence*, one sees at once that there were two very different Miss Perhams, and the volumes should have been divided not in 1949, but in March 1942. The 'first' Miss Perham sprang rather suddenly (at the age of 34) into public view in 1930, during a world tour financed by the Rhodes Trust to study the administration of 'coloured races', when she made her debut in *The Times* newspaper with a series of brilliant articles on Samoa and various parts of Africa. We can say without hesitation that the first Miss Perham was someone whose thought was dominated by ideas of social engineering. That may sound a dull theme, but Margery could clothe it for her readers with all the romance of dominion. In a passage about northern Nigeria, written in 1932, she says:

> The way to see this country is to travel through it on horseback. The political officer on his rounds is, by rigorous tradition, always accompanied by the emir's representative, mounted and robed as fits his position, while behind him in single file will come the local

21

district head and village head, a couple of mallams and one or two other anonymous horsemen, all with flowing, embroidered robes and bright saddle cloths, the leather of their harness brilliantly dyed and hung with coloured fringes and tassels. To ride with such a company, turning in perhaps on the homestead of some half-naked peasant, who with all his family falls prostrate to the ground, is to understand what it meant to be a horseman in feudal Europe.[1]

In relation to Nigeria, she was fair enough to point out that in Lagos at the same period there were half a dozen newspapers owned, written and printed by Africans, and that the African bourgeoisie of the southern towns demanded British sympathy and attention 'not only because the standards they are following' are *our* standards, 'but because the fact that they are just beginning to understand us gives them power to help or hinder us in the business of government.'[2] But the social formation which really interested her at this time was something she called unhesitatingly the 'tribe', and which she visualized as a kind of force or current, which could be harnessed to all sorts of modern purposes by those who understood the system. 'The organized vitality of the tribe', she wrote in 1930, 'of which the highest concentration was once expressed in war, can now be harnessed to economic production, to education, hygiene and a dozen other constructive activities, with results which ... may astonish the world in another 50 years.'[3] Much of her early writing amounted to a kind of Malinowski for the Million. 'The aim of our administration must be to find the true foundations of native society, and build upwards and outwards from them. ... We should foster tribal society into an all-embracing organ of local government, through which all, and not merely a few, of our administrative activities would be expressed ... and turn officers of all departments into teachers.'[4] The fundamental notion was that one was working on communities, not individuals. One should be nice to those Africans who had improved themselves as individuals and passed beyond the compass of their own communities, but colonial government was about the improvement of communities as such.

The first Miss Perham mounted no campaign to include the educated Africans into colonial government, even to its central, proto-national functions. She believed that this kind of work was best done by impartial outsiders, and preferably by graduates of Oxford and Cambridge. Although she never formally took herself outside the Christian camp in which she had been brought up, these years of the 1930s were those in which she was most detached from it, viewing Christian missions with a good deal of suspicion, as organizations which existed to disrupt her tribal communities. This after all was the view of most of those with whom she mixed at the time. Most telling, perhaps, was her attitude to the South African Protectorates. In 1934 she argued for their retention by Britain, but mainly so that they could be licked into shape as shining examples of actively developmental indirect rule. At some later date they could possibly be transferred to the Union of South Africa 'in a state in which they would be a credit to us and to themselves'. The Union, she argued, need have no reason to distrust the success of such an experiment. 'Successful administration on tribal lines touches no controversial issues; all parties [in South Africa], and most of all the segregationists ... desire to see the utmost possible development of native institutions in Reserves.'[5]

The 'second' Miss Perham, who was the one I knew personally, came into existence very suddenly, following the fall of Singapore to the Japanese in February 1942. She was deeply affected by the war on a personal as well as on an intellectual level; one of her sister's sons was killed and another taken prisoner. It seems that it was also a spiritual crisis, which brought her right back into full Christian belief, and caused her to revise the whole context of her thinking about colonialism. Just four weeks after the fall of Singapore she sent to *The Times* a pair of articles, which expressed her new stance, and which, in her published work at least, is the nearest we can come to the central event in her life.

'The Malayan disaster,' she wrote, 'has shocked us into sudden attention to the structure of our colonial empire. Events such as we have known in the last few weeks are rough teachers, but our survival as a great power may depend on our being able to learn their lesson.' She went on to examine the whole concept of a plural society in the colonial context, as it had existed in South East Asia, and as it still existed in so much of Africa, and stressed how the whole existence of the minority communities – be they Europeans and Chinese in South East Asia, or Europeans and Indians in East Africa – rested upon the illusion that the steel frame of imperial power would be there for ever to hold the ring. She invited her readers to imagine what would be the position in Kenya, if Japanese transports and aircraft carriers were to make their appearance off Mombasa. She suggested that 'even to imagine Kenya in the throes of desperate war is to set us wondering whether it is wisdom to encourage separate communities to develop on "their own lines" upon parallels that will never meet.'

She concluded that a revision of the time factor was needed for all aspects of our colonial policy. 'We regarded empire as part of the order of things, at once beneficent and enduring. We developed towards our backward charges a paternalism that could hardly conceive of their coming of age.'[6] To recall that, at the time she wrote this, India was still five years short of independence, is to understand how radical was her change of outlook. One might wonder if she realized how much of her own past habits of mind she was abandoning – for example, when she remarked that 'Many an officer works and overworks with the utmost devotion for the peasants in his charge, while, in their clubs and residential quarters, he and his wife may live almost wholly insulated from the aspiring educated minority of the country.' It was necessary, she concluded, to achieve 'a new and more intimate and generous relationship with [the colonial] peoples'.[7]

And that meant, of course, the kind of rapid, indiscriminate westernization to which hitherto she had been so much opposed:

> We have got to shift the basis of our empire still more from power to service, change it from a distant, half-forgotten affair which we leave to professionals, to officials. Make it a much more direct contact between them and us. Do you realize that they want almost everything that we have to give ... Parliamentary and local government, trade unions, universities, rural colleges, co-operative systems, penal reform, ideas about architecture, or midwifery, or football.

That was a broadcast talk given in 1943.[8] By 1946, with India still short of independence, Margery was deeply involved in plans for the development of higher education in Africa, and she described the need in this way:

> We are now coming ... to the climax of this relationship; they are on the verge of coming forward as communities fit to govern themselves and they are asking from us this one great essential, the training of their leaders and experts so that they may take back from us the control of their own affairs ... The British universities have now got a more important task than any handled by the Colonial Office itself.[9]

In the following years she was at the heart of that extraordinary movement of intellectual colonization whereby more than twenty universities were established in British colonial and post-colonial Africa, and handed over in less than a generation to local management.

During the years between 1946 and 1954, still well before the independence of any African country, Margery Perham showed quite astonishing wisdom and foresight about the direction things would take. She perceived very clearly the consequences for Africa of the rise of American and Russian power, and, unlike most of her contemporaries, she did not resent it. 'Very important criticisms of imperialism have been made by the two major powers in the world, and these are finding now, particularly among the growing number of literate colonial groups, a very ready echo.'[10] That was in 1946. And in 1947 she said in a radio broadcast: 'The spell of our absolute authority is broken. Quite small groups can challenge our right to govern, and by their political leadership and journalism and the outside support they get, they can undermine the confidence of the people in our government.'[11] It was bootless, she wrote in 1952, to claim that the rural millions in the colonies were still friendly and loyal. Even if true, could they be considered an effective or enduring majority, when the fact, easily verified in London, was that every young African who succeeded in rising above the unconscious mass through education and travel, was filled with bitterness as he contemplated the place allotted to himself and his compatriots in the world scene?[12] But perhaps the most amazingly prophetic piece she ever wrote was in 1954, when in an article for the *Listener* she declared her conviction that:

> Independence is something that cannot be given, but must be taken. And first it has to be demanded, and demanded by more than the first half-dozen lawyers and journalists who have learned to direct against us the civil liberties we wrested from the Stuarts: by more than the first handful of 'nationalists' who have created a miniature copy of the Indian Congress. Before their demand can be taken seriously, before there can be any successor to whom we can hand over power, these first self-constituted leaders have to create at least the appearance of a nation. To do this it seems to be inevitable that they first set about breaking the crust of habitual subservience to the colonial government: their weapons are invective and ridicule. They try to raise the desire for freedom by playing upon every possible cause of discontent. Any concessions by the government, short of the final one, are ignored or condemned ... A high emotional temperature is needed in which they can fuse their diverse human material and hammer it into the rough shape of a nation. And how perfectly natural it is that the readiest emotional element from which to draw the required heat is hatred. There is always a small but responsible group ... who struggle bravely for moderation, but they are often thrust contemptuously aside as imperialist stooges.[13]

Here, more than in any other single text, we have the pointer to the historical significance of Margery Perham. Of course we know that there was a long tradition of anti-imperialism in Britain, but most of it was theoretical, retrospective and condemnatory. When the time for decolonization arrived, the literature of anti-imperialism and its characteristic exponents would not make many new converts to the cause. But Margery, whatever her voting record, was an establishment figure, who had spent fifteen years explaining how to govern colonies, and consorting with men like Lugard, Hailey, Grigg and Cameron. When, in one decisive month of 1942, she had experienced a kind of Damascus Road vision of the future, she had no need to look back in anger, or to denounce the work of her old friends. She was able to address everyone to the left of Genghis Khan, and to explain in her lucid way that the scene was changing, and any sensible person would respond by moving a good deal faster than they had hitherto thought advisable, even if it meant doing business with some rather immature, and possibly disagreeable, people. Of course there were some people who were well to the right of Genghis Khan, including one senior Colonial Office official, who used to go round saying: 'We could have stood up to the Americans. And we could have stood up to the Russians. And we could have stood up to the Labour Party. What we couldn't stand up to was the Labour Party *and* the left wing of the Conservative Party.' That is exactly where Margery Perham's influence was so important.

NOTES

1. 'Nigeria Today', *The Times*, 28–30 Dec. 1932; reprinted in Margery Perham, *Colonial Sequence 1930–1949* (London, 1967) (hereafter *Col. Seq. I*), p. 55.
2. Ibid., p. 64.
3. 'Tribal Rule in Africa', *The Times*, 26–7 Nov. 1930; *Col. Seq. I*, pp. 14–15.
4. 'The Future of East Africa', *The Times*, 13–15 Aug. 1931; *Col. Seq. I*, pp. 42–3.
5. 'The South African Protectorates', *The Times*, 6 July 1934; *Col. Seq. I*, p. 129.
6. 'The Colonial Empire', *The Times*, 13–14 March 1942, *Col. Seq. I*, pp. 225–7.
7. Ibid., pp. 229–31.
8. 'From Power to Service', BBC talk reprinted in the *Listener*, 22 April 1943; *Col. Seq.I*, p. 247.
9. 'Relation of Home Universities to Colonial Universities', address to a Conference of Home Universities, 27 Sept. 1946; *Col. Seq. I*, p. 287.
10. Ibid., p. 283.
11. 'Christian Missions in Africa', BBC programme to Africa for Christians in the mission field, 16 Oct. 1947; *Col. Seq. I*, p. 302.
12. 'A Changing Continent', *The Times*, 28 Oct. 1952; *Colonial Sequence 1949–1969* (London, 1970) (hereafter *Col. Seq. II*), p. 68.
13. 'Britain's Response to the End of Colonialism', the *Listener*, 10 Dec. 1954; *Col. Seq. II*, pp. 94–5.

Margery Perham's Image of Africa

Cherry Gertzel

'I have always seen myself', Margery Perham reflected in a seminar she gave at Nuffield College on the eve of her retirement, 'really as thinking of policy, standing as it were in Britain and trying to realize how policy was made, what influences went to bear upon it', and throughout her career her major preoccupation was with colonial policy and administration. Nevertheless in the same talk she also acknowledged the strength of her attachment to Africa itself: 'but of course I never was [detached]. Beginning with this extraordinary feeling about Africa, I have all the time had it growing so that in a way – I don't know if "emotion" is the right word – there has been this immense as it were investment of myself in these African problems.'[1] Moreover, her contribution to the colonial debate over forty years makes it clear that her concern was not simply with the rulers but also with the ruled, and with the relationship between the two. This paper explores the question of how her ideas about the ordering of that relationship were influenced by what she saw in and learned about Africa.

It is based primarily upon her published work, supplemented by a small selection of unpublished material from the archives. There are limitations of course, for our present purpose, to the use of her published work. Nonetheless, used carefully, this large body of material provides the basis for an exploration of how Margery viewed Africa and the process of change imposed upon its peoples first by colonial rule and then by decolonization. What were the perceptions of Africa that underlay Margery Perham's concern for that continent and which caused her to make such an investment in it of herself?

To explore these questions is to explore the growth of the person, especially as she moved in her passage from young don to formidable dame; and in the context of her increasing involvement in the public as well as the academic arenas. It is thus at one level to reflect on how gender and race determined the boundaries of her perception and influenced her views. We have also to remember that Margery was part of a privileged, ruling class, and in Africa part of the process of class formation itself, and

27

so reflect on how that class position affected her awareness not least of the social forces at work. Finally, any such reflections have also to be set in the context of the wider social and political changes that occurred in the course of her long life: in Britain, in Europe, and in Africa itself. The Africa that Margery first visited in the 1920s and 1930s, and the Africa of her last visit, in 1968, to Nigeria at the height of the civil war, were not the same. The international environment within which she began her studies of Africa also had changed, long before, and with it ideas about development and colonialism. Kenneth Robinson once pointed out, 'how close the study of Africa in (Britain) in the heyday of colonialism was to the perceived nature of our responsibilities and interests', and went on to conclude, 'one cannot step out of history, one cannot evade the consequences of power (or lack of it). But one can and must attempt to be aware of the implications of the social and political institutions of the world in which our intellectual activities take place'.[2] Thus we have to situate the person in the context of changing times, and changing ideas.

This paper therefore seeks to weave what we can glimpse of her African vision into the background and the experiences against which her ideas about Africa were formed. This involves a brief look first at her travels in Africa, both before and after the Second World War, and then at her Oxford years, especially the 1930s and 1940s.

The View from the Field

Margery Perham's image of Africa was originally formed in the months she spent in Somaliland in 1921–22, but was more solidly developed in the five years of the 1930s that Roland Oliver estimates she spent 'roaming around' the continent.[3] The first impression from this early exploration of Africa, as it emerges from the letter-diaries in which she recorded her experiences for family and close friends, is of an intense response to the country itself, to its great beauty and to its wildness and to a 'strangeness and remoteness which Europeans seem fated equally to desire and to destroy'.[4] She seemed to reach out with enormous joy, seeking an almost physical relationship to the landscape around her. Thus, in her journey into the Elgeyo–Marakwet country, as they went into the Rift,

> quite suddenly we were in a different world ... It was a day apart from others. Nearly all my days now seem to be red-lettered but this was gold. I climbed out, marvelling and terrified, to a rock overhanging this monstrous chasm and lay in a kind of dream, beaten

upon by sun and wind and by my own wonder, letting Africa-worship fill my heart and mind.[5]

There are many similar entries.

The same responsive enthusiasm and sense of physical engagement emerges from her accounts of other journeys, such as her enormously exhausting tour through Bornu in the course of which she wrote, of one of many camps: 'It was warm, but we burned some logs for the beauty of their fire in the starlit darkness and, lying in a long chair on cushions, I said my grace for the comfort of true hospitality and friendship and for the strange beauty in which we sat.'[6] Her diaries reflect the same sense of reaching out to Africans, and a similar awareness of human beauty. 'Africans are the best of all races for smiles, so complete, so broad, so human and humorous. As I smile back with my mouth and with eyes looking into theirs, I feel that I am greeting friends and cannot believe that such a wide difference of experience divides us.'[7] There was no doubt of her enjoyment at her encounters in villages and elsewhere, and her meetings and talks, even though always through an interpreter. If her forays into Masai manyattas, her scrambling into dark huts, or her penchant for photography, strike a somewhat embarrassing note, they also reflect an enormous enthusiasm, as well as delight.

This image of Africa was that of a romantic and she used the word herself more than once. On her Bornu journey, when she reached Adamawa she recorded: 'This is certainly the most romantic, the most African part of Nigeria, or of any part of Africa in which I have travelled.'[8] Such a sense of joyous celebration of Africa's physical and human beauty belonged essentially to that first phase of her African career. It never left her completely, although it was perhaps to Somaliland that it was most attached in her memory in her later years.

The next impression about those early years is of the *extent* of her travels, even if packed into a remarkably short time. She covered an enormous amount of ground, across Southern, Eastern and Western Africa, taking in the immense variety of each region, both geographical and human, urban and rural colonies of settlement and colonies of 'administration'. Some of that travelling was done in the relative comfort offered by the railways, and in the company of officials from Governors to District Officers. At the other extreme was the 'immense circular journey' she made by car across Bornu and the far northeast of Nigeria, alone with driver and personal servant, doing much of the driving herself, which in the conditions of 1931 would have been physically exhausting.[9] While she clearly luxuriated in the spacious comfort of various Government Houses in both East and West Africa, she also drove deep into some of the most isolated parts of each region, always with the aim of gathering more information, more understanding to add to what she had read. Most important, she went with a sense of purpose.

We have to remember that she was from the outset studying the administration, and for her the best way to do so was to combine detailed study of the official records with discussions with both officials and others. She acknowledged the importance of the support of officials for her work, not least since they controlled access to the files; as she commented after her arrival in Maseru in 1929, 'the whole success of each enterprise depended upon my reception at the hands of the responsible official'.[10] For the most part that reception was enormously helpful, although in Northern Nigeria she had one very difficult encounter.[11] She did not fail to use every occasion to draw out her hosts, recording many long conversations; however, she relied finally on the documentation with which they kept her supplied, supplemented by observations made in the course of her travel. 'Of course, I draw my knowledge mainly from their own and often unpublished papers', she explained of her links with officials in Nigeria in relation to her study of native administration, 'and I regard what I see and hear as giving – I hope! – some life and colour to the printed and typewritten records, central, provincial and district, which will be the main source for the book I hope to write.'[12] As she put it, when in the Transkei,

> It is of course the ideal way to study [the Transkei system]. You have at hand all the officials to answer questions, to expound policy, and to give you, unconsciously as well as consciously, the spirit and traditions of the administration. Then all round you is the country, spread like a map, with experts to interpret the pattern and the colour and missionaries to give you, from their own distinct angle, their stored knowledge of the dark inhabitants.[13]

Her capacity to interact with officialdom was impressive, in later as well as in the early years – her school and university background was after all very similar. She undoubtedly saw her role as critic and reformer, and it is clear that those officials who most influenced her were men like Cameron, Mitchell in his Tanganyika and Uganda days, Newbold and Robertson in the Sudan, all of whom were, like her, concerned with reform and change.

In addition she visited an enormous variety of government and other institutions, and met a whole range of unofficials, political, professional, mission and others. In Nigeria when researching on the native administration she followed a routine which involved visits at each district or provincial centre not only to native administration headquarters but to police, prisons, hospitals, schools and above all the Native Courts. She walked in the markets and sometimes the fields; she visited economic projects and agricultural schemes; she summed it up herself as 'my usual routine, with its motor-cars, interviews, dinner-parties and heavy programmes of investigation'.[14] She had a habit of taking her notebook with her when she went out to dinner.

The colonial administration was thus a key point of departure in Margery Perham's search for understanding Africa in those years, but from the beginning she made considerable effort to meet and talk with Africans as well. Her antipathy to racial prejudice undoubtedly helped to fashion her response to Africa and persuaded her of the need for Europeans to discover 'ordinary social relations with individual Africans which would overcome the assumptions of backwardness'.[15] She tried hard to make such contacts herself. She was not always successful, and peasants did not figure largely in her record. In Tanganyika and in Northern Nigeria, she had numerous encounters with Native Authority chiefs, and the impressions they made upon her are implicit in some of her articles as well as in the volume *Ten Africans*.[16] More important, at a time of growing African political activity there was no doubt of her determination to meet Africans politically involved; nor should we underestimate the courage often required to do so. A striking incident was the night she spent alone in a Kikuyu hut to demonstrate her trust in Chief Waruhui and his people.[17] And she did in fact engage with significant numbers of African political figures in those early travels. So, in South Africa she visited Lovedale and Fort Hare; but she also made an extraordinary visit in Durban to an I.C.U. meeting of rank and file with the trade union leader Champion, whom she described as a 'native agitator',[18] and of whom she said: 'Watching, I could not like Champion. I suppose it would be hard for any white person to like a native agitator.' Like him or not she conveys her sense of respect. Again, in Lagos, in 1931, after meeting 'the so-called "agitator", Herbert Macauley', she left feeling that 'He is one of the ablest Africans I have met and at once a potentially dangerous yet rather pathetic figure.'[19]

Notwithstanding such encounters, she was conscious of the extent to which her association with the administration separated her from the African world. After six days in Kaduna, in January 1931, for example, engrossed in her regular task of reading files, she commented: 'I stepped once out of the Secretariat into Africa.'[20] More than once in Nigeria she wished she was able to talk with Africans without colonial officials present. She was also conscious on many occasions of being a 'white woman'. She was aware of the restrictions upon women in African society and sensitive, especially in Muslim Northern Nigeria and the Sudan, to her own position and role. So, on one occasion, having evaded the restrictions of her colonial host, and accepted the Shehu of Dikwa's invitation to a great ceremony, she arrived and

> remembering the responsibility that rested upon me as the first white woman to cross the threshold, as well as the need to show a proper manner toward the great, I proceeded with all the dignity I could command, walking very slowly and making grave, unsmiling acknowledgement of the plaudits of the crowd and the efforts of the musicians.[21]

As that occasion as well as her earlier encounter with Champion, and many others, showed, she did not allow the conventions of the day to dictate what she did; rather it was the colonial officials who saw gender as an impediment. Perhaps more important, it does not seem that concern for gender issues, as we would understand them today, determined the direction of her enquiries, as her account of the 'Aba Riots' or Women's War in Owerri in 1929 suggests.[22]

She was obviously constrained by her lack of any African language, a limitation that remained with her all her life. This did not prevent her from seeking out 'ordinary Africans', or from great enjoyment on the occasions when she succeeded in doing so; or from regretting in later life the loss of such contacts. Thus on a much later journey to Kenya, in 1948, when the District Officer took her round Fort Hall District, she wrote home: 'The marvellous thing was that Coutts knows Kikuyu perfectly and talks and jokes and makes all the funny intonations of language with them. This is a marvellous and rare experience and I loved every minute of it', and her final perceptive comment was: 'There sure is something about these Kikuyu – one day they may beat the European at his own game.'[23] Yet that occasion reinforces one's sense of her limited involvement with the great mass of ordinary Africans. She herself was aware of this and realized that she had never spent long enough in one place to become familiar with is inhabitants. So, in Ibadan in 1931, she wrote: 'The conclusion was growing upon me that I did not begin to understand [this people]. Their society was too vast and complex for me to grasp in a short visit'.[24] Looking back, in that same Nuffield seminar quoted above, she felt she had never been able to pierce below the surface of things in Africa. 'I always used to think that it was rather like a sheet of water and that I only saw the top and that you had to dive down to look at all the creatures underneath and all the seaweed and the things I couldn't see.'[25] It was not therefore 'ordinary' Africans into whose world Margery most easily went, but that of the educated with whom she had much sympathy and with whom she had no hesitation in conversing.

At the personal level in such contacts she was conscious of racial differences but not of racial superiority; and there was a warmth and essential equality in the way she responded to the Africans she met and in some cases came to know. 'We managed to communicate', she said after her meeting with Chief Waruhui in Nairobi in 1930, 'as people can where there is both mutual interest and liking.'[26] Of her meeting with Tshekedi Khama on that first visit to South Africa, she later wrote that it 'was perhaps the most important of many impressions made upon me during my time in South Africa. Here I had seen, if only in random glimpses, the problem of black peoples caught within the grasp of a white ruling minority determined upon a lasting maintenance of its supremacy'.[27] On her first visit to Khartoum she had 'ardent and exhausting discussions' with Sudanese political figures about native administration.[28] She found them 'more dignified and self-confident than the negro' but the point was that both were part of the educated élites of the 1930s and, given her interests in administration, education, race relations, it was not surprising that she should seek them out. It was equally natural for her to talk with Native Authority chiefs.

A significant point of reference for the ideas she formed and developed in those early years were thus the educated Africans, and essentially the 'middle class'. She was not unaware of their class location. Sayed Sir Abdel Rahman for example, in Khartoum, she described as 'the formidable person who trebles the parts of fanatical religious leader, cotton king and would-be modern nationalist politician'.[29] Ten years later she recognized him as 'the new Westernized capitalist'.[30] She remarked of Eliud Mathu, the first African member of the Legislative Council in Nairobi in 1948, 'I fear he is a kulak.'[31] She saw the new urbanized societies becoming more class differentiated, as when in Lagos in 1932 she distinguished between an upper class 'of rich traders and of professional men ... ; a middle-class of clerks, retailers and mechanics ... ; and the proletariat.'[32] She did not, however, pursue the question of class, perhaps for two reasons. First, she had begun with a concern about race, and race relations, and justice, and so with racial barriers. Race thus obscured class. In 1930 in South Africa; in 1937 in her evidence to the Commission set up to consider the transformation of the then Makerere College in Uganda into a university; and in 1938 in Khartoum, her objective was to overcome the barriers of race.[33] Second, we have to bear in mind her own ideas about civilization and development at that time, and the world view with which she had grown up which accepted an ordering of society based upon the existence of social class.[34]

An enduring image of Africa was, by her own account, that of poverty; an image to which she returned in later life more than once: in her Reith Lectures in 1961; in the Introduction to the first volume of her diaries to be published; and in her final Nuffield seminar. She remembered the ugliness of poverty whether it was black old age 'withered and filthy' in the villages, or a drought-stricken, shrivelled land and the 'grim realities' of the 1920s and 1930s more generally.[35]

This image sits strangely against her very positive impressions of the development she saw in Tanganyika in 1930. Mwanza she described as a 'prosperous place ... brimming over with cattle and ground nuts, with a crowded and alert population'.[36] She was similarly positive about the agriculture she saw among the Kikuyu[37] or later in Zaria.[38] Nevertheless the awareness of poverty is there. It derived in part from what she saw in her travels into the wilder, more isolated regions and in part from her short encounters with what she called 'basic Africa', 'the real bush village'.[39] She understood the 'stubborn and dangerous poverty of the pastoralists'.[40] But she linked poverty also to the absence of material development, and to long isolation from Western civilization. In the far north of Nigeria, for instance, between Maiduguri and Dikwa, she saw country 'so empty of all the signs of civilization we try to introduce'.[41] At that level poverty was backwardness. 'It was incredibly primitive and backward', she recalled in 1963, 'all these words we are not allowed to use';[42] but in 1936, in the Introduction to Ten Africans, she had explained poverty simply in material terms. 'The very poverty of the Africans is a barrier between them and peoples who have enriched – some would say complicated – their lives with the innumerable products of modern industry.'[43]

The causes of this material poverty she found first in the past; in the conditions of pre-colonial Africa, the 'old, harsh unchanged Africa' which she had found still in north-eastern Nigeria, round Lake Chad in 1931.[44] 'The vast majority are primitives ... moulded by unknown centuries of tribal life, the virtues of which are not ours, nor the vices.'[45] The words she used belong to a different era, but we can recognize that for her in the first place poverty and isolation were historical facts. Hence the need to understand

the formidable, almost insurmountable difficulties with which Africans have been confronted by a unique history for which none of them was responsible ... the seclusion of Africa, above all, Central and Eastern tropical Africa, from the rest of the world, its poverty, its difficult natural environment, its division into innumerable tribes and clans of all kinds and all sizes within which

Africans developed institutions and experiences which were almost
utterly irrelevant to the new world which European annexation had
so abruptly superimposed upon them.[46]

She found much in African society to admire. 'The more African
society is studied,' she concluded in 1931, 'the more there is found in it to
admire ... because it contains certain solid elements which Europe would
be glad today not to have lost.'[47] African society 'is not gossamer, and it is
living and living vigorously enough to stand a great deal of injury and
misuse'.[48] But she had no desire to preserve it untouched. 'That the tribe
will not and should not survive I have now come to believe, and also that
the man, torn from his tribe and thrown into our individualistic civilization, is, and for long will be, a man without a home, literally, politically,
economically, spiritually.'[49]

She was aware also of a second level of poverty derived from twentieth-
century change. She perceived the signs in Tanganyika, Kenya and
Nigeria in her travels in 1931; inadequate lands, poor soils, over-grazing.
'The Kikuyu,' she noted, 'show all the now familiar signs of a crowded
reserve, the over-plentiful sprinkling of grey mushroom roofs and
crowded, uneven patchwork of cultivation on exhausted soil.'[50] While she
may not have appreciated the full ecological implications of soil erosion,
she did show herself conscious of the potential population constraints as
East African populations began to recover from the onslaught of disease
and war that had engulfed the earlier part of the century. Her image
conveys something of the atmosphere of uneven regional development
already in train by that time. She also recognized the exploitation of
urban areas, especially in South Africa.

Consistently she saw the two most disadvantaged elements of African
society in the 1930s and 1940s as labour and the educated class, and she
saw the need for state intervention to overcome exploitation. She saw the
Nigerian women who 'sit all day in the gutter offering for sale fractions of
a box of matches'[51] as evidence of commercial entrepreneurialism rather
than linking them to the process of class change. Similarly she understood
the implications for land ownership in Nigeria of the development of cash
crop production but did not follow through the consequences for peasant
society itself and the poor. Similarly, her awareness of the character of
the Ganda ruling class, and of the capacity of Ganda society to internalize
new influences to its own advantage, stopped short of the consequences for the Rwandese labourers on whom Buganda's capacity to
exploit her fertile soils ultimately depended.[52]

Her later visits to Africa took on a different character. The last of her
early travels was in 1937–38 to the Sudan and then on to East Africa.

Then the war intervened, and when ten years later she returned it was not to undertake safaris of the kind she had made before. She used the occasion of her almost annual visits to Makerere also to spend some time 'catching up' on East African and especially Kenyan political events, and particularly in the 1950s or the Mau Mau emergency. She was able in 1948 and 1953 to tour parts of Central Province with the District Commissioner, but not for any length of time. In 1953 she visited the scenes of Lugard's work in Uganda, but she flew to Ruwenzori and then made her way back to Kampala along his route.

In the years 1935 to 1945 moreover, she had become an 'expert' on colonial administration, and much more directly involved in public affairs. She went to Africa after 1945 almost invariably in an official capacity, as for example to Kampala to attend meetings of Makerere College Council of which in 1946 she became a member. Her return to the Sudan in 1948 was to advise on administrative training, although she stayed on to 'catch up', going on to East Africa to do the same. She went, even more so in the 1950s, not as a young researcher but as the doyenne of 'the increasingly numerous corps of academic experts on colonial affairs'[53] and an influential publicist. She still regarded her travels as enabling her to balance documentary evidence with personal observations, 'to check what I could learn from books, lectures and periodicals with the actualities of administration in the field' as she put it.[54] Nonetheless, she saw herself as a visitor; her study in Oxford was where she did her work. In many ways she had been captured by her official role.

This did not mean that she no longer met or talked with Africans. Far from it. On her visit to Khartoum in 1948 she reported home: 'The pressure of life is fierce. The Sudanese are perpetually after me. Invitations pour in, callers [come to] my office, institutions want to be visited.'[55] She renewed contacts from before the war (although some she confessed to having forgotten); in the case of the Sudan she became much engaged with the Sudanese politicians, as she did later with African figures in East Africa, as well as colonial administrators. What it did mean was that her contacts were increasingly at central government, senior political levels. Her concerns were now focused essentially on the transfer of power. At first she continued the same kind of routine as in the earlier years, working at the files, interviewing officials, talking with leading politicians and other public figures. She still packed an amazing number of interviews into her day. It seems, however, that the enchantment was fading. Now she remembered the insects, the sand-flies, and sadly, back in Khartoum in 1948, decided that 'All the romance of the East was there ... but it no longer had any power to charm me.' Although she savoured the tropics again after ten years, Africa had become 'a place to visit not to live in'. She was of course older, and in 1948 still tired after the war which had been enormously taxing physically as well as in other ways. 'Each year of age', she reflected, 'snips the glamour from the East and increases the recoil from all its conditions and insect hostilities.'[56] She made no more long journeys. Increasingly the view from the field became a restricted one subordinated to the view from Oxford.

The View from Oxford

To understand the 'view from Oxford' we have to set out briefly the main elements of Margery's Oxford life, as it took shape after 1935. First, Oxford provided her with the base from which she studied Africa. As she explained it: 'The University invented posts for me and then Nuffield College gave me a Fellowship which allowed me to combine travel with lecturing and writing at Oxford.'[57] Second, in Oxford she worked incredibly hard. As the late Warden of Nuffield put it, she 'had her own show as founder-Director of the Institute of Colonial Studies' from 1939 until she resigned her post as Reader in Colonial Administration in 1948. She was also 'the first of a very small band of scholars who worked closely together through the war years and after to make the new Nuffield College a reality'.[58] She was centrally engaged in the Colonial Service training, as well as in here academic work. The successive volumes in the colonial series she initiated reflect a major task. She read widely. She corresponded and had many visitors. If she became, as she did, the doyenne of colonial studies, she earned it from hard work.

Third, it was an academic world in which she was engaged. She was from the outset at the centre of a steadily expanding circle of academics engaged in colonial and African studies. That circle was not confined to Oxford, but engaged her with London and Cambridge as well, and with the associations and societies at the centre of the study of the colonial world: the Royal African Society, the International Institute of African Languages and Cultures with whose formation she was involved, the Anthropological Institute. In these and other bodies she was involved in the first place as an academic.

Yet not only an academic, for in the fourth place we have to take into account the links between academics concerned with Africa and the official world. As John Flint put it: 'The inter-war period witnessed the rise of the academics, a curious phenomenon in which university scholars and researchers were listened to with increasing respect, then brought in as special advisers from the mid-1920s, and finally, rather indirectly, formulated the blueprints for colonial reform at the end of the 1930s.'[59] Margery Perham was at the centre of that group, linked into it as a result of her own interest and work, her friendship with Lord Lugard, and her expanding involvement with key actors such as Lord Hailey and Joseph Oldham. So her world was also the world of the 'establishment', both the bureaucrats and the politicians, as her inclusion in Malcolm MacDonald's Carlton Hotel Meeting in October 1939 suggests. Over the years she was a member of a number of official bodies: the Colonial Office Advisory Committee on Education, the Colonial Social Science Research Council, and especially the Inter-University Council for Higher Education in the Colonies. While she may not, after 1945, have had the influence on policy that some have assumed, her continued pre-eminence as colonial expert was highlighted by her role during the 1940s and later as publicist, broadcaster, and influential writer to *The Times*.

The colonial administration remained her major point of reference in Oxford as it had been in Africa. She played a central part in planning the courses for colonial officials, and for many years taught in them. She kept in touch with many officials when they returned to Africa; some became friends. The administration was also her point of reference in a more fundamental sense, since it was central to her whole concern with colonial policy, development and change. Colonial officials in the field kept her supplied with information, but also with ideas. Thus Mitchell, Newbold and Robertson, to name but three, used her as a sounding board for their own ideas on reform as well as keeping her abreast of events.[60] Communication at that level seems to have been a crucial element for her thinking.

Yet, as in Africa, so in Oxford, she remained engaged also with Africans, especially as the post-war years took more of them to Oxford, some to her own courses. Some of them, like Mekki Abbas, became good friends.[61] She acknowledged and listened to African views even when she disagreed with them; for example in her encounters with the young Abu Mayanja, whom Andrew Cohen, then Governor of Uganda, had sent off to Cambridge and whom she met at a World University Conference on East Africa in Oxford in 1954. As she described it, Mayanja 'gave a really horrifying speech in which he dropped carefully distilled poison, drop by drop' but she thought him an 'orator of great effect', and she invited him to tea, even if in the course of their discussion she accused him of being dishonest.[62]

There were other students, and also African political and other leaders whom she met, especially during the 1950s, and with whom she was able to debate in a way that commanded their respect. How far this engagement in 'the ordinary social relations with individual Africans' influenced and changed her perceptions of Africa is difficult to tell. Her own respect for the African students and leaders she came to know was clear. Some of them still invited her to enter into a world that had hitherto

been closed to her. Mekki Abbas certainly contributed to her understanding of the Sudan, as did J.M. Kariuki of Kenya. One is tempted to
see a contrast between her encounter with Clements Kadalie and South
African trade unionists in 1929 and that, nearly thirty-five years later, in
very different circumstances, with Kariuki, of whom she said: 'I had no
predisposition to like a "hard-core" ex-Mau Mau detainee yet I quickly
felt a liking for him.'[63] It had been a learning process.

Finally we have to bear in mind the international environment in which
she lived, and the changes it underwent in the thirty or so years from when
she began her career to when she retired. The 1930s saw the rise of Nazi
Germany, and the emergence of Stalinist Russia on to the world scene,
and of the very genuine fears on the part of people like Margery of a
threat to Western civilization as they understood it. In Oxford she could
not fail to be concerned, but also someone like Philip Mitchell (then
Governor of Uganda) in his correspondence to her linked the events of
Europe to the needs of colonialism and the obligations of trusteeship.
Interestingly, his justification in 1937 for transforming Makerere into a
university was 'to counter the fanaticisms of Nazi, Communist or Fascist
... and the dangers of the suppression of individual liberty, freedom of
speech'.[64] He believed that only education could prevent the destruction
of the British Empire: 'No conception of the trusteeship which we exercise on behalf of many millions of human beings in Africa,' he wrote to her
in 1937, 'can exclude an obligation to protect them from the new tribalism
which is destroying so great a part of the soul and mind of Europe'.[65] He
had also confronted her with questions raised by the Italian invasion of
Ethiopia. But Margery herself read Barnes' *Democracy and War* and
Leonard Woolf's *The Barbarians at the Gate.*[66]

The year 1939 brought the war and the 1940s further change, not least
with regard to the United States and its international role. The 1950s were
the Cold War era, and the height of African nationalism. The 1960s
brought decolonization and independence. Margery's four decades in
Oxford thus saw enormous changes in the international environment of
which she was deeply conscious, as her letters to *The Times* and her
broadcasts point out. Above all, the late 1930s ushered in a period of
remarkable change in British colonial policy.[67] By the late 1940s, with the
acceptance by both the Colonial Office and the influential critics, including Margery Perham, of a far more rapid advance towards self-government than had been envisaged pre-war, there developed a policy of
'social engineering' to prepare Africans to become members of a modern
state, culminating in the post-war years in political change and finally
independence. Margery was engaged in all this, actively so, as teacher,
scholar and publicist. She organized and attended conferences; she spoke

on varied public occasions; she lobbied, and she carried on an enormous private as well as public correspondence about colonial development. It is against that background of activity, as well as her African travels, that her ideas expanded after the war.

Perceptions of Change and Development

The years after 1945 saw Margery Perham emerge as a major advocate of greater recognition of Britain's continued obligations of trusteeship as well as rapid political change for the colonial territories. Whether or not her notion of Africa altered greatly is difficult to determine.

While her perceptions of change were sharpened over the years, the image of Africa that emerged from *The Colonial Reckoning* was in essence that formed by her early travels. It was of peoples caught up in rapid change, itself still the consequence of 'the great facts of history and geography that have exposed isolated and tribal Africa to the sudden, dislocating effects of twentieth-century civilization.'[68] Similarly her notion of development remained remarkably consistent. The direction of change would be towards 'the virtues of civilization'[69] and 'the best Western European experience' as she put it in 1957.[70] Africans would be drawn into the civilized world. She recognized the relationship between urbanization and change in African life, although in the 1930s she had been wrong about the pace at which it would take place. She took it for granted that development required the greater integration of African economies into the global capitalist system via the expansion of the commodity trade and peasant agriculture. These were the liberal ideas of development formed in the context of the 1920s and 1930s when economic development and popular welfare became linked for the first time. They remained central to her ideas of trusteeship even as she struggled for more rapid political advance after 1942. Where they changed, however, was with her greater awareness of the process of marginalization, and of the way metropolitan organizations 'acting at times in combination and exercising considerable control at once over export and import trade [took] private decisions in Britain which deeply affected the lives of colonial peoples.' By 1942 she deplored the way in which 'the welfare of the people often swings helplessly in the tide of world markets or is controlled by strong and remote commercial companies responsible only to themselves.'[71] Her concern at the exploitation underlying international commodity markets, the defects of economic *laissez-faire*, and 'the powerful economic forces [that] allowed their force and devastating impact upon native society' emerged more clearly; and finally she saw African poverty as 'that of a people struggling to tame their own difficult continent, without the knowledge, the organization, often the physique, for the task.'[72]

The third consistent element in her image of Africa was of societies divided between the vast mass and a growing educated class whom she saw assuming the life-styles of the West and demanding 'reform on British lines'.[73] From the time of her first travels in South Africa she saw those élites as remarkably independent in their response to colonial change; choosing what they would and would not accept in the way of new ideas, and with their growing influence seeping down into the larger society itself.[74] Hence in her view the importance of education, which came to take an increasingly large place in Margery Perham's concern for the future of Africa. If government was to be transferred to Africans, there must be enough Africans with not only the technical skills but also the liberal and humane ideals, to provide it with the good government that had formerly been supplied by the Colonial Service.

Where Margery's ideas most obviously developed was with regard to political development. She was concerned above all with the politics of change, and so far as the political consequences of colonial subordination were concerned she displayed a remarkable prescience on numerous occasions in her awareness of a 'smouldering' beneath the surface. Thus she reflected, in South Africa, on 'the opposition, one that can hardly be kept long within such moderate bounds, between the paternalism of the white, both in religion and politics, and the new self-assertion of the Bantu.'[75] In Nairobi in 1930, recording her impressions of the trial of Joseph Kangethe, which she attended, she made the comment:

> What was interesting was that behind us, in a silent bank, were the Kikuyu. Inside and at the doors they were massed, listening to every word, almost it seemed without breathing. It gave me a shiver of apprehension for the future. So they will go on watching, with ever-growing appreciation of the issues, and the Kangethes will multiply as they have in South Africa and the Kikuyu, nearly a million of them, sit at Nairobi's back door.[76]

This awareness, along with her concern for justice, undoubtedly pushed her to argue by 1942 for a more rapid pace of political advance; indeed, there were already indications of this position earlier. In this respect she clearly responded to the changing political environment within which colonial authorities operated in each successive decade, and which she saw through the eyes not only of colonial administrators but also of the new educated élites. She also began to see limits to institutional transfer, as decolonization itself began to draw to a close; compare for example two articles on the Westminster model in Africa: the first in 1949 extolled the virtues of parliamentary government in the Sudan, while the second in 1965 acknowledged 'how strange it was that anyone imagined the Westminster model could serve the new Africa'.[77]

In later life Margery was aware that her image of Africa was not that of a new generation of both scholars and African leaders, concerned to restore a positive image of earlier African civilizations, and to shift to centre stage a more radical tradition concerning the process of development. It is important therefore to bear in mind that the issues forced upon our attention by the radical thrusts of the under-development and Marxist positions were emerging, certainly in Oxford, only as she herself reached retirement. We ask very different questions today, and have a different understanding of the process of change under colonial rule. Margery, in later life, was conscious of the new approach, agreed with some of the altered perspectives but not all. Her image of Africa, from our current viewpoint, was no doubt inadequate. We must nevertheless recognize that she raised many of the issues and questions that continue to absorb us today.

NOTES

 1. Typescript of taped talk to students, October 1963, Perham Papers (hereafter PP), Rhodes House Library, Box 9, file 6, ff 30, 32.
 2. Kenneth Robinson, 'Experts, Colonialists and Africanists 1895–1960' in *Experts in Africa*, Proceedings of a Colloquium at the University of Aberdeen, edited by J.C. Stone (Aberdeen University African Studies Group, March 1980), p.74.
 3. See Roland Oliver, in his address at the Memorial Service, the University Church of St Mary's, Oxford, 18 May 1982.
 4. 'The Sudan', *The Times*, 7 June 1939; reprinted in Margery Perham, *Colonial Sequence 1930–1949* (London, 1967), (hereafter *Col. Seq. I*), p.183.
 5. Margery Perham, *East African Journey* (London, 1976), p.194.
 6. Margery Perham, *West African Passage*, ed. A.H.M. Kirk-Greene (London, 1983), p.141.
 7. Ibid., p.197.
 8. Ibid., p.156.
 9. Ibid., Chapters 6–9. One fact that emerges from the diaries is the frequency with which she seems to have fallen ill on those travels. Mitchell in 1938 told her that his concern for her health was the only reason why he had not put her name forward for the post of Principal of the new Makerere College.
10. Margery Perham, *African Apprenticeship* (London, 1974), p.88.
11. Perham, *West African Passage*, pp.118–19.
12. Ibid., 114.
13. Perham, *African Apprenticeship*, p.73.
14. Perham, *West African Passage*, p.95.
15. 'Britain's Role in a World of Racial Challenge', *Listener*, 3 June 1965.
16. Margery Perham, ed., *Ten Africans* (London, 1938).
17. Perham, *East African Journey*, p.32.
18. Perham, *African Apprenticeship*, p.144.

19. Perham, *West African Passage*, p.52.
20. Ibid., p.54.
21. Ibid., p.125.
22. See Margery Perham, *Native Administration in Nigeria* (London, 1937), Ch.XIV; and *The Times*, 30 Dec. 1932. See also Judith Van Allen, ' "Aba Riots" or Igbo ' "Women's War?", Ideology Stratification, and the Invisibility of Women', in Nancy J. Hafkin and Edna G. Bay, eds., *Women in Africa*, Studies in Social and Economic Change (Stanford, California, 1976).
23. Sudan/Kenya Diary, 1 April 1948, PP 53/2.
24. Perham, *West African Passage*, p.35.
25. PP 9/6, ff.29–30.
26. Perham, *East African Journey* , p.33.
27. Perham, *African Apprenticeship*, p.210.
28. Khartoum Diary, 29 Dec. 1937–9 Jan. 1938, PP 50/5.
29. Ibid.
30. Khartoum Diary, 2 March 1948, PP 53/2.
31. Kenya Diary, PP 53/2.
32. 'Nigeria Today', *The Times*, 30 Dec. 1932; reprinted in *Col. Seq. I*, p.63.
33. See Perham, *African Apprenticeship* e.g. pp.44–52, 146–52; Evidence to Makerere Commission, 5 Feb. 1937, PP 516/1, pp. 21–34; Khartoum Diary, 12 Jan. 1938, PP 53/2.
34. Uganda Diary, 14 April 1948, PP 53–2.
35. Perham, *West African Passage*, p.149; Perham, *Col. Seq. I*, xv.
36. Perham, *East African Journey*, p.63.
37. Ibid., p.186.
38. Perham, *West African Passage*, p.55.
39. Ibid.
40. 'A Prospect of Nigeria', *Listener*, 20 Oct. 1960, reprinted in Margery Perham, *Colonial Sequence 1949–1965* (London, 1970), (hereafter *Col. Seq. II*), p.215.
41. Perham, *West African Passage*, p.122.
42. Nuffield Seminar, PP 9/6, f.31.
43. Perham, *Ten Africans*, p.10.
44. Perham, *Col. Seq. I*, xv.
45. Perham, *African Apprenticeship*, p.240.
46. 'Rhodesia: A Search for Fundamentals', *Listener*, 16 June 1966, *Col. Seq. II*, p. 319.
47. 'Native Administration in Tanganyika', *Africa*, 4. 3 (1931), *Col. Seq. I*, p.33.
48. Ibid., p.32. And see her Introduction to Margery Perham and J. Simmons, eds., *African Discovery* (London, 1942), in which she seeks to redress past distorted views of Africa as a 'place of complete and anarchic savagery'.
49. Perham, *African Apprenticeship*, p.240.
50. Perham, *East African Journey*, p.143.
51. 'Nigeria Today', *The Times*, 29 Dec. 1932, *Col. Seq. I*, p. 61.
52. 'The Model Baganda', *The Times*, 25 Aug. 1938, *Col. Seq. I*, pp. 169–73. Cf., for example, Audrey Richards, *Economic Development and Tribal Change* (Cambridge, 1954).
53. David Goldsworthy, *Colonial Issues in British Politics 1945–61* (Oxford, 1971), p.56.
54. Perham, *African Apprenticeship*, p. 27.
55. Report of Visit to East Africa and Sudan, 1953, PP 54/4.
56. Sudan Diary 21 Feb.– 22 April 1948, 1 March, PP 53/2.
57. Perham, *African Apprenticeship*, p. 27.
58. D.N.Chester, Memorial Address, 18 May, 1982.
59. J.E. Flint, 'Macmillan as a Critic of Empire', in Hugh Macmillan and Shula Marks (eds.), *Africa and Empire* (London 1989), p.218.
60. See, e.g. PP 514/3 for Mitchell's correspondence, and PP 536/6 for Newbold's.
61. See Robert Heussler, *Yesterday's Rulers* (London, 1962), *passim*.
62. Perham to Keith Hancock, 15 March 1954, PP 514/6.
63. J.M. Kariuki, *Mau Mau Detainee* (London, 1963), p.xi.

64. Mitchell to Perham, PP 514/3.
65. Ibid.
66. Diary, Pond's Farm 1939, PP 50/9.
67. J.E. Flint, 'Macmillan as a Critic of Empire', pp. 229–30.
68. Foreword to O. Awolowo, *Path to Nigerian Freedom* (London, 1947), p.12, *Col. Seq. I*, p. 308.
69. 'Tanganyika Now', *The Times*, 5 Aug. 1937, *Col. Seq. I*, p.168.
70. 'Kenya after Mau Mau', *The Times*, 18 March 1957, *Col. Seq. II*, p.148.
71. 'The Colonial Empire', *The Times*, 14 March 1942, *Col. Seq. I*, p. 288.
72. 'Britain's Role in a World of Racial Challenge', *Listener*, 3 June 1965.
73. 'Nigeria Today', *The Times*, 30 Dec. 1932.
74. "A Changing Continent', *The Times*, 28 Oct. 1952, *Col. Seq. II*, p.68.
75. Perham, *African Apprenticeship*, p.72.
76. Perham, *East African Journey*, p.36.
77. 'Parliamentary Government in the Sudan', *The Times*, 20 June 1949, *Col. Seq. I*, p.329; 'Britain's Role in a World of Racial Challenge', *Listener*, 3 June 1965.

Margery Perham's Initiation into African Affairs

Deborah Lavin

Margery Perham's associates in African affairs in the 1930s were for the most part distinguished, a good deal older than she was, enlightened and established. Her earliest lectures reflect her interest in Buell's 'exciting' notion that Africa was one of the few regions of the world where the course of developments might be influenced by human reason. London teemed with groups studying Africa: the International Institute of African Languages and Cultures, Chatham House, the Royal Empire Society, the Royal African Society, the Conference of British Missionary Societies at Edinburgh House, the Colonial Empire Union section of the Overseas League, the London Group on African Affairs, the Imperial Institute's Africa Circle among others. She was in touch with many of them, with every opportunity to discuss the application of research to policy. Miss Perham moved between Oxford and Whitehall, Chatham House and Fleet Street. She was to become famous for taking the African standpoint against the settler view in East, Central and South Africa, and as the advocate of the form of African policy and development summed up in indirect native administration and economic development through African peasant production. She first studied this on the ground in East Africa: her ideas were most fully expounded after her visit to West Africa, which became the subject of her first major work. Yet South Africa and its problems shaped her outlook more than she was later prepared to acknowledge. One of the interesting features of her work in the 1930s is to see how she attempted to square the South and West African circles.

Yet her own commitment to the continent was also rooted in emotion, and this article will seek to bring out some of the strong emotional currents which gave direction and meaning to her ambitions. Her papers reflect the qualities she brought to the study and service of Africa – woman, academic, well-informed commentator and natural writer. These qualities were recognized and encouraged in the late 1920s and the 1930s by some of the key figures in London's Africa establishment as well as by prominent critics of African empire. Her enthusiasm for African research settled her future in ways she can hardly have imagined when she wrote *de profundis* in her 1927 diary of the bouts of despair that drove her to bed in a darkened room at St Hugh's College, Oxford. 'I have no religion and no principles .... Will anything else come? Shall I find a purpose, and some hope and happiness?' Three things only seemed to give her pleasure: strenuous physical exercise especially in mixed doubles at tennis, the dream of a natural physical life 'as some kind of nymph in perfect harmony against a natural background', and her work. 'Success comes with concentration – one idea, one branch of work, one unflagging effort ... Is it too late to begin – in ten years something might be achieved ....' 'It was not cold-blooded choice which sent Joan of Arc to Orleans or Lawrence to Arabia. No, but it sent Disraeli to Downing Street.' Restlessly, she thrust these away as, for all their gifts, 'essentially adventurers. I could not achieve such success nor in my soul relish it if I could.' Nevertheless there was still the yearning for a different life: 'my body longed', she wrote, 'to throw off the despotism of my brain.'[1] Even as she embarked on her first major research tour, she dreamed of being 'a happy spectator of life' in a house on the Cotswolds or the Berkshire Downs, recognizing 'I shan't get very far at this rate.'[2] In fact, the end of the next decade was to see her well advanced on the road to academic and public recognition.

The South African Starting Point

Margery Perham had travelled to Somaliland in 1921 and had observed the Permanent Mandates Commission in session in Geneva in 1927 and 1929. Under the auspices of Reginald Coupland, Beit Professor of Colonial History at Oxford and pioneer of the academic study of race, she lectured on 'British policy towards native races' in 1928 – bringing passion to her survey of the rise of the humanitarian spirit, the abolition of slavery, the South African, American and New Zealand race problems:

> Apart from being vast and complex, the subject is also hot with the heat of life; more than that it is a subject that unless carefully handled, becomes painful, dangerous, dealing as it does, with conflicts that cut at the root of men's material interests, their religious and social code, issues which have been and may still be very literally, of life and death.

It was South and Central Africa, she argued, that epitomised 'the native problem'. She challenged the assumption that because the African acquiesced in being 'the perfect unskilled labourer, strong and patient', it should follow 'that all blacks are capable only of labour' (a view she later, erroneously, attributed to the Round Table). She found no incongruity in commenting that 'the Hottentots are not a very attractive people' (adding 'reedy legged and pot-bellied'). Of Hertzog's policy of racial differentiation, whereby the black 'must not be Europeanised and industrialized but kept in the old framework – agricultural and communal – self-governing in his own areas by progressive stages and in harmony with his own tradition which has no affinity with the ballot box', she observed that it 'undoubtedly has a great deal to commend it'. This she qualified with appropriate scholarly doubt: was it unpopular with Africans? Was it practicable? Could it be said to conform to Article 22 of the Covenant of the League in preparing Africans in South Africa 'to take their stand in the strenuous conditions of the modern world'?[3] She amplified these thoughts the following year in four lectures on the Mandates system in which she juxtaposed, conventionally enough, 'Europe's need of Africa as a great farm and a great mine' with 'the danger which is caused by rooting people out of the background of centuries'.[4]

Oxford, then as now, was full of intellectual recruiting-sergeants and hidden persuaders. Margery Perham was recruited for Africa in the first place by the white Commonwealth idealists whose ideas she was later to oppose. She wrote of Lord Lothian, Secretary of the Rhodes Trust, 'It was due to his faith in me that my career was completely changed.' He came to see her early in 1929 when she applied to the Trust for one of the Travelling Fellowships designed to give Oxford dons experience of life in the overseas world so that they could be of more use to Rhodes Scholars. He struck her as 'tall, boyish of face, unlined by conflicts or intense thought' but 'fearless almost to unscrupulousness'. He seemed less keen to hear her plans than to impart his own views on the native problem: the influence of the Protestant woman at the root of all racial discrimination; the contribution of the white settler. She noted that he talked of native concubines quite openly, without apparently first testing her for shock. He advised her to begin in South Africa, and provided introductions. 'Without them I am blind and stupid, seeing only the outside of things.'[5] Thus armed, she travelled by way of America and the Pacific to South Africa. She collected Homeric amounts of information, assiduously recorded in notes gathered in compounds and docks, schools and Joint Councils, universities and meetings of the Industrial and Commerical Workers Union, in slums, mines, law courts, government departments and assemblies, as well as countless individual interviews.[6]

Ironically, her South African experiences were partly responsible for her enthusiasm for indirect rule. She debated the issue of settler versus African rights with Lothian from 1930, when he had sent her in South Africa a copy of Joseph Oldham's *White and Black in Africa*.[7] Lothian wrote of the inevitability and rapidity of African transformation and industrialisation and the need for safeguards, not to delay or curb the transformation but so that the African should benefit from the good and be protected from the implicit evils. Miss Perham replied some months later, having extended her tour to East Africa, with a lengthy piece of argument entitled 'Economics and Politics in Africa in the next 50 Years'. 'When I had read a few pages of Mr Oldham's book ... I shut it, as I saw my head was full of the same arguments ... and I thought it better to write this letter while independent of his influence.' She believed Lothian had exaggerated the effects of European assimilation. There would be more economic development if the African was kept on the land, with peasant production and the techniques of indirect rule to evolve modern African societies out of tribal societies. She was struck by the Council system in the rural Transkei and by the contrasting resistance to European assimilation in neighbouring Ciskei:

> Ciskei is the area where contact has been longest, and the inter-penetration most complete. Yet here, within a stone's throw of the rich European farm upon which he works, and his grandfather before him, the native lives in his little Rondeval, which is all but empty of the products of machinery, kills his land by overstocking it, acting on his traditional conception of cattle, while his wife is a 'red' heathen, and smears her face with clay.[8]

The essential conservatism of her approach was to become clear from her lecture to Oxford's Ralegh Club in 1933 where she argued that the success of indirect rule 'demands that a ring be put round native societies so that their integrity may be preserved and the ... development controlled'.[9] In a lecture to the Imperial Club later the same year she credited Hertzog with 'forcing the Union to face its native problem – curious term – in the most vital and practical way'. Segregation was a means of holding the ring – so long as it was seen as a temporary, special measure and did not 'degenerate into mere stagnation'. It would, she thought, 'help the tribal African through his transition period and to develop even on lines that compete with the European' before eventually he was admitted to citizenship on equal terms.[10] She came to reapply her South African experience to the Southern African Protectorates at the time of her debate with Lionel Curtis in 1935–6. While she accepted their eventual incorporation in South Africa as a proper goal, this should be only after an interim phase of indirect rule, and only when the Union's own black reserves were consolidated along the lines of the Transkeian Council system leading to a federation of Councils in which 'the Africans could do something to build up a genuine local government of their own and train themselves for effective partnership in such central Councils as may open out for the whole Union.'[11]

It was also in Southern Africa that the particular African sphere to which she was to devote herself had been revealed to her; when in 1929, from 'a sordid hotel with painted mirrors in Johannesburg' she looked back to an idyll of love on horseback on safari with an Assistant Commissioner in the mountains of Basutoland ('a dream, a beautiful dream – but a dream').[12] Here was another powerful influence upon her: the long romance with District Officers and other colonial officials. She absorbed their rule-of-thumb administrative beliefs and protective attitudes to tribal societies against the disintegrative effects of white settlement and industrialization which inspired her rationalization of indirect rule. In her review to Lothian at the end of her tour she told him that whereas in Kenya 'the air is distracted with politics', Uganda proved to be 'the turning point of my enquiry' which 'supplied the unexpected evidence that the native can receive civilisation and ... economic development ... without white settlement' and on the basis of his own institutions.

> All this is under the Colonial Office, through a system of indirect rule, with the assistance of mainly Mission Education. In political matters calm and confidence reign. The administration, with all its specialist officers, concentrates with a single mind upon native development ... the health and happiness of the peasant upon whose production the revenue depends, is the object of all policy, and to him, uninterrupted, undiminished, like Mrs Gaskell's circle of blessing, the revenue returns in services.[13]

Philip Mitchell, Native Secretary in Tanganyika, recognized her conservatism: 'The blessed word "native" and the horrible phrase "indirect rule" are more obstructive of logical thought than anything else,' he warned her in 1932. 'You are a sad offender yourself and would really in your heart much prefer an African dressed in skins and plumes, waving spears and generally "King Solomon's Mineral" – a sort of variety entertainment for tourists and an outlet for the romantic.'[14] In Tanganyika the governor, Cameron, had given her the support that enabled her to conduct her enquiries and had allowed her to tour with Mitchell to see a version of indirect rule working in practice. Like Mitchell, she believed Cameron to be a great man, though he shocked her by denying any debt to Lugard in his own version of indirect rule.[15]

She was to explain in her Ralegh Club lecture in 1933 why she accepted indirect rule as 'healthy' in a way that could not be matched by 'a half dozen technical departments imposing their unappreciated benefits from without'; it had become an article of faith.

> I believe in indirect rule . . . because there really is no other solution.
> . . . It works and works well (1) because of the amazing adaptability
> of the African which compensates equally for their difficulties and
> our mistakes. (2) because of the presence of men of sympathy,
> imagination and ability in the Col. service. I do not only believe in it
> but I believe enthusiastically, partly because, if we can carry it
> through well, we shall allow a healthier development in Africa than
> in India, building up from small historic units of local government
> towards larger and larger federations. . . . [16]

This was the essence of the Colonial Service strategy, based on the Indian
model, of using indirect rule to contain the threat of African nationalism,
just as the preservation of the indigenous basis of native authorities was a
pragmatic necessity adopted by a small number of British officials ruling
vast territories through existing traditional authorities. Similarly, her
idea of nation-building through the federating of traditional authorities
was a rationalization of the Colonial Service strategy of defending
colonial control against the emergence of a possible nationalism, as
Guggisberg's Provincial Councils had been designed to do in the Gold
Coast; or Maffey's Native Authorities in the Sudan, conceived as so many
aseptic glands against the spread of infection from Egyptian nationalism.

Widening Horizons: towards the *African Survey*

It was a remarkable achievement that despite her official connections
Margery Perham retained her sympathy for the African point of view
as she understood it. She returned to England early in 1931 convinced
that Africa stood in danger from 'half-informed generalisations and
decisions',[17] and determined 'now to get as far as I can towards an
understanding of the African',[18] perhaps by studying a single tribe. At this
point her attention was fixed on Kenya. Officials and unofficials among
what Mitchell called 'the Sahib-log' spoke the same language and had
attended the same schools; the government would have preserved more
detachment if the settler community had consisted of immigrant
Afrikaners. What was needed was 'intelligent imperialism': the officials
were conscientious, but generally more idealistic than instructed.

It was on the basis of their shared preoccupation with 'putting the
welfare of the native first' in Kenya that she first began her close cooperation with the veteran administrator Lord Lugard, and her association
with the missionary spokesman Joseph Oldham. 'I am a back number, old
enough I imagine to be your grandfather!' Lugard told her. 'I hope much

tor Africa from your enthusiasm – with youth, intellect and charm of person to help you.'[19] She agreed with Lugard and Oldham that the only way forward in Kenya would be to separate black and white areas, with separate budgets and administrations, but she argued for a Council representing all interests to legislate for central economic services.[20] Oldham thought hers 'much the best memo I have ever seen on the East African question'.[21] While working with Lugard she wrote for *The Times* a series of articles critical of Kenya policy.[22] Sir Edward Grigg, Governor of Kenya, complained to Lothian lest this denigration of the ideals of Rhodes and Milner redound unfavourably on the Rhodes Trust which had sponsored her; Lothian dismissed his protest as absurd.[23]

It was not only in the development of her practical views on native administration that Margery Perham was indebted to her South African initiation. The white Commonwealth idealists whom she came to oppose were also much involved in the ferment of intellectual enquiry, which embraced the whole range of African policies. Her more radical contemporary, the South African W.M. Macmillan, remarked in his autobiography that to his generation growing aware of African problems in the 1930s, there had been two sources of interest in England – the philanthropists and the ideological imperialists, and that it was a mistake to distinguish too sharply between them.

> Although latter-day students of history are inclined to class the missionary pressure-groups (who did indeed get some support from agnostic socialists) as left-wing and the ideological imperialists as right-wing, there seemed to be no such clear-cut division of emphasis when one was dealing with the glimmerings of light which came from either of their fires. The missionaries, mainly concerned to protect the weak against exploitation, could be reactionary, over-paternalistic and downright old-fashioned; the imperialists made some practical contribution towards progress through the introduction of technology and the colonial service. In a naive fashion, as it now seems, I tried to ride both horses. ... [24]

In her article for the *Round Table*'s Diamond Jubilee Number in 1970,[25] Margery Perham glossed over this important point. She had crossed swords with Lionel Curtis over the Southern African Protectorates, with Grigg in East Africa and Dougal Malcolm over Rhodesia, and she thought in terms of an unrelieved contrast between the defenders of African rights and those who aligned themselves with white settlers. The reality had been more complex. Curtis spanned two colonial worlds, and had she but known it he and Philip Kerr (Lothian) had as early as 1912 identified the race question as '*the* question'. In writing *The Problem of the Commonwealth*[26] (with which Miss Perham disagreed violently) Curtis had accepted advice to play down the race question in order to establish the idea of a federal Commonwealth. Miss Perham concluded – wrongly – that he had no interest in tropical Africa. Her heroes were the defenders of African rights, Lugard and Oldham, and she described how 'I flung myself into battle as a junior aide to Lugard and Oldham who were working for a Joint Select Committee [on Closer Union in East Africa]'.[27] She did not know, or had forgotten, that her mentors had begun their campaigns by relying on Curtis as an ally for his tactical advice and contacts, and that the idea of applying research to policy in Africa owed much to the work of Curtis as well as Oldham in the 1920s and 1930s.

Her links with Curtis went back as far as 1928 when she had been invited to join a Chatham House study group convened by Lugard and Oldham, and including Sir Humphrey Leggett and the educationalist Hanns Vischer, to debate the economic development of East Africa. Out of it had grown the idea of government-sponsored research in East Africa on the model of the Balfour committee for civil research in England, though the Kenyan budget was too small to run to a permanent research department and Mitchell always blamed Curtis and the Hailey Survey for pre-empting his own plans for African civil research in Tanganyika, in which he had hoped to involve Miss Perham on the political side. Oldham came to regard Lothian's and Curtis's view of African research as over-directed to economic development – the study of soils, products and economic possibilities. In 1929 Lothian and Curtis had followed up the Smuts lectures by returning to the theme of research into the African economic revolution. 'Africa is broken up into a number of territories none of which is financially able to undertake a thorough and comprehensive study of the native peoples,' Curtis wrote to the head of the Carnegie Corporation:

> We must learn what administrative activities, education, and physical science directed by government and private agencies can do to enable them to gain instead of lose by the changes which are being forced upon them. But there is in existence no instrument for gathering the information upon which such studies can be based, or for indicating to the government what information ought to be gathered for comparative purposes. To design such an instrument requires a couple of years' work ... [28]

This scheme, which had grown out of discussions at Rhodes House and a meeting at Chatham House chaired by Baldwin (and attended by the familiar Africa nexus of men like Lugard, Oldham, Lothian, Amery and Ormsby-Gore), had the added advantage to Curtis of improving Oxford's 'amateurish, unauthoritative and unorganised' approach to political science and the growing field of international relations: 'a University like Harvard has money to do this and sends out men like Buell to Africa ... whose results, sound or otherwise, are in fact influencing public policy; Oxford is doing nothing of the kind.'[29] However, in the event the big African research project was based at Chatham House in London, not in Oxford.

Miss Perham was considered with thirty or so others as a candidate to conduct the Survey. She was in distinguished company. Among the names suggested were civil servants (George Schuster, William Marris, Arnold Wilson), Americans (Jerome Greene, Whitney Shepardson), and some younger academics: Leakey, Firth, Roxby, Richard Pares, W.M. Macmillan, John Maud. Oldham put her name forward – 'She has proved that governors and political officers are ready to give her access to their files with a freedom they might not so willingly accord to a man. It will probably not be desirable that a report should be made under her own name since a certain number of people would discount its value if it were written by a woman'.[30] The study of Africa, like anthropology and imperial history, was to attract an unusually large professional interest from women, but recognition was hard won: Sir Malcolm Hailey was appointed to write the Survey. Nevertheless Miss Perham was a member of a consultative planning committee and played an important part in correcting Hailey's perspective by trying to persuade him to get to know West Africa first, as she regretted intellectually she had not done herself: 'I have always felt that a far truer perspective of Africa could be formed by starting on the West Coast.'[31] Hailey saw 'the root problem in Africa as the Bantu problem'.[32] At an informal conference with those already in the field (Lothian, Curtis, Julian Huxley, Lugard, Malcolm MacDonald, Macmillan, Maud, Oldham, Salter, Tomlinson of the Colonial Office and Ivison Macadam of Chatham House) it was agreed that he should call in research assistants to produce specialist volumes on particular questions arising from the contact of black and white. Macmillan was dismissed as being 'undiplomatic, personal and dogmatic' – 'had we given him the job we should have at once had against us the Union government in South Africa and all the settler elements in East Africa'.[33] Margery Perham was invited in his stead to 'Buellize' recent developments in the field of administration.

But while Miss Perham was thus becoming confirmed in her association with the establishment, she was determined that the view taken by the Survey should give due weight to the West African setting. In 1931–2 she had made her second African research journey, to Nigeria, and the plan of study she now proposed in connection with the Survey was not conceived as an answer to any 'Bantu problem'. Under the heading 'Native Administration in Tropical Africa', half of a seven-page draft was devoted to indirect rule in West Africa, Uganda and Tanganyika; one page to the problems of the Sudan, Nyasaland and Southern Africa; two lines to 'a brief comparative summary of French and Belgian methods'; the rest to 'general problems of native administration in Africa' including 'the anthropology of native administration' and 'the forces of assimilation'. The proposed final chapter – 'the future of native administration' – began with a seven-line summary on indirect rule and ended with the notes: 'Native administration as a training for self-government. This end implicit in our Imperial traditions'.[34] The book was never written as planned. The Nigerian chapter was expanded into *Native Administration in Nigeria* (Oxford, 1937), a classic exposition of indirect rule which drew plaudits from Colonial Service giants like Cameron, Bourdillon and Syme and cogent criticism from the ex-Nigerian district officer, Walter Crocker: 'There cannot be a Governor or Secretary or Head of a Department who would not be gratified by your book. This seems to me a very severe indictment.'[35]

Her West African journeyings revealed that her personal adaptation to Africa had its own hazards. She embarked on an anthropology course in 1932 to explain not only Africa but herself. 'You are not to go and study under Malinowski,' Philip Mitchell advised, 'he has a destructive Polish mind – very brilliant and wide; but he will leave you incapable of believing in anything.'[36] Not all her correspondents were as disinterested in their advice as they were assiduous in supplying the official administrative material on which her research depended. One letter from Nigeria read: 'I wish your adopted mission in life, though I would not have it different, were not so tiresomely incompatible with filling your natural mission in life.'[37] Sir Edward Grigg had found it difficult to 'conduct long safaris in the company of a young woman'; something of her isolation appears in a note to Walter Crocker: 'You don't realise how few oases there are in the desert I am travelling. Indeed, I think one has to travel alone before one realises that human relationships are the only things that matter ... '[38] In months of illness and introspection in late 1932 on her return to England her activities seemed no more than 'the buzzing of a fly against a window pane' and love (like religion) only a temporary palliative. Henceforth she would 'expect no more of what I have hitherto meant by happiness'; the study would be her sanctum. But the self-doubt probably never left her. This fragmentary diary runs for twenty years, ending in 1951. She took it up again in 1938, writing, 'I have only one plane. My work is my philosophy, my religion, my whole life.' But the challenging philosophy of a friend left her at sea, adrift on historical and philosophic uncertainties about the relation of philanthropy and imperialism. By instinct and upbringing she felt herself aligned with the philanthropists, but she now began to suspect that individuals and communities did more for themselves 'under the goad of oppression than in the managing, almost suffocating grip of altruism'. 'I am a play-actor, with sex at war with a cautious ambition, with an intellect harnessed to an emotional yet practical philanthropy ... used as a form of self-expression,' she wrote.[39]

Public Recognition and Debate

Despite her doubts, Margery Perham was by the mid-1930s making her name in a number of interlocking Africa circles. The Rhodes Visiting Fellowship had come to an end, but support with funds for her researches was forthcoming from the International Institute of African Languages and Cultures, underwritten by the Rockefeller Foundation and dedicated to furthering what Oldham called 'the almost sacred subject of anthropology'. At the Imperial Institute she joined Lugard, Oldham, Leonard Barnes, E.W. Bovill, Leggett, Ormsby-Gore and others in studying papers on native agriculture, the case for native cooperatives and statistics produced from Chatham House by I.M. Judd. She was in demand from groups studying slavery, the colonial question, Abyssinia, Bechuanaland, native taxation, peaceful change in Africa. In 1934 she publicly opposed the transfer of the High Commission Territories to the Union of South Africa. She joined the London Group on African Affairs, formed to assist the work of the Joint Councils of Europeans and Africans in their protest to the Secretary of State for the Dominions against the transfer. From the London Group sprang the Friends of Africa; at one time it seemed likely that, with W.M. Macmillan, she would throw herself into working with more radical political movements in company with Winifred Holtby, William and Margaret Ballinger, MacGregor Ross, Leonard Barnes, Malinowski and Arthur Creech Jones.

She had moved to defend the High Commission territories, for which in any case she had a special personal affection, after Tshekedi Khama brought Bechuanaland into the news in late 1933. She remembered his welcome to her on her first trip to Serowe – 'small and lithe, resolute and intelligent';[40] he became the first African whom she knew on terms of personal friendship. Once Hertzog had requested their transfer, Margery Perham's stand on the Protectorates epitomised the contradictions inherent in liberalism and humanitarianism, and the squaring of the West and Southern African circles. To begin with she accepted that the Union would be the 'ultimate legatee', but thought that in the meantime the Protectorates would provide a point of contact between Britain and

South Africa and should at least be handed over as going concerns. The application of indirect rule might facilitate 'an administrative and psychological break from the past', even provide 'a great opportunity to contribute to the solution of South Africa's major problem'.[41] She drew up 'Notes upon a programme of reform for the South African Protectorates'[42] on unimpeachably West African lines, with training and newly defined powers for the chiefs, more scope for commoners in tribal institutions, native treasuries; South African Rhodes Scholars were to be drafted in as political officers. Many of those objecting to transfer would have dissociated themselves from the terms of her enthusiasm for the 'magnificent material' for indirect rule 'in these people in their unbroken pride and tribal patriotism'.[43]

Nevertheless, she carried the war into the columns of *The Times* so effectively that Lionel Curtis suggested that 'as an expert on native affairs and one to whom governments will listen' she should publish her views together with his as a contribution to the debate.[44] He had returned to South Africa in 1935 and had been convinced that the Fusion government of Hertzog and Smuts epitomised the true spirit of conciliation and equal rights of the Union of 1910. He supported transfer of the Protectorates, arguing that the territories were stagnating (a scandalous and, he thought, characteristic example of official neglect); that in a new era of South African reform, unless the reformers received the recognition due to them as an independent Dominion by the transfer of the territories promised in 1910, the hard-line followers of Malan would in the long run prejudice both native interests and British-South African relations.

In their collaboration over *The Protectorates of South Africa*[45] confrontation was conducted politely, in terms of mutual goodwill. 'I cannot forget the charm and generosity he showed in our relationship,' Margery Perham recalled.[46] 'I was especially touched by your personal references to myself,' Curtis wrote.[47] 'The book will stand as a confutation of Kipling's saying that "the female of the species is more deadly than the male". Your reference to George Eliot surprised and delighted me. I thought that your generation never opened those Victorian pages.' The old brigade swung in behind Miss Perham. Lugard worked on the House of Lords; Oldham offered to bring in the Archbishop of Canterbury and talked to Geoffrey Dawson; Coupland advised on tactics ('I have had a long talk with Curtis. I know him of old, and the symptoms are unmistakable. *Nothing* will now change his mind. He is launched on his crusade . . . . His main immediate move is a Joint Committee of both Houses . . . . This is satisfactory as far as it goes. It entails full publicity, no secret wire pulling, and the airing of all opinions').[48] Her campaign brought her wide recognition. She saw Hertzog and wrote to J.H. Thomas; she advised Sir

William Clark, the High Commissioner, on policy, and after the Hertzog-Thomas Agreement she was supplied with material for further *Times* articles by Clark and the officials of the Dominions Office.[49] The debate with Curtis evoked much curiosity and interest: Curtis was asked at an Oxford party who had won and was heard to reply, 'O well it was the kind of race where everybody gets a prize!'[50] But the general verdict went decisively in her favour. Dawson wrote to say that she had wiped the floor with him.[51] Crocker wrote, 'I am sorry you had to rip up dear old Lionel like that, but you did it in as gentle a way as possible';[52] her success was noted in *West Africa* ('It is no light matter to differ from Mr Curtis')[53] and the *Spectator* commented that she was 'in no sense *impar congressa Achilli*'.[54] Congratulations flowed in from African circles – John Harris and Charles Buxton, Julius Lewin and W.M. Macmillan. The most uninhibited tribute came from an Oxford colleague: 'Well done, Marjee. I'm so glad you sloshed that Curtis creature. I should think you have considerably loosened his underpinnings.'[55]

In 1937 Miss Perham, visiting East Africa, was able to become an observer of the De la Warr Commission on Higher Education and gave evidence about Mitchell's cherished university project, Makerere. The following year Mitchell even floated the idea that she might be appointed Principal of the new African university college, but dropped this on hearing that she had been invited to assist in the foundation of Nuffield College where Oxford academic research was to issue in policy-making. This would give her, Mitchell urged, 'an active and effective part at the centre of a movement which has as its real – if unavowed – object no less than the rediscovery of the spirit and faith of those who established the system we call the Empire . . . .' Here at last was the chance to break down 'the outworn, timid flat-foot bureaucracy'. 'There is not likely to be for a generation an opportunity like the present,' Mitchell continued: 'The Hailey Report, the Nuffield foundation . . . . You are in a very special sense the key to all this . . . . The Oxford work is really exciting if it can be got going; through it you might get the CO pulled together one day and completely recast and all sorts of things might be done.'[56]

The letter was a positive stimulus encouraging her to seize the moment to promote 'intelligent imperialism': she had taken to heart Hailey's observation that in Africa, unlike India, there was no fundamental study of the principles upon which administration was being built up. She had always valued research free from what she called 'the embarrassment of officialdom', and had looked for more focusing of public attention on Africa, for 'still more contact between the theorist and the practical man, still more influence of opinion upon the Colonial Office'. She espoused both research and reform. She did not, however, become drawn into the

London protest lobby although she was in touch with the London Group over their opposition to the Morris Carter Commission on land in Kenya and over the Southern Rhodesian Bills of 1936, and she opposed amalgamation of the Zambesian territories in evidence to the Bledisloe Commission on the familiar grounds that 'white settlement injures the present interests and future prospects of African peoples'.[57] But she could not share the protesters' doubts about the doctrine of indirect rule. Lugard had perhaps laid on her a heavier burden than he knew when after the death of his wife he acknowledged Miss Perham as 'the inspiration which has helped and encouraged me',[58] and wrote in 1937: 'There is real satisfaction in feeling that I hand over to you the torch which I received from [Sir John Kirk] and that it will be in hands so much more capable than mine.'[59] She had become an established figure on research committees and commissions concerned with the application of research to social and educational policy in Africa. But Norman Leys considered research a mere alibi for inactivity on reform, while Macmillan thought her predilection for fact-finding 'had a blurring effect' on the report of the sub-committee of the Committee on Education in the Colonies dealing with the education of women and girls.[60] Like other radical critics of empire, he suspected that indirect rule 'was a device for driving advancing Africans back into the tribal life from which they were escaping'.[61]

His suspicions were justified: Miss Perham, though she had portrayed some westernized individuals in *Ten Africans*,[62] did not find it easy to fit educated Africans into indirect rule. She admitted from 1930 onwards that they would have to be given equal citizenship with Europeans, in South Africa as elsewhere, and that it would be difficult to assimilate them into their traditional local societies. Nevertheless, her faith in the adaptability of African institutions was such that she continued to expect the African editor, lawyer and clerk to go back to his rural homeland to serve the development of his own community and to energize local native administrations. In her Ralegh Club talk she claimed that the educated African had to be saved from 'a life of predatory individualism'. 'I believe he will go back not to live in a barren and frustrating exile in no man's land as a lawyer or a politician, but to the service of his own people.' Indirect rule, she asserted, 'is *assimilation from within*'. But when she met Dr Azikiwe the following year she wrote to Oldham: 'I deeply regret that he is already somewhat embittered. What is to be done with such a man – above all things in Ibo country? He will indeed be a pike among the minnows.'[63]

Yet her early South African experiences had given her some perceptions far ahead of her time. Roland Oliver has rightly pointed out that what he calls 'the "first" Miss Perham mounted no campaign to include the educated Africans into colonial government'. He quotes 'the most amazingly prophetic piece' written by the second Miss Perham in 1954: 'Independence cannot be given but must be taken. It has to be demanded, and demanded by more than the first half-dozen lawyers or journalists.'[64] However, as far back as 1930 she had already argued that in South Africa at least the process of political self-assertion could not be halted. She had written to Lothian: 'It is too late to turn back: ... the half educated units are there; we must go on educating them, and if we are making Editors of anti-European newspapers, secretaries of black trade unions and the like, we must still go on, for we have lost the time when it lay with us to give and reached that when it is for them to take.'[65] This was a path to independence which, at this time, she was hoping that the British colonies could avoid by the development of federations of traditional native authorities. The educated African, however, was not content to remain integrated in his rural community; the outcome of the indirect rule doctrine was the British West African nationalists who had been alienated by it. Margery Perham had glimpsed this in her Ralegh lecture: 'while we have borne the heat and burden of the day and been, I strongly believe, the best administrators of primitive peoples we shall lose our grip during the period of assimilation and the leadership and the rewards will fall to the [assimilating French] who have been bad administrators [of primitive peoples].' She was right, though she did not then draw the correct inferences from her own insights. French colonial practice assimilated educated Africans into central administration and retained their cooperation, whereas the indirect-ruling British had excluded them to hold the ring for the African rural communities to adapt, and so lost their enthusiastic cooperation.

The End of the Decade

In 1939 Margery Perham was among the pundits on Africa – including Hailey, Coupland, Lugard, and W.K. Hancock – whom Malcolm MacDonald assembled to ask how indirect rule was contributing to the development of democratic parliamentary government in the African territories. Miss Perham argued that the tribes represented 'reality' as opposed to the 'artificial' state system imposed from above. Her proposed remedy was to speed up the political education of the native authorities 'to head off the intelligentsia from the state system'.[66]

Within the ten years she had set herself in 1927, Margery Perham had achieved acknowledgement and recognition. She was accepted in London's Africa circles – academic, administrative, journalistic, philanthropic, reforming. She had been fortunate, perhaps, in her patrons, but she had maintained views independent of them. She was a recognized authority in the field of colonial administration, a silver medallist of the Royal African Society, called on to advise at the highest level. Lugard wrote to her in 1939: 'The influence of an exceptionally charming and attractive woman is very real, and when this is combined with an outstanding brain – an almost unique combination – the effect is wonderful.'[67] She fully reciprocated the devotion with which Lugard and the indirect rulers had accepted her into the official and professional African circles where she felt most at home: indirect rule became for her a morality, embodying the essential African point of view. But if it is true that 'a second Margery Perham' was later to embrace westernization as a reality, it is likely that the analysis of Lothian and the white Commonwealth men stressing the need for economic change in Africa played an essential, though largely unacknowledged, part in her conversion.

NOTES

1. Private diary, 29 July, 1 August 1927: Diary 1927–30, 'College, Rhodes Trust, Basutoland', Perham Papers (hereafter PP) Rhodes House Library, Box 34 file 6.
2. Private diary, 25 June 1929, PP 34/6.
3. Introduction to lectures on 'British policy and the native races', 1928, PP 227/11.
4. Lectures on 'The Mandates system', 1929, PP 228/5.
5. Private diary, 25 Jan. 1929, PP 34/6.
6. South African notebooks, 1929–30, PP 80–86.
7. J.H. Oldham, *White and Black in Africa: a critical examination of the Rhodes Lectures of General Smuts* (London, 1930).
8. Lothian to Perham, personal, 11 Feb. 1930 and Perham, 'Economics and politics in Africa in the next 50 years', PP 9/5.
9. Notes for a lecture to the Ralegh Club, 5 March 1933, PP 229/3, f 11.
10. 'The two main political problems of Africa', Notes for a lecture to the Imperial Club, 18 Nov. 1933, PP 229/6, f 11.
11. Discussion on native administration in South Africa, Nov. 1935, PP 229/10, ff 21–2.
12. Private diary, 22, 26 Dec. 1929. PP 34/6.
13. 'Economics and politics in Africa', PP 9/5, pp.11–12.
14. Mitchell to Perham, 20 Nov. 1932, PP 491/2.
15. See e.g. Margery Perham, *East African Journey* (London, 1976), p.209.
16. See note 9, ff 20–1.
17. Perham to Lothian, 13 May 1931, PP 9/1.
18. Perham to Oldham, 29 Oct. 1931, PP 9/1.
19. Lugard to Perham, 13 June 1931, PP 22/1.
20. Perham to Oldham, 17 May 1931, Oldham Papers (Rhodes House Library) 5/8.
21. Oldham to Perham, 20 May 1931, loc. cit.
22. 'The future of East Africa', *The Times*, 13, 14, 15 Aug., and (leading article) 16 Aug. 1931, reprinted Margery Perham, *Colonial Sequence* (London, 1967), pp.35–52.
23. Grigg to Secretary of the Rhodes Trust, 14 Sept. 1931, and Lothian note, PP 9/1.
24. W.M. Macmillan, *My South African Years* (Cape Town, 1975), p.196.
25. Dame Margery Perham, 'The Round Table and Sub-Saharan Africa', *The Round Table*, Diamond Jubilee number, 1970, pp.543–55. See also PP 329/11.

26. L. G. Curtis, *The Problem of the Commonwealth* (London, 1916).
27. Perham, 'The Round Table and Sub-Saharan Africa', p.549.
28. Curtis to Keppel, 20 July 1931, MSS Lothian GD40/17/121.
29. Curtis to Feetham, 14 Oct. 1930, MSS Curtis 3; see R.L. Buell, *The Native Problem in Africa* (New York, 1928).
30. Oldham to Lothian, 8 May 1933, Oldham Papers 2/5.
31. Perham to Oldham, 23 Oct. 1934, Oldham Papers 1/2.
32. Notes of an informal discussion which took place at Blickling Hall, Norfolk, on Saturday and Sunday 15 and 16 July 1933, MSS Lothian GD40/17/122.
33. Curtis to Carr-Saunders, 29 June 1933, Lothian papers GD40/17/122.
34. Draft plan of proposed book 'Native Administration in British Tropical Africa', PP 329/2.
35. Crocker to Perham, n.d. [1937], PP 287/4.
36. Mitchell to Perham, 14 Feb. 1932, PP 491/2.
37. Hunt to Perham, 2 July 1932, PP 395/4.
38. Perham to Crocker [n.d.], PP 26/4. This note refers to one from Crocker in 395/2.
39. Private diary 1932–51, *passim*, PP 33/4.
40. Paper on Bechuanaland [n.d.], PP 377/2.
41. Perham, 'Note on Pim Reports', 11 June 1934, PP 285/3.
42. Perham, 'Notes upon a programme of reform for the South African Protectorates', 1934, PP 382/2.
43. Annotation by Perham on Pim to Perham, 2 July 1934, PP 381/1.
44. Curtis to Perham, 30 April and 4 May 1935, PP 285/2. The Perham articles were published in *The Times*, 5 and 6 July 1934, and 13, 14, 15 and 16 May 1935, together with leading articles on 10 November 1934 and 11 April 1935.
45. M. Perham, and L. Curtis, *The Protectorates of South Africa* (Oxford, 1935).
46. Perham, 'The Round Table and Sub-Saharan Africa', p.552.
47. Curtis to Perham, 15 May 1935, PP 285/2.
48. Coupland to Perham, 26 April 1935, PP 382/4.
49. Clark to Perham, 21 July 1938, PP 383/1.
50. B. Gwyer to Perham, 1 June 1935, PP 382/4.
51. Dawson to Perham, 16 May 1935, PP 382/4.
52. Crocker to Perham, 21 May 1935, PP 382/4.
53. *West Africa*, 25 May 1935.
54. *Spectator*, 14 February 1936.
55. Correspondence on the transfer of the Protectorates, 1934–7, PP 382/4.
56. Mitchell to Perham, 31 Oct., 1 Dec. 1938, PP 514/3.
57. 'Draft memorandum on the effect of white settlement on Africa, written at the time of Bledisloe, c.1938', PP 606/1.
58. Draft dedication for a new edition of *The Dual Mandate in British Tropical Africa*, 1935, PP 317/1.
59. Lugard to Perham, 5 Dec. 1937, PP 22/2.
60. M. Macmillan, *Champion of Africa: W.M. Macmillan, the second phase* (Long Wittenham, 1985), p.135.
61. Ibid., p.136.
62. Margery Perham, ed. *Ten Africans* (London, 1936).
63. Perham to Oldham, 23 Oct. 1934, Oldham Papers 1/2.
64. See above, p. 25
65. 'Economics and politics in Africa', p.9, PP 9/5.
66. 'Future policy in Africa', report of meeting at the Carlton Hotel, 6 Oct. 1939, PP 685/2.
67. Lugard to Perham, 16 Jan. 1939, PP 22/2.

Forging a Relationship with the Colonial Administrative Service, 1921–1939

Anthony Kirk-Greene

Even in a society where male predominance was general, the British Colonial Service was unusual in the degree to which it embodied masculine values. This is apparent both in the many reminiscences of empire published in the past twenty years,[1] and in the more academic studies (as yet fewer) of gender and office within the hierarchy of imperial bureaucracy.[2] It was marginally affected by the contribution of women in certain limited capacities, as in nursing and education, and by the appointment, at the very end of the colonial period, of a small number of Women Administrative Officers.[3] To quote Helen Callaway, the service was 'a male institution in all its aspects: its masculine ideology, its military organization and processes, its rituals of power and hierarchy, its strong boundaries between the sexes'.[4] Yet for many years, from the publication of her first major academic book in 1937 to her retirement and the closing down of the Colonial Office in the mid-1960s, one woman was more widely known to members of the Colonial Service, across the Empire but above all in Africa, than any single colonial governor – with the possible exception of Lord Lugard. This was Margery Perham. It was perhaps her major personal achievement in a many-sided career.

The modern Colonial Service can be credited with a putative family of honorary relatives. Sir Ralph Furse (1887–1973), in his long-serving and influential role at the Colonial Office, first as Private Secretary (Appointments) in 1910 and finally as Director of Recruitment from 1931 to 1948, is generally acknowledged as its father. There is also a case for looking on Joseph Chamberlain (Secretary of State for the Colonies 1895–1903) as its grandfather – he it was who had called for the first and far-reaching enquiry into the structure and conditions of the Colonial Service. Two men might qualify for recognition as its uncles: Charles Jeffries, long associated with the Personnel Division of the Colonial Office; and Leo Amery, who as Colonial Secretary between 1924 and 1929 pushed through the unification of the diverse territorial services[5] and initiated the setting up of the committee responsible for the

1930 Warren Fisher report on recruitment,[6] – 'the Magna Carta of the modern colonial service'.[7] In its final years Alan Lennox-Boyd could be regarded as its godfather: in the decolonizing 1950s and later, he did much to maintain morale by securing compensation terms for premature termination of career and setting up resettlement programmes for members of the Colonial Service as they were overtaken by rapid localization and independence, first as Secretary of State for the Colonies and then as President of both the Overseas Service Resettlement Bureau and the Overseas Pensioners Association. Within such an honorary kinship group Margery Perham must be cast in the role of godmother to the Service during the last thirty years of colonial rule.

The earning of such a reputation was the product of many years of intensive study of the practical working of British colonial administration, of identifying its weaknesses and proposing means for its improvement. The purpose of this article is limited to exploring the essentially personal aspects of how she won the admiration and affection of the Colonial Administrative Service; how in the years before the Second World War she got to know individually, and often closely, so many of its members, as frequently Assistant District Officers in the bush and Provincial Commissioners in the boma (government station) as the incumbents of Government House; how this generated in them the belief that they knew her well and the faith that she, at least, recognized the worth of what they were doing and the dedication with which they did it; and how this honorary status as godmother to the Colonial Service enabled her to do so much in Britain for its betterment in terms of training and performance, recognition and reward.

This account is also limited in time. Margery Perham's career, insofar as it was concerned with the Colonial Service, falls into two substantial and more or less equal parts, each marked by a major innovation in which she was closely involved. It is with the first phase, which spans almost exactly the inter-war period, that the present paper is concerned. It starts with her pioneering venture to British Somaliland in 1921, and closes with the organizing of the two inaugural Summer Schools on colonial administration held at Oxford University on the eve of the Second World War. The second phase opens in 1943 with her close cooperation with Sir Ralph Furse at the Colonial Office and with Sir Douglas Veale, Registrar of Oxford University, in preparing a memorandum whose recommendations were to inspire and shape the government's new ideas and plans for the recruitment and training of the Colonial Service in the post-war world. This was drafted for the Devonshire Committee, and resulted in the reformed 'Devonshire Courses' which began to operate in 1946.[8] It closes with her retirement in 1963 and, during the early 1960s, with three retrospective contributions: her BBC Reith Lectures on the end of Britain's African empire in 1961; the encouragement of her American pupil, Robert Heussler, whose *Yesterday's Rulers* (1963) discusses Oxford's contribution to the making of the British Colonial Service between 1920 and 1945, telling much about Perham, Furse and Veale;[9] and her initiative, along with others, in founding the Oxford Colonial Records Project (at first under the direction of J.J. Tawney, a former District Commissioner), which over nearly twenty years did sterling work in collecting and preserving the personal papers of colonial administrative officers.

Each twenty-year period is also characterized by an outstanding publication, which furthered her claims to be recognized as first *a* (for Lord Lugard died only in 1945 and Lord Hailey in 1969) and then *the* British authority on African administration. Each reflected her thinking about the Colonial Service. One was *Native Administration in Nigeria*, published in 1937 and for subsequent generations of colonial probationers at Oxford, Cambridge and London the preferred standard text over Lugard's *The Dual Mandate in British Tropical Africa* (1922, 4th ed. 1929) and his *Political Memoranda: revisions of instructions to political officers on subjects chiefly political and administrative* (1906, 1919). The other was the second volume of her life of Lord Lugard, *The Years of Authority*, which appeared in 1960. In each instance, it was impossible to separate the name of Margery Perham from an intimate understanding of colonial administration and its politico-executive Colonial Service. It was a career to which she had brought 'the historical scholarship which set the contemporary problems of African government in the wider context of the history of British imperialism throughout the world' to, *inter alia*, her teaching of cohorts of colonial administrators, 'whose work has always been close to her interests and to whose training in the academic disciplines relevant to their tasks so much of her life has been devoted'.[10] Her status was publicly confirmed first by Oxford University's creation of a Readership in Colonial Administration for her in 1939, and finally by the British government's recommendation to the sovereign in 1965 to honour her by investing her with that distinctively Colonial Service award of membership in the order of chivalry of St Michael and St George (DCMG), whose Chancery resided in the Colonial Office.

Somaliland Beginnings

In 1911, Margery Perham's elder sister Ethel set the seal on a shipboard romance of the previous year, while sailing to Mombasa to undertake mission work in East Africa, by marrying a New Zealand cotton planter settled in Jubaland, in the East Africa Protectorate. Major Harry Rayne had served with the New Zealand contingent in the Boer War and had been political officer on the Nandi expedition of 1905, where he had been mentioned in despatches. It was in 1911 or 1912 that Margery first met her brother-in-law, who was to be influential in beginning her life-long interest in the Colonial Service. At the end of the First World War, like so many young British officers who had successfully held commissioned rank over African troops,[11] Rayne was the kind of man the Colonial Office was looking for. He was appointed a District Commissioner in Somaliland; and described his experiences there in a book subtitled 'Leaves from the Note-Book of a District Commissioner'.[12]

Whether it was the excitement of seeing Africa, the magnet of being with her sister, or the thrill of travelling up-country with one of Britain's stereotype 'lone DCs', there is little doubt that Margery's visit to stay with her married sister in Hargeisa in 1921–22 proved not only, in her own words fifty years later, to be 'The Time of My Life', but also a genuine turning point in that life. How right she had been when, following a breakdown of health at Sheffield University while teaching ex-servicemen undergraduates, many of them restless and poorly qualified academically, she had dismissed her mother's suggestion of a protracted convalescence in Switzerland or the Lake District and opted instead for recuperation in the remoteness of British Somaliland.[13]

Not only was this the beginning of Margery Perham's fifty-year love affair with Africa, it was also the origin and inspiration for her lifelong interest in colonial administration and her growing familiarity with its practitioners, the District Officers. Two years later, after being appointed to a tutorial fellowship at St Hugh's College, Oxford, her research and the new course of lectures she designed in the mid-1920s were centred on colonial administration, first of the Indians by Sir William Johnson in eighteenth-century North America and then, in 1928–29, by other imperialist powers in exercising their responsibilities under the League of Nations mandates, including the USA and New Zealand in the two Samoas.[14]

But it was in fiction, however thinly disguised, and not in the typical academic study, that Margery Perham poured out her perceptions and enthusiasms about the British Colonial Service as she first encountered it. As she reminisced years later, 'there was no routine of the D.Phil. in those days ... no one to tell me how to use my knowledge of the nature and problems of Somaliland ... so, needing an outlet for my deeply felt impression, I wrote a novel'.[15] *Major Dane's Garden* was published in 1925,[16] amid tributes, for instance, to the 'soundly written, vivid and convincing [story], obviously by a man [sic] who knows intimately the

land of which he writes'. At least one American reviewer got it right
when, despite his Philadelphia colleague's titillating headline of 'Honor
Triumphs Over Sordid Passion', he concluded that here was a story which
'deserves the extensive reading it will never receive'.[17] *Major Dane's
Garden* presents Margery's sensitive portrayal of the classic Colonial
Service clash between the two contrasting temperaments which bedevil
so many a situation of hierarchic leadership, the ruthlessly ambitious
careerist and the more humanitarian subordinate. In this case, it is the
conflict between Colonel Cavell and Major Dane; in between, a 'weak'
Governor ('intelligent ... a thruster ... unsure')[18] and a lightweight
Colonial Secretary ('one of those men who cultivate a well-bred bois-
terousness of manner ... a godsend at a chilly dinner-party ... a sure way
with women, whom he called "dear ladies"').[19] Margery Perham, of
course, is on Dane's side. She leaves us in no doubt about her approval
both of his mind, which was constantly active, and also of his self-control:
'altogether a weather-beaten but reflective person, who looked as though
he knew how to keep silence'.[20] Naturally – for is this not a novel? – Dane
falls in love with the young wife of the man-of-action Cavell, and it is into
Rhona's mouth that Margery Perham puts her belief, already forming, in
those complementary and indivisible aspects of what, forty years later,
she was to sum up as 'the civilizing qualities of the ideal DC'.[21] Rhona is
passing the same fundamental judgement when she tells Major Dane:

> You can do for [this country] what no other man can do. You
> understand its people – don't pretend to me that for all their
> wildness, you don't love them. You are a first-class administrator.
> You can fight for this country; but that's not all. You can water it
> and plant it. That's why it has your allegiance, an allegiance you can
> never take back.[22]

Few Colonial Service readers will follow the clash of personalities in
Major Dane's Garden without recognizing and assigning their own cast of
real-life colonial characters.

Getting to Know the Colonial Administrator in the Field

If Margery Perham's 1920s perceptions of the District Officer and his
superiors are to be found in fiction, the empirical evidence of her continuing interest in the facts is abundant throughout the 1930s. For this is the
decade when, with characteristic resolution, she decided to explore for
herself on the ground some of the topics she had been working on at
Oxford during the years since her return from Somaliland. To undertake
the study of colonial administration meant above all to get to know the

colonial administrators inside out and, just as important, from top to bottom.

The opportunity for this came when, in 1929, she was awarded a Rhodes Trust Travelling Fellowship, with the aim of studying 'the colour question' and 'British Native Policy'. She was helped in her preparations by the Secretary of the Trust, Philip Kerr (later Lord Lothian) with appointments to meet the experts at home (Lord Lugard, Sir Donald Cameron, Dr J.H. Oldham, Professor W.M. Macmillan)[23] and introductions to those abroad. Although she had seen only a handful of Colonial Service officers in action, she had been studying and lecturing on the subject, and reading the Mandates Commission's reports. Her tour took her from America to the Pacific, and thence to Africa. In Western Samoa she had little hesitation in condemning the inferior quality of middle-ranking officials sent by New Zealand to administer its mandated territory.[24] At the same time she was ready to hold forth in detail to C.A. Berendsen, New Zealand's Secretary of External Affairs, on the superior merits of the carefully selected and university-trained career Colonial Service initiated by Britain in 1926. On the strength of what she knew, she put forward proposals for co-operation between the two services.[25] She had carried away the same impression of a less than adequate service from American Samoa,[26] and was to go on to commend Australia for the training in anthropology given to the new cadres of its Papua service. 'We want anthropologists by the dozen,' she declared, 'part of every Colonial Service.'[27]

Margery Perham, then, was continuing to formulate what she wanted from the Colonial Service. Already, too, she recognized and romanticized over what she liked about the best representatives of the British Colonial Service. From San Francisco to Fiji, for instance, she rejoiced, not necessarily uncritically, in the company of a young cadet, 'Petronius' [A.E.P. Rose], 'strikingly handsome, tall and slim ... well-set grey-blue eyes ... well-cut English flannels, correct, restrained, ... I wondered whether ... his character could match his appearance'.[28] On the other hand, Margery was unable to discover anything to commend in the behaviour of the half-dozen Colonial Service cadets who entertained her at the communal 'Batch' in Suva. She found the evening a great strain, admitting, however, that her Oxford don's 'attempt, as the only woman, to be bright, social and interrogative' had undoubtedly contributed to the failure of the dinner party.[29]

It is when Margery Perham reached Africa, towards the end of 1929, that her cultivating of the District Officer as a man to be studied and understood is evident in every boma she visited. After seeing something of the South African 'native administration', she reached Basutoland, with its British officials. There, she immediately felt in rapport with Hugh Ashton, the Assistant Commissioner of Maseru District, the 'good trek-comrade' at hard work as much as at play,[30] establishing an empathy with the Colonial Service which was to be as influential to her thinking in the long run as it was important in the short. His superior, the Resident Commissioner (J.C.R. Sturrock) also comes out well: 'The R.C. is a good man. ... One does not expect, nor generally find, saints at the head of an administration, and the R.C. seems almost that. Quiet, modest, simple, earnest, sympathetic, thoughtful – I have chosen all the adjectives carefully.'[31] If this was the Major Dane image revived, it was nevertheless a yardstick which Margery never let drop.

Her constant evaluation of the Colonial Service officials in southern Africa was not confined to those in the field. She was no less 'interrogative', forthright, appreciative and generally at home with colonial governors. Her encounters with Sir Cecil Rodwell in Government House, Salisbury, and with H.M.G. Jackson, his formidable Chief Native Commissioner ('pretty stiff going at first');[32] the time spent with Sir James Maxwell, the Governor of Northern Rhodesia,[33] standing up to the 'stiff character' of his Secretary for Native Affairs, the 'barking' Moffat Thompson,[34] present revealing cameos of how Margery handled, maybe harried but generally won over, the senior officials too.

From Central she moved northwards to East Africa. In Tanganyika her enthusiasm for the policies being initiated by the governor, Donald Cameron, doubtless smoothed her relations with his subordinates in the field. Among them were young Donald Troup (who had crossed swords with her when he 'interfered at Oxford with the studies of one of my pupils' but 'now seemed inclined to overlook the past')[35] and D.K. Daniels, both just down from Oxford and its new Colonial Service training course, the latter with a hockey blue; and Graham de Courcy Ireland, 'a handsome, long-lashed, lustrous-eyed cadet ... being sent alone, apparently inexperienced as a babe, into the heart of Masailand'.[37] Then there was A.T. Culwick, an anthropologically-minded ADO,[38] T. A. G. Buckley and E.C.R. Richards, both Tanganyikan Provincial Commissioners, and a reunion with Margery's brother-in-law, Major Rayne, now D.C. Washamba. In Dar es Salaam there were triumphs, both personal and research, in Government House, conspicuously with the admired Cameron. There were also earnest encounters with the Chief Secretary, Douglas Jardine ('furious arguments');[39] and wonderful tutorial days with Philip Mitchell, then Secretary for Native Affairs, 'a man of very high ability, brilliant and masterful ... who for me proved an ideal travelling companion and exponent of the system'.[40]

It is perhaps hardly surprising that in Kenya her relations with administrators in Nairobi were less cordial, since she disagreed with the policy of the governor, Sir Edward Grigg, who was working towards the transfer of power to the European settlers – but she recorded his courtesy, and her long talks with him. Less happy were her dealings with his private secretary E. Dutton – 'disapproval' (he once minuted that she should be boiled in oil).[41] She found more congenial companions, however, such as the Chief Native Commissioner, G.V. Maxwell (from whom she heard derogatory comparisons with policies in Fiji),[42] and, away from Nairobi, Provincial Commissioners C.M. Dobbs and O.F. Watkins, and District Officers, such as D.C. Boulderson (Kavirondo) and especially C.E.V. Buxton (Masai).[43]

It was to be a similar story, of intensive investigation and extensive getting around, when Margery made her second major field visit, to West Africa in 1931–32. If anything, with fewer missionaries and no settlers to talk with, her close acquaintanceship with the Colonial Service proved to be even more rewarding and more revealing. Not only was she fortunate in that Cameron had been promoted from the governorship of Tanganyika to that of Nigeria ('my hopes of being able to study this vast country', she noted on the opening pages of her diary, 'depend mainly upon one man, Sir Donald Cameron'),[44] but the Chief Secretary in Lagos, Sir Alan Burns, in whose care she was placed, was the brother of a family friend. In the southern half of the country Margery continued to find it simple to win the cooperation of the officials; she established particularly helpful and mutually admiring relations with, for instance, H.L. Ward Price, the Resident of Oyo Province (she noted how Nigerian Residents were 'bigger men' than their counterparts in East Africa, the Provincial Commissioners),[45] and William Hunt, deputy Lieutenant-Governor of Eastern Nigeria;[46] and she spoke warmly of F.W. Carpenter in Buea, 'casual in manner, kind and thoughtful behind it . . . deadly serious about his work'[47] (and a hockey international). But in Northern Nigeria, the territory in which Lugard had created his system of indirect rule, she found relations were not so easy. This was because Cameron was attempting to impose more central control on the somewhat ossified form of provincial administration in the North, and, as she later recalled, she was frequently regarded as 'the governor's spy'.[48] She found the Resident (and uncrowned emperor) of remote Bornu, P. de Putron, one of the North's 'characters', particularly difficult: 'my heart sank as I looked at de Putron, as I could see in a minute how he regarded my visit'.[49] On his instructions, as she supposed when she won them over, two of his subordinates were initially unhelpful: D.F.H. Macbride, 'extremely intelligent, well-bred and cultivated. I admire the way a young man of his type tackles this rough and arduous work and seems keen and happy in his loneliness',[50] and P.E. Lewis at Dikwa, who was trying to fortify himself with drink against this visitation by a female guest from Government House.[51] In the major northern city of Kano she established cordial but, she felt, reserved relations with the powerful Resident, H.O. Lindsell, former Fellow of All Souls, 'a very important man for me ... he is wary and has not yet decided how much he can tell or show me';[52] but had closer contact with the Senior District Officer, Commander J.H. Carrow (later to become famous as Resident), 'one of those vital, dominating, apparently genial people with, I expect, a storm quick to blow up behind the sunshine once they are crossed'.[53] In both south and north she got to know District Officers by the dozen, from senior ones like F. de F. Daniel and G.S. Browne, 'one of the ablest men in Nigeria',[54] down to cadets like J.A. Calder and W.R.R. Ffrench in Katsina, R.C. Stanley and D.A. Percival in Zaria, and the two unnamed ex-Oxford cadets who dined with her at the Residency in Oyo and were 'so shy that it was almost cruelty to speak to them'.[55] One cadet in Kano whom she found exceptionally interesting was W.R. Crocker, 'quite the most intelligent person I have met in Nigeria, except the Governor'. Finding him 'intellectually starved' and acting as little more than 'an office-boy under men who may distrust a brilliant subordinate and think he needs teaching his place', Margery advised him to resign from the Colonial Service.[56] But she had no scruples about enlisting him to devil for her after hours in the Resident's office:

> While in the middle of my lunch at 3 o'cl. – i.e. 1/2 hour after we lock up and call it a day – a messenger brings me 6 or more pages of stuff to be typed from the Resident for you. Though weary and a slow typer do I curse or blaspheme? Not I! With a smile on my face I rapidly rise from my lunch and sally forth to the Office with only one thought in mind – 'It is all for her!' Was there ever such devotion?
>
> Don't forget if there is ever any more or less inside stuff you are wanting from here – e.g. from our files – just say the word ... [57]

Their correspondence continued warmly until shortly before her death, and one of his later letters to her sums up the enthusiasm she invoked in so many colonial administrative service men: 'What a life of service and mastery and achievement you have to look back to! I can think, dear Margery, of no woman contemporary of yours with such a record.'[58] In his memoirs, Crocker was to return the compliments she had paid him.[59] He did, however, blame her for having persuaded him to tone down parts of the extremely critical book he wrote on Nigerian administration.[60]

Kenya and Nigeria were two territories which she studied in detail; the third was the Sudan. The Sudan Political Service was under the Foreign Office, and not, of course, part of the Colonial Service; yet the administration of the country was carried out through a comparable structure of Provincial Governors and District Commissioners, and the evidence of her cordial relationship with, and compelling respect for, many of the Sudan Political Service officers is such that the extraordinarily rich Sudan dimension must be included. She maintained a warm and serious correspondence both with Douglas Newbold, the man who 'showed to me the highest standards I had ever seen in colonial administration',[61] and with Hugh Boustead. Not only did Boustead, like so many officials, send her copies of confidential circulars and reports even after he had transferred to Aden,[62] but he wrote with enthusiasm both of her recent visit to Darfur – 'a superbly delightful week with you in the mountains and on the road' – and of reading her *Native Administration in Nigeria*: 'My God, you know how to express things in a very living way – seeing all so clearly.'[63] Margery in fact paid more visits to the Sudan than to any other African country between 1929 and 1949. The pleasure, like the profit, was two-way. 'I had one particularly interesting visitor from outside the Sudan,' records G.W. Bell in recalling his tour of duty in Kordofan in 1937. 'Margery Perham stayed with me for several days and I took her round and showed her how our administration worked and what we were hoping to achieve. She was an expert – informed, perceptive, sympathetic and stimulating.'[64] Here was just one more administrative officer who kept in touch with her throughout his life.[65] It may also be recalled that it was primarily of the field administrators in the Sudan that she wrote that glowing tribute to 'the civilizing qualities of the ideal District Commissioner', an epitaph that the whole cadre of African Colonial Service administrators would like to have earned:

> The many British Officers, indefatigable, versatile, and humane, in the Sudan and in other dependencies, who grew to the stature of this opportunity, created one of the supreme types of their nation, that of the colonial District Commissioner. But nowhere else in Africa, it seemed to me, was the tradition of these officers so high, or the friendliness and even affection towards them of the people so widespread, as in the Sudan.[66]

Thinking about Colonial Administration

With so much African experience behind her and so much practical knowledge of colonial administration and personal knowledge of the District Commissioners (few other scholars could claim so much first-hand Colonial Service knowledge at such an early age), Margery devoted much of the 1930s, between her African visits, to theorizing, lecturing and writing about what she had seen and learned. She was beginning to make her name as the leading authority on colonial administration.

From 1929 she became a close associate and admirer of Lord Lugard. She was a frequent guest at his house at Abinger in Surrey, where she helped him with, and learned much from, his Permanent Mandates Commission papers and his ceaseless revision of the *Dual Mandate*, even though he never completed another edition after 1929. There, too, she met many of his former colleagues from Nigeria who came 'in a continuous procession' to pay their respects to 'The Chief', men like W. Gowers, R.P. Nicholson, C. Orr, G. Tomlinson, H. Vischer.[67] In 1930-31 Margery met colonial administrators from East Africa when she covered the sittings of the Joint Select Committee for Closer Union in East Africa for *The Times*. At such public lectures as those she gave on 'Native Administration' before the International Institute of African Languages and Cultures in 1931, or on 'Indirect Rule' before the Royal Society of Arts in 1934, the audience contained a number of colonial administrators. Newspaper articles and letters, especially in *The Times*, and from 1933 onwards her growing involvement in broadcasting, helped to keep her name before the public. In 1936 she was invited to serve as research consultant to Lord Hailey for the *African Survey* which the Royal Institute of International Affairs had commissioned. When in Africa the following year, she was an observer of the De la Warr Commission on education in East Africa, and in 1939 she became a member of the Colonial Office's Advisory Committee on Education in the Colonies. Oxford, too, began to recognize its own. Though she had had to give up her tutorial Fellowship at St Hugh's College in 1930 in order to stay on in Africa, the college elected her to a non-stipendiary Research Fellowship. In 1935 she was appointed to a university Research Lecturership, and four years later to a Readership, in Colonial Administration.

In 1937 Margery Perham published her first major book on colonial government, *Native Administration in Nigeria*, derived from her intensive field work there five years earlier. While its evaluation lies outside the scope of this article, mention must be made of her advocacy, in the concluding chapter, of the 'scaffolding theory' of colonial administration, which caused misunderstanding, right down to the days of Nigerianization of the Civil Service in the mid-1950s, by its assertion that Africans should not be allowed to enter the administrative service. This service, she said,

> should aim at being increasingly advisory in its functions. It should be regarded as the temporary scaffolding round the growing structure of native self-government. African energies should be incor-

porated into the structure: to build them into the scaffolding would be to create a vested interest which would make its demolition at the appropriate time very difficult.[68]

Getting to Know the Colonial Service in Conference and Lecture Room

Apart from her direct encounters in Africa, there were two other contexts in which Margery Perham learned to know colonial administrators at first hand: as cadets in pre-service training and in the Summer Schools on Colonial Administration. Oxford played a leading role (jointly with Cambridge, later complemented by the London School of Economics) in the general training programmes for the Colonial Service between the wars. In 1926 the two universities had agreed to the Colonial Office invitation to mount an annual Tropical African (later Colonial Adminis-trative) Service course for its probationers. Margery lectured regularly to the courses both in Oxford and Cambridge,[69] and her other talks and writings must have constantly brought her into touch with members of the course.[70] The Colonial Service Club records at Oxford show how several hundred administrative cadets attended the course between 1926 and 1939 (by 1937-38 the annual intake had risen to 45), once again pre-dominantly destined to serve in Africa. She herself acknowledged the value of this clientele when she came to look back on colonialism and the Colonial Service in her Reith Lectures.[71]

In 1937, the Social Studies Research Committee of Oxford University organized its first Summer School on Colonial Administration.[72] Though its Chairman was the Beit Professor of Colonial History, Reginald Coup-land, the Vice-Chairman (and the moving spirit) was Margery Perham. She made sure, too, that the conference was held, for a whole fortnight, at her own college. 'It was intended,' we are told, 'primarily for the benefit of officers of the colonial administrative service, and mainly for those serving in Africa', but officers of the Sudan Political Service were also eligible to attend.[73] Margery saw the Summer Schools as 'a sort of intellectual refresher' for the serving members; whereas the initial courses should stimulate the cadets into seeing what native administra-tion was all about and could achieve. Once again, it was the mind she was after: 'They can be given a serious *intellectual* approach to their work.'[74]

A successor fortnight's conference was held in 1938, this time at Lady Margaret Hall (whose principal was the sister of a retired colonial gover-nor, Sir Selwyn Grier). Again, the aim was 'to enable officers to review and discuss problems of colonial administration'.[75] Once more, the Vice-Chairman was Margery Perham, and the Secretary of State, Malcolm MacDonald, singled out her and Professor Coupland for special thanks.

'They have both already given much to the Colonial Service,' he noted, 'but the conception of this School was one of their happiest efforts.'[76]

At both Schools, the colonial service 'brass' ('You're firing off a barrage of big guns' was Newbold's comment to Perham)[77] was out in full force, an achievement which Margery Perham was influential in ensuring. In each year the Secretary of State for the Colonies gave the opening speech and on both occasions the inaugural address was given by Lord Lugard. The Parliamentary, Permanent and Assistant Under-Secretaries of the Colonial Office all dined or lunched with the School and made further speeches. As for the formal speakers, no less than 31 in 1937 and 25 in 1938, their roll-call reads like an extract from the 'top table' guest list at the Colonial Service's pre-war Corona Club annual dinner: Sir Donald Cameron, Lord Hailey, Sir John Shuckburgh, Sir Selwyn Grier, the Marquis of Lothian, and Sir Alan Pim (Douglas Newbold wrote to Margery asking whether he could come for only three days – 'it's a triumph to have got it going at all' – and later, 'it broke my heart to have to leave the School')[78]. All spoke, along with nearly every leading academic in one or more of the fields and including speakers on the French, Belgian, Dutch – and the Roman empires. Margery's own lectures were two in 1937, on 'British Native Administration in Africa: I Policy, II Application' and, in 1938 (again a double-barrelled performance: only Lord Hailey and Professor Coupland also gave more than one paper) 'British Native Administration: I Problems, II Prospects'.[79] There could be little doubt in any of the colonial administrators' minds, 101 of them in 1937 and 100 in 1938 (out of a total of some 300 attending the two conferences) about who, next to Lord Lugard, really was the expert on colonial administration – and hence on the Colonial Service.

The Summer Schools, then, were an effective means whereby Margery Perham extended her knowledge of individual Colonial Service officers gained in the field. At that time the total strength of the Colonial Administrative Service in the whole of Africa was about 1,200. Recruitment was still recovering from the brake of slump followed by the miseries of retrenchment, and had fallen, for the whole of the Empire, from 133 in 1928 to 20 in 1931. It was not to reach the 100 mark again until 1945. In 1947 the African establishment rose to 1,390 administrators and had reached 1,782 by 1957. Throughout, Africa accounted for something like 75 per cent of Britain's colonial administrators, so if Margery Perham was able to bring 200 colonial administrators to Oxford in 1937 and 1938, predominantly from Africa, she was in a position to meet on these occasions and, perhaps more influentially, to be known to, in between 15 and 20 per cent of the Colonial Administrative Service working in Africa. These were mostly from the District Officer level; as Newbold noted in a letter to Margery urging that the 1939 School should not be cut to less than 80 nor allowed to exceed 120, 'we don't want the hierarchic principle to invade a democratic school. It was noticeable there were no Provincial Commissioners or Residents from Africa'.[80]

Two of her favourite themes in lecturing to both cadets and Summer Schools were indirect rule and native administration. But for all her idealism, her lecture notes show that she kept her feet on the ground. She warned the Summer School of 1938 of the dangers inherent in a situation of non-accountability by a Colonial Service which had 'practically no responsibility towards the administered ... we ignore and override their objections ... the influence from below is still negligible.' She warned, too, against Britain's complacency with its imperial character: 'When we come to consider how the harness of our power fits upon our subject people, we should not step back to admire the sight presented but try to look underneath for galls and saddle-sores.' She also emphasized the two-way nature of the exchange:

> The self-criticism of thoughtful members of the Service can be collected and distilled. I presume therefore to come before you not ... as one commenting from some detached position of superior eminence which I believe myself to inhabit, but as an instrument collecting and reflecting your own ideas – the mirror of yourselves, in fact – your better selves as I may hope.[81]

Other themes, often in note form, to be put across to cadets and the Colonial Office alike were: 'Danger of inferiority complex of most administrative staff', 'Staff College: fear of pemmican [sic] instruction' and, characteristically, 'Lack of sense of spiritual and aesthetic values – something to learn from the French'.[82]

Conclusion

By 1939 Margery Perham was, uniquely, able to supplement her reputation as the leading academic authority on colonial administration through an unrivalled knowledge, in both depth and spread, of the field agents of colonial government, above all the backbone District Officer cadre.[83] In one or another context she had met perhaps up to a quarter of the officials in that grade serving in Africa. Little wonder that, whether it was based on a tutorial at Oxford, correspondence from the field, a day's visit to an up-country boma, a week's encounter in a provincial headquarters, or a whole fortnight in the relaxed intimacy of a Summer School, so many District Officers could feel and give expression to their confidence that they too, in common with pro-consuls like Lugard, Cameron and Newbold, knew and were known to Margery Perham, and were thus justified in asking of the new cadet entry just down from Brasenose, Corpus or Clare as they disembarked at Lagos or Takoradi, Dar es Salaam or Mombasa, 'And how is dear Miss Perham?'

What is constantly revealed by her correspondence is how frequently those District Officers kept in touch with her. Two themes stand out clearly: the allusion to a tutorial or to a visit in the field, and the diffidence with which so many of them, high or low, opened their correspondence. 'Little did I think (as they write in some autobiographies),' wrote Peter Canham thirty years later, 'when I sat at your feet in Rhodes House in 1937 ... that I would ever be addressing you by your first name.'[84] 'I don't suppose you remember', read Sir James Robertson's opening sentence, 'coming to stay with us in El Dueim in the distant years before the war.'[85] 'I do not suppose you will remember me. We met in Enugu when you first came out to Nigeria,' was Frank Bridges' introduction thirty years on.[86] It was the same with other overseas civil servants, like Richard Cashmore, Sir Miles Clifford, Hugh Elliott and Robin Hodgkin.[87] The letters from Philip Snow and Terence Gavaghan may be held to typify the many: 'You could not possibly recall me', wrote the former, 'but I used to attend your lectures at Cambridge in 1937 ... and I was privileged often to have talks with you after your lectures which I still remember with pleasure', while the latter expressed his feelings thus: 'You will see [in forwarding something he had written] the long-range persistence of your own influence on the development of some of my attitudes ... It is now thirty years since I first attended your Seminars ... but, as with many others, they left their mark on me.'[88] No governor and few Colonial Office officials could claim as wide a circle of acquaintances within the Colonial Service.

Margery took the opportunity of the Reith Lectures, looking back on the colonial period, to sum up many of her observations of the Colonial Service officers whom she had met, taught and got to know over the past forty years. 'No attempt to reckon up the uses and abuses of Britain's colonial rule,' she stated, 'could be complete which did not try to evaluate the agency through which it was carried out',[89] namely the Colonial Service. The élite of that corps was the administrative service. Her list of 'desirable qualities' in the District Officer – an amalgam of her own and those set out by the Warren Fisher Committee in 1930 – reads more like the description of an impossible, even unlivable-with, paragon rather than of an ordinary mortal: 'vision, high ideals of service, fearless devotion to duty born of a sense of responsibility, tolerance and, above all, team spirit, [with] courage and physical prowess'.[90]

True, he had his weaknesses, which Margery Perham was too honest and forthright even to wish to gloss over. Disdain for his technical colleagues and an inflated sense of hierarchy were faults, even if intellectual isolation and the lack of comparative experience were handicaps for which he could not be blamed. Accurately, she pointed to the regrettable fact that the Colonial Service officers were 'nearly always too few in relation to the African numbers, and perhaps too British, to cultivate an intimate social relationship with its charges', above all with the educated élites. However, she often found that the defects of the service were due less to the faults of its members than to the lack of direction given to it by its masters, all the way from the colonial governors to the British public: 'A service can respond to a lead and can sustain a tradition, but it cannot create policy.' The impression she regularly brought back from Africa was how nearly every Colonial Service officer she met revelled in his work. 'It was certainly a man's job,' she recorded. 'It could take all he had to give, with every faculty employed at the stretch.' Her conclusion was idealistic: the office of District Commissioner deserved to stand forth in history as 'one of the supreme types developed by Britain to meet a special demand'. For Margery Perham, 'if the Colonial Service was not a task for the genius, the marvel is that it attracted so many men of high standards of character and education'.[91]

A full biography may give a more complete explanation of how a woman could break into such a male-dominated and male-oriented circle as the Colonial Service. Yet from the Service perspective, several indications have already been established. For instance, Margery regularly came to the field armed with acquaintanceship with, and letters of introduction from, the highest authorities – such letters were a feature of empire travelling between the wars, and normally brought offers of hospitality. Her introduction to Lord Lugard, before she left on her world tour, opened many doors. Another 1929 introduction, this time to Sir Donald Cameron, led to invitations to stay in his Government Houses of Tanganyika and Nigeria. In the Colonial Service, a visitor with such a pedigree of Government House status could hardly go wrong up-country (with the exception that has been noted in Northern Nigeria). For her part, she backed up these credentials with qualities of her own. One of them was her basic respect, and indeed admiration, for the strong element of ritual which was ingrained in British colonial rule – the formal etiquette of administration. The other was the solid research and application with which she matched her intense interest in the subject. Taken all together, these powerful recommendations were generally enough to break through the normal constraints upon women in colonial society and to enable her to make use of her femininity as an asset rather than a liability in her work. She herself wrote of 'that degree of magnetism from the ardour of my interest, which enabled me to influence men and to gain their help and information. I have always played the woman . . . '[92] More prosaically, it might be added that she was attractive, sporting, and a good mixer – always a refreshing kind of visitor to an up-country station.

There are two entries – in no way unique – from her diary which encapsulate the Perham strategy for getting to know the Colonial Service in the field. The first is from her Pacific diary, where she sums up her recipe for success. In Wellington, she discovered the advantages of going at once to the top, 'never to the junior man first'. Margery found there that she had no need to wait for the chance 'to gather a few crumbs' from some underling or to look 'with awe at the titles on the doors behind which the supermen of administration direct the world's affairs at high pressure'. She knocked on the door of the man in charge and found that 'no official . . . seems ever too busy to talk about his own work. The difficulty is not to get in to him, not to start, but to stop him.'[93] The second comes from Tanganyika, where, having gained the sponsorship of the 'top men' – Cameron and Mitchell – she wrote: 'I was thus able to visit a number of districts, to stay with administrative officers, and watch them at work upon the structures covered by the term "Native Administration" '.[94]

Finally, on her research visits she never gave any impression other than that she was there to work and to learn. Whether in Lagos or Dar es Salaam, in Suva or the Sudan, her diaries are full of terse entries about how she had just spent a rewarding day with the office files: 'Work all day until five, and then a walk along the shore with Mrs Jardine, wife of the Chief Secretary' – 'I got in a last morning's work at the office'.[95] 'Next day, Sunday, I worked hard and in the evening went to tea with Major Jackson, who motored me out to his brother, the Chief Native Commissioner' – 'I had an interview with the Governor, he was much better in his office than in his house;'[96] and, most evocative of all, this description of herself at work:

> Here I am writing . . . sitting in the Governor's chair at the Governor's table, with the arms of England emblazoned above my head. No Secretariat staff could have been more friendly. I was introduced to the senior officers and all the documents I asked for were piled on the table around me. I am now beginning the task of trying at close quarters to understand Nigeria.[97]

No other academic researcher got so close to the context of African colonial administration, or got to know so many of its practitioners, their strengths and their weaknesses, as intimately as did Margery Perham.

This, then, is an outline portrait of the Colonial Service's first – and last – godmother. Like the ideal godmother, she could be more approachable than a parent, for discipline did not have to be her concern. The fact that she was not herself a member of the Colonial Service was very much an advantage to her in her dealings with the service. District Officers could – and did – confide in her what they would never have dared or wanted to tell their Provincial Commissioners, the Governor or the Colonial Office. Moreover, she could censure and rebuke as well as congratulate and inspire; nor did she hesitate to point to a weakness or pounce on a fault. Like the best of godmothers, Margery Perham is remembered by her adopted godchildren for that mixture of affection, mutual respect, high standards, and a sense of romantic idealism, which gained her such a special place in Colonial Service circles.

NOTES

1. The genre includes Charles Allen, *Plain Tales from the Raj* (London, 1979), *Tales from the Dark Continent* (London, 1983); Ronnie Knox Mawer, *Tales from a Palm Court* (London, 1986); and Derek Hopwood, *Tales of Empire: the British in the Middle East* (London, 1989).
2. For example, Kenneth Ballhatchet, *Race, Sex and Class under the Raj* (London, 1980); John G. Butcher, *The British in Malaya, 1880–1941: the social history of a European community in colonial South-East Asia* (Kuala Lumpur, 1979); Joan Alexander, *Voices and Echoes: tales from colonial women* (London, 1988); Janice Brownfoot, 'Memsahibs in Colonial Malaya: a study of European wives in a British Colony and Protectorate, 1900–1940', and Beverly Gartrell, 'Colonial Wives: villains or victims?' in Hilary Callan and Shirley Ardener, eds., *The Incorporated Wife* (London, 1984); Claudia Knapman, *White Women in Fiji, 1835–1930: the ruin of empire?* (Sydney, 1986); and Helen Callaway, *Gender, Culture and Empire: European women in colonial Nigeria* (London, 1987).
3. See, for instance, 'Nursing Sisters in Nigeria, Uganda, Tanganyika' and 'Women Administrative Officers in Colonial Africa', bibliographical essays sponsored by the Oxford Development Records Project, Rhodes House Library.
4. Callaway, *Gender, Culture and Empire*, p.5.
5. *Colonial Office Conference 1927*, Cmd. 2883 and 2884, and *Colonial Office Conference 1930*, Cmd. 3628 and 3629, along with CO Misc. 385 and 416 (Confidential).
6. *The System of Appointment to the Colonial Office and Colonial Service* (Fisher), Cmd. 3554, 1930.
7. Charles Jeffries, *The Colonial Empire and its Civil Service* (Cambridge, 1938), p.55.
8. *Post–War Training of the Colonial Service* (Devonshire), Col. No. 198, 1946.
9. Heussler's *plus royal que le roi* attitude towards the Colonial Service continues to be a matter of debate, though nothing should dim the depth and thoroughness of his research. His unpublished autobiography [personal knowledge] reveals the encouragement he derived from working with Margery Perham. She noted, when writing to congratulate him on and thank him for a copy of *Yesterday's Rulers* (London, 1963), that her 'main [comment] is satisfaction that an American observer could pass such a favourable opinion'. However, she added, 'I think you are too kind.' In reply, Heussler argued that his fault lay not in being too kind but 'rather in not being British and not having been close to Africa and the Colonial Service, as you have been'. Perham to

Heussler, 14 Jan., and reply, 21 Jan. 1969, Perham Papers (hereafter PP), Rhodes House Library, Box 27, File 1.

10. Kenneth Robinson and Frederick Madden (eds.), *Essays in Imperial Government presented to Margery Perham* (Oxford, 1963), p.vi.

11. This was an experience and qualification to be widely replicated in the Colonial Service recruitment between 1945 and 1949 of wartime officers who had served in the Indian Army, Royal West African Frontier Force and King's African Rifles; see PP 244/1. Rayne had served with the K.A.R.

12. H. Rayne, *Sun, Sand and Somals: leaves from the notebook of a District Commissioner* (London, 1921).

13. Margery Perham, *West African Passage*, ed. A.H.M. Kirk-Greene (London, 1983), Introduction, p. 9.

14. PP 227/10,12, 228/2,4,5.

15. 'The Time of my Life', the *Listener*, Jan. 1970, PP 352/4; reprinted as the Prologue to Margery Perham, *African Apprenticeship* (London, 1974).

16. M. F. Perham, *Major Dane's Garden* (London, 1925); republished in 1970, with an error in the alleged date of the first impression.

17. *Saturday Review of Literature* (New York) and *Philadelphia Public Ledger*, both reviews being quoted on the dust-jacket of the 1970 reprint (London) and retained in PP 283/2.

18. Perham, *Major Dane's Garden* (1970 ed.), p. 3.

19. Ibid., p. 11.

20. Ibid., p. 61.

21. Introduction to K.D.D. Henderson, *The Making of the Modern Sudan: the life and letters of Sir Douglas Newbold* (London, 1953), p. xiii; see below, p. 71. A few years later she rephrased her encomium of the ideal DC as one who 'could be relied upon to be humane, uncorrupt, diligent, even when left alone quite unsupervised in the outer regions of a very testing continent'. Margery Perham, *The Colonial Reckoning* (London, 1962), p. 125.

22. *Major Dane's Garden*, p. 359. A comparison of the characters of Major Rayne and Major Dane might start with the diaries in PP 34/1 and 2. There is nothing relevant to this in her 1923 lecture notes on her Somaliland visit, PP 227/2.

23. See the introduction by A.H.M. Kirk-Greene to Margery Perham, *Pacific Prelude* (London, 1988), pp. 14–17, which is based on the Rhodes Trust files and PP 9/6.

24. Perham, *Pacific Prelude*, pp. 103–4.

25. Ibid., pp. 150–4.

26. Ibid., p. 89.

27. Ibid., p. 188.

28. Ibid., p. 69.

29. Ibid., p. 113.

30. Perham, *African Apprenticeship*, p. 129. For forty warmly written pages he remains simply 'the A.C.' For an integrated version of printed text and original typescript, see PP 39 and Patricia Pugh, *Catalogue of the Papers of Dame Margery Perham*, Bodleian Library, Oxford (1989), p.56.

31. Perham, *African Apprenticeship*, p. 88. His anonymity also is preserved in the diary.

32. Ibid., p. 248–9.

33. 'I count those long nightly talks with him as one of the most interesting events of my journey.' Ibid., p. 238.

34. Ibid., p. 235.

35. Margery Perham, *East African Journey*, (London, 1976), p. 201. Again, for a comparative text, see PP 42–44, and *Catalogue*, p. 52.

36. Perham, *East African Journey*, pp. 101, 105–6.

37. Ibid., p. 48.

38. Ibid. He returned to Oxford shortly afterwards to take an advanced degree in anthropology and co-authored a number of books. After settling first in Kenya and then in South Africa, he published a partisan memoir *Britannia Waives the Rules* (Cape Town,

1963).
39. Perham, *East African Journey*, pp. 43–7.
40. Ibid., p. 17.
41. Ibid., pp. 155 ff.
42. Ibid., p. 29. Maxwell had previously served in Fiji.
43. Ibid., pp. 21–3, 140–4, 154, 171, 193.
44. Perham, *West African Passage*, p. 23. For a comparative text, see PP 46–8.
45. Ibid., p. 31.
46. Ibid., pp. 170, 182. The hundred or so letters exchanged between them in 1932, often on a daily basis (PP 395/4), reveal a very affectionate relationship. The Hunt papers are now in Rhodes House Library.
47. Ibid., p. 212.
48. Talk to Nuffield students at the time of her retirement, 1963, PP 9/6.
49. Perham, *West African Passage*, p. 118.
50. Ibid., pp. 152–5.
51. Ibid., pp. 122–3. Understandably, Margery's visits were not always welcome (e.g. Dutton and de Putron, above) or a success (cf. notes 41 amd 49). Of a dismal dinner-party at Bauchi, when the D.O. invited the whole station (six men) to meet her, she wrote ' I can't think I was a social success' (*West African Passage*, p. 164). One of the party, an Education Officer, remembered fifty years later how she was 'subjected to the utmost rudeness from one of our own number, an A.D.O., ex-Gurkha captain, and did her very best (helped by some, not all of us) to laugh it off.' (B.A. Babb to writer, 30 Dec. 1983). Kenneth Robinson (personal communication) recalls one colonial governor referring to her as 'Aunt St Margery'.
52. Perham, *West African Passage*, p. 62.
53. Ibid., p. 61.
54. Ibid., p. 213.
55. Ibid., p. 31.
56. Ibid., pp. 86–7. Crocker was one of a small number of cadets recruited from Australia.
57. Crocker to Perham, 26 January 1932 , PP 395/2.
58. Crocker to Perham, undated, ?1968, PP 26/4.
59. W.R. Crocker, *Travelling Back: Memoirs* (Melbourne, 1981), p. 85.
60. W.R. Crocker, *Nigeria: a critique of British colonial administration* (London, 1936); Perham, *West African Passage*, p. 87n.
61. Introduction to Henderson, *The Making of the Modern Sudan*, p. xxvii. Much of the Perham/Newbold correspondence is reproduced verbatim in the text. See also her Sudan diaries in PP 50, 53 and 54, including the typical entry of 7 March 1938: 'Newbold is marvellous. He ... was as idealistic as ever. It renews my faith and my hopes for Africa. We could not stop talking.' PP 50/7.
62. For example, Boustead to Perham, 8 March 1950, with enclosure, PP 26/2. Cf. Parr to Perham, 8 April 1938, with enclosure, PP 27/8, and Newbold to Perham, 1 June 1938, Henderson, *Making of the Modern Sudan*, p.83.
63. Boustead to Perham, 2 and 20 March 1938, PP 26/2.
64. Gawain Bell, *Shadows on the Sand: Memoirs* (London, 1983), p. 77. As Governor of Northern Nigeria when Margery visited Kaduna in January 1960, he allowed her to read his secret despatches to the Colonial Office on the political situation (PP 58/3) in the same way as, a decade earlier, his senior colleague in Khartoum, the Civil Secretary, Sir James Robertson, continued Newbold's practice of sending to Margery a copy of the secret intelligence reports which he received from Provincial Governors. PP 536/7.
65. In addition to PP 26–9, already cited, PP 536/1–7 indicate the range and depth of her correspondence with Sudan Provincial Governors and District Commissioners, including Reginald Davies, R.C. (Ned) Mayall and Martin Parr as well as Newbold, Boustead, Robertson and Bell.
66. Introduction to Henderson, *The Making of the Modern Sudan*, p. xiii.
67. Margery Perham, *Lugard: The Years of Authority* (London, 1960), p. 694.
68. Margery Perham, *Native Administration in Nigeria* (London, 1937), p. 361. When

Hugh Boustead first read this 'heresy', he immediately wondered how the Khartoum establishment would react to her views! (Boustead to Perham, 20 March 1938, PP 26/2). Margery may not have ever reconciled herself to Africanization of the District Officer grade (cf. PP 249). On her first encounter with the 'new venture' of local training at the Residency, Zaria, in 1960, she was unimpressed by the two Northern Nigerian cadets invited to dinner (PP 58/3). See below, Chapter 9.

69. Address to African Studies Association, 1964, reprinted in Margery Perham, *Colonial Sequence 1949–1969* (London 1970), p. 270.

70. For example, her lecture notes in PP 227–31, especially 228/3, 'Notes for the final lecture [on Native Administration] in a series given to Colonial Service Cadets at Oxford' (1929), or 229/8 (1935) and 229/11, with a plan and notes for lectures on Indirect Rule for Oxford Colonial Cadets (1935–6).

71. Perham, *The Colonial Reckoning*, pp. 16 and 126.

72. The Perham Papers are disappointingly slight on these two Summer Schools. For a proper study, one would need to start with the Colonial Office files. PP 242/1 is worthless on the organization of the two Schools (in any case, the 1937 is missing altogether, and neither summary of the proceedings has been retained). The important papers catalogued as 'Oxford and Cambridge Summer Schools and Conferences' (PP 250–2) do not start until 1947.

73. *Oxford University Summer School on Colonial Administration: summary of lectures, July 1937* (privately printed, Oxford, 1937), p. iii.

74. Notes on proposed schemes for Summer Schools and Colonial Service Courses, PP 244/2.

75. *Oxford University Summer School on Colonial Administration: Second Session, 1938* (privately printed, Oxford 1938) p. v.

76. Ibid., p. 1. PP 242/2 refers to the rival Cambridge Summer School of 1938, held in mid-August.

77. Newbold to Perham, 13 June 1938, printed in Henderson, *The Making of the Modern Sudan*, p. 84.

78. Newbold to Perham, 11 March and 4 July 1938, ibid., pp.82, 85.

79. A fuller version of the 1939 lectures is in PP 242/3.

80. Newbold to Perham, 4 July 1938, in Henderson, *The Making of the Modern Sudan*, p. 85. The list of those registered shows that he was not quite right, as there was one PC from Kenya and one Resident from Nigeria.

81. Lecture to 1938 Summer School, PP 242/1.

82. Memorandum on Colonial Service training, 1935–6, PP 244/1, ff. 14–15, 29.

83. Her nearest contenders, as it were, were also women but anthropologists rather than historians: Lucy Mair and Audrey Richards. Even a latter-day colonial governor could say to Margery when she wrote to congratulate him on his promotion: 'There are not many people from whom I would value a complimentary and encouraging word more highly.' Sir Richard Luyt to Perham, PP 27/4.

84. Canham to Perham, 4 Nov. 1967, PP 26/3.

85. Robertson to Perham, 16 May 1945, PP 536/7.

86. Bridges to Perham, 1 Feb. 1966, PP 26/2. Cf. his *So We Used To Do* (Edinburgh, 1990), p. 78.

87. PP 26/3, 26/6, 27/1.

88. Snow to Perham, 15 Jan. 1974 , PP 28/2, and Gavaghan to Perham, 12 Sept. 1978, PP 26/8.

89. Perham, *Colonial Reckoning*, p. 119.

90. Ibid., p. 124.

91. Ibid., pp.125–8.

92. Private Diary, 18 Jan. 1941, PP 33/4.

93. Perham, *Pacific Prelude*, pp. 26 and 152.

94. Perham, *East African Journey*, p. 17.

95. Ibid., pp. 46 and 47.

96. Perham, *African Apprenticeship*, pp. 248–9, and 250.

97. Perham, *West African Passage*, pp. 24–5.

Margery Perham, Christian Missions
and Indirect Rule

Andrew Porter

'the missionary question is not to be dissociated from the future
of the African natives, and so the subject must be touched on ...'

[Mary Kingsley, 1897][1]

'Their ignorance of the usages of the world, their efforts to please
and their damned bad tea. Their unconscious assumption that
nothing matters except themselves, ...'

[Sir Frederick Lugard, 1913][2]

The quotation above from that earlier traveller in Africa, Mary Kingsley,
has a significance which is more than decorative. Margery Perham's
outstanding concerns – the proper valuation of African societies and their
constructive adaptation to the modern world, the right development of
colonial administration, the importance of education, and the ethics of
empire – overlapped at many points with Kingsley's. In their lecturing
and writing, and their influence with those in authority (or at least their
capacity to compel official attention), the two can be seen as playing
similar roles.[3] Both, moreover, developed firm views on the place of
Christian missions in their relation to the state and society in Africa.
Kingsley's highly critical opinions are, of course, well known. Her out-
spokenness infuriated much contemporary missionary opinion, and it
might be thought that at this point any reference to the similarities
between the two careers should give way to the contrasts. Mary Kingsley,
'brought up an agnostic ... a "staunch Darwinian" to the end' and
showing 'evident unfamiliarity with the procedure of the Sunday Service',[4] seems at first sight far removed from the Margery Perham whose
interest in missions took her in 1963 to the presidency of the Universities
Mission to Central Africa, and to responsibility for its merger in a
strengthened enterprise with the Society for the Propagation of the

Gospel. It is one purpose of this article, however, to suggest that this divergence is easily exaggerated. In many ways, one may suggest, Perham in the 1920s, while less strident and impetuous, took up not so very far from where Kingsley had left off: for Perham too, at that time, concern for Africa's future had little obvious place for missionary enterprise. The process by which this came to change deserves exploration. The gradual clarification and modification of her views on 'the missionary factor' involves not only Perham's personal odyssey, but the fortunes of her other preoccupation, indirect rule, as well as the broader transformation of imperial relations which culminated in decolonization.

I

It is difficult to construct an unequivocal picture of Margery Perham's attitude towards missions in the years immediately before she began her African travels in 1929. The views taken of Perham's background and later life are remarkably consistent in their stress on the Anglican Christianity which underpinned them. There are, for example, her own summaries – 'High Church schools, women's colleges and middle-class idealism generally', 'by nature ... a woman and by education ... a religious woman'.[5] These are echoed by later commentators, who have recalled her uncle (a missionary in Malaya and archdeacon of Singapore), her Woodard Foundation schooling, her sister Ethel's early missionary inclinations, her own style of churchmanship and her 'robust faith ... [that of] a simple and singularly cheerful Christian'.[6] By upbringing, therefore, one might be tempted to assume on her part a predisposition to sympathy with the work of at least Protestant missionaries. Yet even if the examples of Anglicans such as the Reverend Sydney Smith and the 3rd Marquess of Salisbury were insufficient to raise doubts over it, such an unqualified assumption would be rash.

For Mary Kingsley, severe general reservations about missionary methods and the results of their work were perfectly compatible with admiration and affection for individuals. One such was Mary Slessor, the United Presbyterian Church missionary at Calabar. Perham not only clearly shared that particular respect, but also something of Kingsley's general attitudes.[7] There is no ground for thinking that in the 1920s Margery Perham would have seconded Kingsley's more extreme fulminations; and she was in any case too conscientious an academic to do other than 'speak only of what I know'.[8] Yet, in the fragmentary evidence available, it is possible to sense a distinct indifference or coolness towards the missionary fraternity during this period. It is dangerous to place much weight on a simple lack of material; strangely, however, no signs seem to exist of Perham having taken any serious interest at this time in the educational initiatives of the mid-1920s, in which the more forward-looking missionary leaders were involved – the Colonial Office Advisory Committee on Education, the Institute of African Languages and Cultures, and the 1926 Le Zoute conference. Perhaps this is explicable in terms of her other preoccupations, first the resumption of her post at Sheffield and then the start of her career as a tutorial fellow in Oxford. Nevertheless, there are other pointers in the same direction. In a draft she prepared on 'The Basel Mission' or a reference like that to the Paris Evangelical Mission's 'long and honourable task of bringing Christianity and western education to the Basuto', there is at most a detached interest and that essentially in their contribution to the wider complexities of contemporary politics.[9]

Such comments may, of course, reflect Perham's immediate and passing concerns rather than a more general outlook on her part. A brief on the Cameroons Mandate, or a response to the continuing discussion of the High Commission Territories, hardly called perhaps for decided expressions of personal commitment. However, one might also suggest that reasons for this distance lie deeper than an ordinary scholarly detachment; they were in part personal and also more widely characteristic of her generation. Many in the wake of the First World War felt their religious faith weaken, and Perham was no exception. As she later recorded, the influences were several. Spurred on not least by books such as Lecky's *History of Rationalism* and Bury's *History of the Freedom of Thought*, 'I began to doubt when in Oxford, especially in the period after Edgar's death.' The result was that from 1917 on 'I treated religion with respect because I felt the great sincerity of some of those who lived it ... and because I could still see that it played a very useful if not an absolutely necessary part in sweetening and even sustaining society.'[10] This attitude of personal and utilitarian respect, it would seem, was not proof against evidence of both individual failings and a wider functional inadequacy detectable in many missionary efforts, evidence which her early travels provided in plenty.

The general problem of relations between the West and non-European societies, of which for Mary Kingsley missionaries had been a part, was one equally apparent to Perham and her contemporaries. Even before setting out on her Rhodes Trust Travelling Fellowship in 1929 she had herself been very struck by a Maori's passionate criticism of the West's destructive influence in New Zealand:

> As she spoke it was impossible not to burn with the feeling of guilt ... Races are defaced, distorted, demoralised, displaced, and as

such live on, pitiful perhaps, more often crippled, soulless, be-
wildered until they learn their own history and turn to hatred, and
from hatred to revenge. And the oppressing race lives on ... building new frailties into its character, living to feel, perhaps, useless
regrets, living to suffer retribution. Meanwhile something has been
lost to the world, the individuality, the spontaneous force of a
people, which ... might under proper guidance ... have enriched
the world ... Instead of that a Maori has learned English, and we
have learned a little wisdom only that she may say and we may
understand her when she says 'It is too late'.

Only in Africa, she concluded, was it 'not too late' to prevent the
disintegrating impact of western penetration.[11]

This experience may have done no more than reinforce directly the
general lessons of her historical studies and work on the Mandates
System, but it did so both powerfully and in a way which was essentially
confirmed by subsequent first-hand investigation initially in the Pacific
and in southern Africa.[12] Her notes on visiting Polynesia later in 1929
reveal her continuing consciousness of the fragility of local societies and
the mounting threat posed by western culture. With their long history in
the Pacific, missions were a part of the problem. 'Like other Pacific
islands Samoa early attracted the attention of intrusive Europeans, adventurers of all kinds, whalers and other exploiters – and missionaries!'[13]
That the missions' impact in the islands had been generally benign
seemed to her to owe more to the constraints under which they operated
than to newly-constructive thinking by missionaries themselves. There 'is
really little you can teach these people. They have, and they know, nearly
all they need; the missionaries bring the Christian religion and so add a
new interest and depth to village life, plus the hobby of churchbuilding.'
The fact that 'All this seems to have little or no disruptive results' was also
due to the Polynesian's striking ability 'to show a certain resistance, or
rather a power of assimilating Christianity to his own religious ideas'.[14]

II

Evidence of a more carefully defined outlook slowly emerged as Perham
developed her first-hand experience of Africa, subsequently imbibed
some systematic anthropology, and reflected on her observations and
notes made in the field. Little that Perham encountered between 1929
and 1932 in South and later in both East and West Africa, either allayed
her religious uncertainty or persuaded her that missionaries had much of
an answer to the problems of the colonial world. In the Union she was at
first hesitant in passing judgement. Conscious of the long history of

missionary work, particularly in the Cape, she felt it 'almost insolent to pass any criticism'. Yet from Fort Hare to Buntingville she encountered everywhere an oppressive paternalism as well as 'overmuch complacency'. Visits to Lovedale and a Cowley Fathers' mission in the Transkei impressed her in part, but prompted a general conclusion: 'it is impossible not to feel that the missionary too often gives just what is ready in his hand to give, without more careful adaptation to the needs of the native'.[15]

Her recorded encounter with missionaries training teachers in Central Kavirondo brings to mind later recollections of her as 'always calling attention to the best and fighting against the shoddy'. 'They were Mill Hill, and like all Mill Hill I have seen, just a little dingy. But then cleanliness is only next to godliness and they certainly have that.'[16] On other occasions her strictures recall phrases from the Anglican confession. White Fathers at Biharamulo in Tanganyika were found wasting their opportunities, clearly leaving undone the things which they ought to have done. In Kenya, others worked only too readily at things which they ought not to have done, and had 'just been stopped quietly encroaching beyond their borders, a way many missions have in these parts.'[17]

Missionaries' proprietorial attitudes towards 'their' Africans irritated her, and were hardly more defensible or attractive when applied to spheres of territory.[18] Characteristics such as these seemed in East Africa only to point up the inadequacy of missionaries claiming, or being used, to represent African interests. Her observations on Canon H. F. Leakey, who had this task in the Kenya Legislative Council, carry a double irony: 'an apparently meek little man who looked rather unfit for his strenuous function of voicing the opinion of the two and a half million natives'.[19]

Even for the wholeheartedly sympathetic, the daily realities of life on most mission stations were often likely to seem drab, and their very worthiness carried elements of disillusionment. For the young Margery Perham the attractions were probably still fewer, as she relished

> the fascination of Africa with the sheer fun and interest of travel and the enhancement of my own position which my experience gave me. The self-importance [?and] pseudo-romance of this woman traveller were a comforting change – with all the male company thrown in – from the chill corridors of a women's college.[20]

However, there was more to her mental reservations than disquiet over details compounded by the counter-attractions of official entertainment.

At root she was working towards the conclusion that missionaries were pursuing a mistaken strategy. The education which they provided was not only limited but too often wholly inappropriate. Feeling herself able to appreciate why 'the missionaries tried, at any cost, to transform selected individuals into some semblance of themselves', nevertheless she could not condone it. Individualism was linked in her syllabus of errors with a westernized literary education, with pupils' incomprehension of the Dickensian workhouse of Oliver Twist or with the 'meaningless recitations' and striving after 'perfect handwriting' which she encountered in Roman Catholic missions in the Congo.[21] 'It is almost pathetic how the missionaries as pastors struggle to repress discontent with one hand while, as teachers, they give the African the fuel for this fire.'[22]

Here were the seeds of her sense that missionaries could be a seriously debilitating and even destructive force, at one in many ways with white settlement or large-scale mining enterprise. Margery Perham relearned lessons imbibed earlier by Mary Kingsley and, like her, expressed them for her own generation. The case was not only to be progressively sharpened in her writings during the 1930s, but reinforced from various directions. There were the wrecks of individual missionaries and the disillusionment with the minimal standards of so much missionary education expressed by teachers in government schools. Clearly there were incompatibilities between the missionary record and Perham's vision of an Africa in fifty years' time, quite possibly 'covered with happy peasants contributing more and more to world trade and still keeping their land and their pride'.[23] She disliked the tendency of early missionary efforts in matters of church-state relations to work for the development of non-European governments, as she later put it, 'dependent upon their advice and as far as possible immune from other interventions'. Perham was referring here to missionary policy in mid-nineteenth-century Abeokuta, but its echoes persisted. Observing that in Samoa 'the missions keep severely neutral in the political conflict', she felt obliged to offer an immediate qualification. 'That is to say they do nothing to help the [colonial] Government and I suspect that any benevolence in their neutrality finds its way to the native side.'[24]

As Perham's knowledge of colonial administration, her affection for administrators, and her confidence as a commentator on indirect rule grew, her criticisms of the missions were clarified and became more public. In 1931 she was writing in *Africa* of the need to counteract the generally undermining and corrosive effects of western civilization, not least those of education and Christian teaching.[25] By the time she published her classic account of Nigerian administration in 1937, it was her view that among her 'Disintegrating Influences', 'Chief, and generally first in time ... has been that of the missions'. The spread of Christianity had opened up 'what to Africans is a deep and unnatural rift ... between old and young', while conversion had brought about 'deracination' and the destruction of a sense of civic duty.[26] In a self-consciously modern and progressive world, and with the additional security of that wider Oxonian confidence wherever questions of imperial management were involved, she thus secularised a common Anglican disdain for evangelicalism, low or high.[27]

III

There was, it must be said, little that was original in all this. Perham was swimming with the tides and charting the prevailing currents as she went. Roland Oliver has shown how, complementing strands of self-examination within the missionary world itself, they had begun to flow strongly against hitherto dominant forms of missionary activity with the publication in 1922 of both Lugard's *Dual Mandate* and the Report of the Phelps-Stokes Commission'.[28] Confidently aware of the scale of the African challenge in the wake of her first interviews with Lugard and Sir Donald Cameron, Perham had herself by May 1929 made up her mind on two counts, that 'white settlement is not good for the African', and 'The ideal would be government by the colonial service'.[29] Where Kingsley's counterweight to disintegration was provided by the traders, so Perham found her organizing class in a body of enthusiastic and systematically-trained administrators, formed according to British models – unlike the American 'naval men' she encountered that same year in Pago.[30]

Like her early travels, so her continuing contact with the leading lights of the Colonial Service reinforced these preliminary conclusions. There can be no doubt, for example, that Lugard's influence, interest and friendship assisted the definition of Perham's priorities in the 1930s, as she herself was only too willing to confess. Their correspondence shows their increasing intimacy, especially in the autumn/spring of 1932–3, as well as the very wide range of their practical cooperation. As Lugard laboured on successive sheaves of her drafts and proofs for *Native Administration in Nigeria*, she wrote to him:

> I think you know what it means to have you living so near and to be able to see you and share your work ... I feel the bond between us there all the time. I cannot begin to tell you what a difference your encouragement and affection have made to my work and my life.[31]

Perham was aware of the difficulties this caused and fought hard to retain her objectivity and independence of judgement.[32] Nevertheless, the balance of her opinions on missions and government, tipped already by the drift of events and her own colonial experience, was held in place by the weight of the Lugard connection.

Active government could alone stop the rot in Africa; missionaries were too numerous to be ignored, but needed to be controlled within a clearly-established administrative framework. A system of indirect rule – 'a system by which the tutelary power recognizes existing African societies, and assists them to adapt themselves to the function of local government' – could provide the answer.[32] This alone held out the prospect of allowing 'change by growth rather than mere substitution – growth of familiar tribal institutions into more modern forms to suit modern conditions', and could 'preserve a fair field within which Africans can strike their own balance between conservation and adaptation'.[34] Disintegration on one hand, the 'mere policy of preservation' on the other, were juxtaposed as the Scylla and Charybdis to be negotiated. Officials liable to the 'besetting disease' of administrations, namely 'ossification arising out of complacency', had to be criticized and cajoled to bring them into line: so too missions and their products. It was not their work but that of local councils and treasuries which 'would allow the cooperation of educated and Christian people who are at present often left outside', and would introduce 'the authorities and ultimately the people into the modern world as nothing else can do'.[35] The proper task was to define the place of the missions in the new structures now being erected.

As she felt her way towards such a definition, she again drew heavily on the ideas of others. The British government's own interest after the war in taking the initiative to put relations with the missionary fraternity on a new footing was evident in the establishment in 1923 of the Advisory Committee on Native Education, and in the latter's 1925 report on Education in Tropical Africa. Again the link for Perham eventually came above all through Lugard, who had been there as a member from the start and was its active chairman from 1926–37.[36] She also gradually came to see that the missionary response to those early moves had been no superficial flash in the pan. The Christian missionary movement between the wars was no more at one in itself than at any other time. It was increasingly difficult for an intelligent observer not to recognize that significant sectors of it were changing, and were doing so not least in response to the leadership of J.H. Oldham and the International Missionary Council.

Oldham had been an influential figure at least since 1921, but it is not clear that Perham paid much attention to his activities before she first met him in 1929.[37] His publications and his work on the Advisory Committee on Native Education (from 1929, on Education in the Colonies) provided an effective barometer of the way in which ideas about purpose and methods in missionary headquarters were changing. Of particular relevance, perhaps, to the development of Perham's ideas were Oldham's efforts to rebut all charges that missions were a force for the disruption of African society. He pressed constantly for the definition of missionary goals, for 'the progressive evolution of a coordinated policy of Christian education, thought out in the light of the Christian meaning of education and the missionary purpose and closely related to the living forces in modern Africa'.[38]

Oldham was anxious to avoid both the forced withdrawal of missions and the mere dictation to missionaries by governments. Not only did he express sympathy with the aims of Sir Donald Cameron, who was prominent alongside Lugard as an occupant of Perham's administrative pantheon: he also believed that Cameron's views 'have solid roots in Christian theology'. 'The religious meaning of the doctrine of creation necessarily implies a reverence for the institutions which a race has evolved in the historic process of its growth. ... [Cameron] asserts as strongly as any wise missionary ... that existing institutions are a means and not an end.'[39] Oldham therefore aimed at achieving constructive cooperation between missions and administrations based on clear missionary plans for the future. He thereby contributed decisively to the process through which, by the end of the 1930s, mutual understanding had greatly increased and the missionary societies were well able to respond collectively and in detail to major departures in imperial government policy.[40]

There is room for an extended investigation not only of developments in missionary thinking and policy in the 1930s, and of Oldham's influence upon them, but of the extent to which Perham took account of such changes. In this connection it is still unclear to what extent she was involved with others in Britain during the first half of the decade, like Margaret Wrong and J. W. C. Dougall, who supported the cause of African missions. There are, however, at least circumstantial reasons for thinking that these changes became important to her because of their increasing relevance to her other developing concerns. In particular they had a bearing on her mounting involvement with East African policy, and with educational matters. Following the debate over closer union, she was from 1935 in close touch with the Governor of Uganda, Philip Mitchell. Alongside him she was busily preoccupied with the work of the De la Warr Commission on higher education, the report of which placed great emphasis on the future importance of mission-government cooperation in educating Africans. Just as Uganda also contributed to her enthusiasm for indirect rule, so East Africa as well as West seems likely to have influenced her constructive thinking about missions.[41]

Thus by 1937 Perham, while often critical of the missionary record, was also able to see promise in these signs of movement and cooperation at the top. They were, she felt by the mid-1930s, just beginning to have an impact on what was being done in Nigeria.[42] She seems, however, not only to have regarded their practical implementation from the missionary side as often the essentially reactive response to government initiatives, but to have felt that a constant administrative challenge to missionaries on the ground was also necessary. Only under this spur would missionaries 'weave their influence deeply into the life of the societies they serve and close, at any rate in the lower stages of education, the gap which still exists between their methods and the policy of indirect rule.'[43]

IV

The gap between Perham, the missions and the 'indirect rulers' thus never became unbridgeable however much it widened on particular questions. As her sense of the problems matured, practical answers to them rarely seemed to be very far behind. Common external pressures were also in part responsible for this.[44] It is difficult now to recapture the passion with which in the 1930s issues like closer union in East Africa and the future of white settlement were fought over. In trying to do so, it is important to understand how fearful many liberals and humanitarians were that they would lose their battle on behalf of the African. In such circumstances all parties needed every friend they could muster. The flow of questions which called for organized representation and political pressure – amongst them the work of the Mandates Commission, the future of the South African High Commission Territories, the Abyssinian crisis, German colonial claims – held together initially shaky allies and forged a farreaching network of cooperation.

In this setting, it is argued, as challenges to indirect rule also began to crystallize and its practical shortcomings impinged increasingly on policy-makers' consciousness, Perham gradually discovered the extent of the coincidence between her own and many missionary opinions. By the spring of 1941, she was wondering how to 'write a book upon Africa according to the old standards, with old facts which are falling so far into the past with present events racing ahead at their present mechanised speed'.[45] At about the same time she had begun to collect in a newly systematic way material on missionary activity, and to build up what were to become her regular contacts with the Conference of British Missionary Societies and the Church Missionary Society.[46] Reflecting on the Christian past, she wrote: 'True, other religions had [sic] and do offer a social cement to other societies, but they are mostly helped by the setting of static conditions and strong pressures and unspoken historical traditions.' Now, in an ever more self-evidently secular and rapidly changing world, Christianity alone seemed capable of offering new hope.[47] As the certainties which had so recently underpinned thinking about indirect rule crumbled, this perception provided the basis for a new slant to her activities.

This process was aided not a little by the tragic and desperate experiences of the Second World War; these led to a revival of Perham's own religious beliefs.

> It was the full realization of the character of Nazism ... that first made me doubt my own doubts. It stood out as the antithesis of Christianity, quite literally anti-Christ and it was destructive of the entire social and spiritual life of man. It showed the full logic of materialism. And I saw it as created in part from our own failures to follow the Christian values.[48]

At a more personal level, just as her earlier scepticism had arisen to some extent from her brother's death, so this rediscovery of faith 'was deepened by the sorrow caused by Wilfrid's death and Robert's imprisonment'. 'Nothing less than the Christian religion', she concluded, 'could hope to answer the horrifying return of a supposedly Christian people to deliberate savagery'.[49]

Recent scholarship has explored in considerable detail the devastating impact of the 1939–45 war on Britain's colonial system.[50] In response to the fundamental upheavals of these years there emerged both nationalist ambitions and administrative responses, the latter variously designed to check if possible the speed of political change. Attuned to the worlds of both the Colonial Service and, increasingly, Africans themselves, but belonging to neither, Perham moved in a different direction. Perhaps Lugard's death in 1945 helped to make this possible.

She recognized that by 1947 there had taken place 'a revolution in methods and in attitudes of mind', but it was one which created more problems that it solved. These were far less technical and material than personal and moral, for the commitment to self-government and the management of progress towards it called for uncommon powers of sympathy, patience and restraint. '[W]e shall not succeed in all this, or even approach success, unless many more of us who are concerned with this great enterprise find our purpose and our strength in Christ.'[51] Even allowing for the tastes of her audience and the rhetoric of the occasion, this seems a far cry from the Perham of the 1920s and 1930s. Her position, moreover, became steadily more clear-cut. From looking to missions in 1947 'not only to humanize policy but to construct something on a deeper level than policy or even the existing imperial connection', she had moved by 1954 to the point where she could write: 'It is so clear that whatever politics may do in the short-term, it is the work of the Missions alone that could save Africa in the long run from all the dangers and demoralization that threaten so many of her people.'[52]

Perham's passage from the administrative frameworks of indirect rule within which the primarily educative activities of the missions would be tightly constrained to a free-for-all firmament into which Christian teaching should be infused wherever possible, was also spurred on by the anxieties of the Cold War and fears of communist propaganda. While Africans were being offered 'a clear dynamic wholly non-Christian alternative', it was incumbent on the West to reemphasize the essentially Christian nature of its own liberal democracy.[53] This was certainly a task for the new recruits to the Colonial Service, and perhaps Perham's personal commitment to their education needs to be seen in this light. Lugard's agnosticism in matters of religious faith would no longer suffice. At the level of colonial societies themselves the problem had to be tackled too in those spheres where hitherto missionary bodies had played only a small role. To this end, Perham was actively involved, from 1948, in the discussions within the Inter-University Council for Higher Education, on religion in colonial universities; she was also in touch with the Church Missionary Society about questions of staff recruitment and the provision of chapels.[54] Where haste was important, the elements of self-sacrifice and economical operation (which had always been liable to endear missions to others) gained a newly-heightened significance.[55] Perham also found that, even from a purely practical point of view as with people like A. S. Cripps in the 1930s, missionaries continued invaluable allies in pursuit of particular causes, such as her opposition to the Central African Federation.

In re-evaluating the Christian and missionary contribution to Africa's present, Perham seems also to have reconsidered their past record with greater tolerance or sympathy. As she explained to Canon Kingsnorth of the UMCA in 1963,

> I feel that the early missionaries were faced with an almost impossible problem. I know it is not fashionable now to refer to the state of savagery which they found in most parts on their arrival, but I hardly see how they could have worked, in those early days, except by making these areas of peace, order and civilization'.[56]

Her sketches for talks and lectures increasingly stressed the clear and inevitable phases of missionary work, as well as the need for a balanced assessment of their record. 'No need', she noted, 'in order to please Africans or the humanists to agree that the older missionaries worked on wrong or mistaken lines'.[57] Others will know perhaps how such reconsiderations may have spilled over into her teaching; but it would appear that, as in the 1920s and 1930s, so in the twenty years after the Second World War, Perham's historical study and first-hand experience played upon each other in ways crucially affected by the changing filter of her own religious commitment.

Finally, it is possible to observe how, in distancing herself from her earlier preoccupation with indirect rule, Perham came to advocate a strikingly changed vision of the right relations between church and state. Where in the 1930s she had emphasized the need for subordination and control, she became steadily more preoccupied with the possibility that this would encourage African rejection of a religion which seemed little more than 'a buttress of imperialism'. Promoting Christianity as a vital social cement was one thing, but 'It is not a very distant shift of intention for Christianity to be used to stifle discontent, to draw off nationalism and oppose communism, for the state in the form of colonial governments and education departments to work in with missionaries and support them.'[58] Thus she came to echo the view which Oldham had expressed years before, that it could not 'in the long run be to the advantage of Christianity to be treated as an economical substitute for a police force'. For Perham in the 1950s, 'What seemed once to be an advantage to Christianity, that it was the faith of the rulers, has now become a handicap', became an insistent refrain.[59]

Missions, missionary churches, and African Christianity would fulfil their inestimable potential, for both solving the problems of race relations and easing the transition to eventual independence, only by keeping their distance from the state.[60] Close links had at times in the past been inevitable, most recently as 'the idea of the welfare state grew on the secular side' and the state looked to the resources of the missions for assistance in areas such as health and education.[61] Increasingly, however, these needed to be broken, not only in the interests of securing a continued existence for the churches themselves but also as a means of retaining independence and power sufficient to check the drift towards secularism, especially in education, of the new African governments.[62] Her renewed belief in Christinaity as vital to social stability and mores thus prompted the re-emergence of a high Anglican view of the state and secular society open to redemption by independent Christians and religious institutions.

V

It is no wonder that as her perspectives and activities shifted Margery Perham was drawn into close official links with the missionary societies.

She also joined forces with campaigners such as Michael Scott in the Africa Bureau.[63] It seems likely that this process was part cause part effect of the fact that while her relations with the Colonial Office remained close under the Conservative government, she became progressively less influential there during the 1950s. Well aware of the lobbying power of the missionary societies, she became a vice-president of the Universities Mission to Central Africa late in 1960, and only shortly afterwards president. It was a difficult time, for she was called in to officiate at the society's demise by merger with the Society for the Propagation of the Gospel. Yet her appointment was nevertheless a most fitting one, for her own knowledge of Africa and explicit commitment enabled her both to justify the new departure to many supporters and to overcome some of their reluctance to abandon much-loved historic forms. However, there was also historical irony in the fact that the person once seen by Lugard as taking up his torch should be the promoter of a scheme to increase the power and independence of a missionary fraternity against that of civil governments.[64]

At the same time, it can be seen as historically appropriate for Perham as Lugard's heir to work for new administrative arrangements which would help to keep government on the right progressive road, so contriving still to avoid the ossification and disintegration which had worried them both thirty years before. In the circumstances, sensitive to the limitations of Christian influences, Perham might even have felt inclined to apply afresh Mary Kingsley's lament of sixty years before as she fought to prevent the traders being edged aside. 'I am a pessimist about the future of [West] Africa now it is falling so completely into the hands of this official class'.[65] However, Perham was at least able to temper pessimism with her consciousness that the missions had changed for the better, not least since those days in 1913 when Lugard had been wearied by their self-absorption.

In exploring the interplay of Margery Perham's ideas on religion and government, the historian not only comes close to the heart of problems likely to perplex any biographer, but confronts issues central to the development of the humanitarian tradition in the twentieth century. There is no doubt that to some historians her concerns and the reinterpretations of 'trusteeship' which they involve will seem not only naive but at best peripheral.[66] Judgement, however, should perhaps be reserved for the time being. In what degree these patterns of thinking affected many other individuals, the extent to which they shaped either the 'moral disarmament of African empire',[67] or the moral rearmament of anti-colonial radicalism and colonial radicals, and the contribution which they made – as eventually Perham and her friends hoped they would – to the dismantling of colonial rule, have still largely to be charted. That Margery Perham's career, and the papers which she and others have left in Rhodes House, provide a basis for such investigations is, however, not in doubt.

NOTES

1. Mary Kingsley, *Travels in West Africa* (London 1897; 5th ed., Virago Press, London, 1981), p.659.
2. Lugard to his wife, 6 Feb. 1913, in Margery Perham, *Lugard: The Years of Authority 1898–1945* (London, 1960) (hereafter Lugard II), p.404.
3. 'Present tendencies of African Colonial Governments', draft by R.S. Rattray, Perham Papers (hereafter PP), Rhodes House Library, Oxford Box 688, file 6.
4. Kingsley, *Travels*, p.x.
5. Margery Perham, *East African Journey* (London, 1976), p.165; Private Diary, 5 Dec. 1938, PP 33/4.
6. Anthony Kirk-Greene, 'Margery Perham and Colonial Administration: a direct influence on Indirect Rule', in F. Madden and D.K. Fieldhouse (eds.), *Oxford and the Idea of Commonwealth* (London, 1982), pp.139–40; Roland Oliver, 'Margery Perham, 1895–1982: Three Memorial Addresses' (typescript, SOAS Library, University of London, 1982). One might nevertheless suggest that her frequently introspective diaries call into question Oliver's emphasis on the 'simple and singularly cheerful' Christian.
7. Kingsley, *Travels*, p.659 and *passim*; Deborah Birkett, 'An Independent Woman in West Africa: the case of Mary Kingsley', (unpub.Ph.D. thesis, London, 1987), pp.146–50; Margery Perham, *Colonial Sequence 1949–1969* (London, 1970), (hereafter *Col. Seq. II*), p.347.
8. [1?] May 1929, Notes 1929–1931, PP 80.
9. For developments in the 1920s, see Roland Oliver, *The Missionary Factor in East Africa* (London, 1951; repr. 1970), and J.W. Cell, *By Kenya Possessed; the correspondence of Norman Leys and J.H. Oldham 1918–1926* (Chicago/London, 1976); 'The Basel Mission', ms draft (n.d. but late 1920s), PP 329/3; 'The South African Protectors', *The Times*, 5 July 1934, reprinted in Margery Perham, *Colonial Sequence 1930– 1949* (London, 1967), (hereafter *Col. Seq. I*), pp.120–1.
10. 'What do I believe?', Private Diary, 14 Nov. 1943, PP 33/4; Edgar, youngest brother and three years older than Margery Perham, was killed at Delville Wood on the Western Front in 1916.
11. 31 Jan. 1929, Notes 1929–31, PP 80.
12. Margery Perham, *East African Journey*, Introduction, p.17.
13. Margery Perham, *Pacific Prelude: a Journey to Samoa and Australasia 1929*, ed. A.H.M. Kirk-Greene (London, 1988), p. 92.
14. Ibid., pp.76, 91, 101–2.
15. Margery Perham, *African Apprenticeship* (London, 1974), pp.43–65, 70–2, 75–7. Cf. Michael Scott's later recollections of his similar South African impressions in 1927–28, *A Time To Speak* (London, 1958), pp.43–5.
16. Norman Chester, in 'Three Memorial Addresses'; *East African Journey*, p.147.
17. Ibid., pp.73–4, 150.
18. Margery Perham, *West African Passage*, ed. A.H.M. Kirk-Greene (London, 1983), pp.26, 36.
19. 'The Future of East Africa', *The Times* 15 August 1931, *Col. Seq. I*, pp.48, 52; May 1930, *East African Journey*, p.24.
20. Private Diary, 14 Nov. 1943, PP 33/4.
21. Perham, *African Apprenticeship*, pp.52–65, 229.
22. Ibid., p60.

23. Perham, *West African Passage*, pp. 88, 41; *East African Journey*, p. 69.
24. Perham, *Lugard II*, p. 448; *Pacific Prelude*, p. 102.
25. 'The System of Native Administration in Tanganyika', *Africa* (July 1931), 310–11.
26. Margery Perham, *Native Administration in Nigeria* (London, 1937), pp. 238–40, 279–80.
27. For introduction to the Oxford background, see Madden and Fieldhouse (eds.), *Oxford and the Idea of Commonwealth*; and Richard Symonds, *Oxford and the Empire: the last lost cause?* (London, 1986).
28. Oliver, *The Missionary Factor*, p. 265.
29. 'General on Africa', [1?] May 1929, PP 80.
30. Perham, *Pacific Prelude*, p. 89.
31. Perham to Lugard, 18 Aug. 1936, PP 22/2.
32. Perham to Lugard, 29 Oct. 1936, PP 22/2; to Creech Jones, 2 Sept. 1945, PP 23/1, f. 54–5.
33. 'Some Problems of Indirect Rule in Africa', *Journal of the Royal African Society* (1935), reprinted from *Journal of the Royal Society of Arts* (1934).
34. 'The Colonial Empire XI: Future Relations of Black and White in Africa', the *Listener*, 28 Mar. 1934, 522; 'A Restatement of Indirect Rule', *Africa* (July 1934), 331.
35. 'The System of Native Administration in Tanganyika', *Africa* (July 1931), 305; Some Problems of Indirect Rule in Africa', *Journal of the Royal African Society* (1935), 14.
36. Oliver, *The Missionary Factor*, pp. 266–9; Perham, *Lugard II*, pp. 657–62. See also Cell, *By Kenya Possessed*; Andrew Roberts, 'The Imperial Mind', and J.R. Gray 'Christianity', in Andrew Roberts (ed.), *The Cambridge History of Africa Volume VII: from 1905 to 1940* (Cambridge, 1986), chs. 1 and 3.
37. Notes 1929–1931, PP 80.
38. J.H. Oldham and B.D. Gibson, *The Remaking of Man in Africa* (London, 1931), Introduction. See also J.H. Oldham, (ed.), *The Modern Missionary: a study of the human factor in the missionary enterprise in the light of present day conditions* (London, 1935).
39. J.H. Oldham, 'The Educational Work of Missionary Societies', *Africa* (1934), 47–59.
40. See for example Conference of Missionary Societies in Great Britain and Ireland to Lord Lloyd, Secretary of State for the Colonies: A Memorandum inspired by a *Statement of Policy on Colonial Development and Welfare*. Cmd 6175 (London, 1941), copy in PP 738/1.
41. This paragraph rests heavily on the very stimulating comments by Alison Smith on my original conference paper. Relevant material is to be found, for example, in PP 516/1, 616/2, and the Diaries of Sir Philip Mitchell, Mss.Afr.r.101, Rhodes House Library, Oxford.
42. Perham, *Native Administration in Nigeria*, p. 282.
43. Ibid., pp. 281–4. Cf. the view of a recent historian of the Church Missionary Society on the 1920s: Jocelyn Murray, *Proclaim the Good News* (London, 1985), p. 203.
44. See K.E. Robinson, *The Dilemmas of Trusteeship: aspects of British colonial policy between the wars* (Oxford, 1965); R.E. Robinson, 'The Moral Disarmament of African Empire, 1919–1947', *Journal of Imperial and Commonwealth History*, 8 (Oct. 1979), 86–104.
45. Private Diary, 24 April 1941, PP 33/4.
46. See Religious matters: press cuttings 1940–77, PP 739/1, and missions: press cuttings 1941–48 PP 739–2; correspondence in PP 738/1.
47. Private Diary, 14 Nov. 1943, PP 33/4.
48. 'What do I believe?', Ibid.
49. Ibid. Wilfrid and Robert Rayne were her nephews.
50. For introductions to recent research, R.F. Holland, *European Decolonization 1918–1981: an introductory survey* (London, 1985); A.N. Porter and A.J. Stockwell, *British Imperial Policy and Decolonization 1938–1964* (2 vols, London, 1987, 1989); J.D. Hargreaves, *Decolonization in Africa* (London, 1988); John Darwin, *Britain and*

Decolonization: the retreat from empire in the postwar world (London, 1988).
51. 'Christian Missions in Africa', talk in a BBC programme to Africa for Christians in the mission field, 16 Oct. 1947, *Col. Seq. I*, pp. 302–5.
52. Perham to Canon Max Warren (CMS General Secretary), 22 Feb. 1954, PP 738/1 f. 20.
53. See also Notes for talk to missionaries serving in Africa (c. 1963), PP 240/12.
54. See correspondence in PP 719/2.
55. Cf. Perham's emphasis in January 1953 on the value of this 'to the pagan tribesmen [of the southern Sudan] with the result that many of them are now Christian', *Col. Seq. II*, pp. 75–6.
56. Perham to J. S. Kingsnorth, 21 Jan. 1963, PP 15/1 f. 11.
57. Notes for lecture, 10 May 1966, PP 241/6 f. 6; see also 'A historical sketch of missions, past and present – esp. in Africa', n.d., PP 241/6, ff. 1–2; and Notes for a talk at Stuttgart on the cultural and spiritual life of colonial peoples, 17 Feb. 1954, PP 238/6.
58. Notes for 'Religion as a buttress of Imperialism?', talk to UMCA, 23 May 1950, PP 236/10 f. 5.
59. Oldham, *Africa* (1934), 56; 'The Struggle against Mau Mau', April 1953, *Col. Seq. II*, p. 109; and ibid., pp. 47, 204, 235.
60. 'Christianity and Colonialism', July 1959, *Col. Seq. II*, pp. 172–9; also ibid., pp. 11, 107, 226; Notes for talk to missionaries serving in Africa, n.d. [c. 1963], PP 240/12.
61. Notes for Address to UMCA General Meeting, 12 May 1964, PP 240/18.
62. Perham to Kingsnorth, 21 Jan. 1963, PP 15/1 f. 11.
63. Scott, *A Time to Speak*, pp. 271, 286.
64. Lugard to Perham, 5 Dec. 1937, PP 22/2.
65. Kingsley to John Holt, 21 April 1898, cit. Birkett, pp. 254–5.
66. For contrasting attitudes, see J. E. Flint, 'Scandal at the Bristol Hotel: some thoughts on racial discrimination in Britain and West Africa and its relationship to the planning of decolonization, 1938–47', *Journal of Imperial and Commonwealth History* 12 (October, 1983), esp. 81–3; and D. A. Low, 'The End of the British Empire in Africa', in P. Gifford and W. R. Louis (eds.), *Decolonization and African Independence, 1960–1980* (Yale, 1988).
67. Cf. R. E. Robinson, 'The Moral Disarmament of African Empire' in n. 44 above.

Margery Perham and *Africans and British Rule:* a wartime publication

Michael Twaddle

Margery Perham was a student of empire whose writings, from the 1930s onwards, often appeared in British newspapers. She was also a keen supporter of the British Empire. On both counts she was therefore extremely annoyed when she heard from her publisher, Oxford University Press, in June 1942 that her little book on *Africans and British Rule* had been banned by the British colonial authorities in Kenya. She promptly kicked up a fuss and the book was soon unbanned. This paper is mainly about that fuss; about this little book and its successive banning and unbanning; and about the way in which the incident illuminates different wartime attitudes to British rule in Africa. It is based principally upon information about these matters preserved in the Perham archive, now superbly catalogued and housed in Rhodes House Library. Use has been made also of confidential correspondence on the same subject in the Kenya National Archives, which came to light by chance when scanning censorship files in Nairobi for quite another purpose.[1] Though not one of her major publications, this short work does provide further evidence of the aptness of Thucydides's ancient remark about war being a forcible schoolmaster, as well as minor additional evidence for that socio-biological history of Nuffield College, Oxford, which must surely also one day be written.

Oxford University Press planned the book in mid-1940 as one of its 'African Welfare Series': booklets designed to help create an informed public opinion among Africans in British colonies. The title suggested to Margery Perham by the series' editor was 'Colonial Government'; the length should be 15,000 words, and the vocabulary limited to 2,000 words, in order to make it intelligible to Africans with some secondary school education. Miss Perham sent him a draft synopsis, which she said had the general endorsement of Eliud Mathu, the first Kenyan to study at Oxford, though he had urged her not to talk down to Africans 'as to children'. The OUP editor disagreed:

> We are not writing for him and his like ... but for just those 'children' of Africa, in mind if not in years, to whom any book in

English is a serious enough study ... Concrete example and practical illustration wherever possible, I say, and avoidance of abstract philosophy and ideals. I hope we can suggest practical ways by which Africans can enable the British government to give them more authority and a greater share in administration.[2]

Margery Perham, writing against the background of the fall of France, saw the task as part of her contribution to the war effort. She had, in the previous years, opposed any concession to Germany's claims for the return of its colonies. She now explained that

the European situation [had] brought the position of the colonies and especially of Africa so much into the front of men's minds. ... The main purpose of her book [was] to present Africa not as a name or a map in European diplomacy, but as a problem of government, a rich variety of persons and peoples, and a stern test of our high claims, much repeated in these days, to a peculiarly altruistic form of trusteeship.[3]

Meanwhile she felt it necessary to decline another request for a pamphlet to assist the war effort – on trusteeship in the Commonwealth – from an Oxford colleague seconded to the Ministry of Information:

I think I told you I was pushing through now a short book for Africans on the whole question of British government in relation to their ambitions. You will agree this is badly needed at the moment. ... I shall write it as a direct answer to questions that I know are troubling the minds of English-speaking Africans all over British Africa.[4]

She wrote quickly and more than doubled the 15,000 words indicated; the study eventually ran to 35,000 words and filled nearly one hundred small pages. It is not surprising that factual errors crept in; one, stating that the Kabaka Mutesa of Buganda, rather than his successor Mwanga, murdered Christian converts in the 1880s, was queried by the editor, but still appeared in the first impression.[5] The argument of the book is of interest chiefly as illuminating Margery Perham's own underlying approach to issues of colonial rule in the early part of the Second World War. The injunction to keep to simple language caused her to be unusually forthright. A quarter of the volume is devoted to setting the problem of Africa's 'backwardness' – and of how far it might have been racially determined – in the context of Britain's own early development from tribal kingdoms into a twentieth-century democracy. The length of these two introductory chapters was the main question raised by the editor about the text.[6] Three chapters examine, against the test of Britain's claims to 'altruistic trusteeship', the rights and wrongs of the acquisition and rule of its African dependencies. The remaining pages raise very briefly questions of the future: how far indirect rule provides an adequate basis for development towards self-government; how far such development can be reconciled with white colonization; and the role of education as the great solvent.

Africans and British Rule, a title agreed only at the final stages, was published while the course of the war was still critical in mid-1941, and went through three impressions. The notices it received were generally favourable, though Norman Leys, in *Time and Tide*, thought it too sympathetic to colonial rule,[7] and *West Africa* considered that its tone was 'too much *de haut en bas*'. However, almost immediately, trenchant criticism of the the book came from the West Indian economist, W. Arthur Lewis. This was in the League of Coloured Peoples' *Newsletter* for September 1941:

> What questions must an African ... ask himself about the effects of British rule over his country? As a boy he sees that his school is a shambles compared with that reserved for white children – if indeed there is in his area any school at all for blacks. As he grows up he realises how inadequate are the lands on which his people live, and learns how they have been pushed into small and barren reserves to make room for white settlers; or he finds his father a tenant on a European farm, compelled by law like a medieval serf to do at least three months' labour on the farm by way of rent. As a young man he goes away to work in the mines, and finds that however intelligent he may be, a colour bar (whether enforced by law as in South Africa, or by custom as in Northern Rhodesia) prevents him from getting any skilled job. He finds, too, that if he tries to make any organised protest he is held up for sedition and imprisoned, or branded as a communist agitator and hounded from job to job. It does not take him long to see that if he had had the luck to be born of white parents in Africa all doors would be open to him: to be born black is to be born already half-strangled by economic and racial bonds.

To the question of why this should be so, Lewis continued that Margery Perham had produced eight chapters of argument of which he proceeded to present a summary, brutal but not inaccurate, which it is worth quoting at length:

Chapter I: 'The Growth of Britain's Government.' You Africans must realise that you are backward. We English, too, were once slaves like you, and you must realise that it took us many centuries to reach our present high state of civilisation. For our progress we, like you, owe much to foreign rulers, the Romans and the Normans, and much to the Tudors, strong rulers who stood no nonsense from our tribal chiefs, the barons, or from Parliamentary democrats.

Chapter II: 'Africa as it was before European Occupation.' You Africans when we discovered you were even more savage than we had ever been. In fact so savage that some of us wondered whether you were not really an inferior biological specimen, incapable of advancement. There are a lot of reasons [lengthily enumerated] for thinking so, but science has not yet advanced sufficiently to prove it, so for the time being we must give you the benefit of the doubt.

Chapter III: 'How British Africa was Gained and How it is Governed.' Don't believe people who say we went to Africa solely for selfish reasons. Sometimes we did, but in other cases our motives were humanitarian. For instance, having been the leading slave power in the eighteenth century, we took over some territories in the nineteenth century in order to stop the slave trade.

Chapter IV: 'Uses and Abuses of Imperialism: I. Political.' What would you do with freedom if you had it? You are much better off without it. 'I want to emphasize this point, for I believe it is important to face it once and for all. Subjection was the only way by which, on account of her backwardness, and the nature of Europe's nineteenth century system, Africa could have been brought into the civilised world' (p.59).

Chapter V: 'Uses and Abuses of Imperialism: II. Economic.' It is true that your people have been severely exploited by British capitalists – mining companies and trading combines. Well, we have now decided to allow you to form trade unions and co-operatives, but be careful not to use them irresponsibly.

Chapter VI: 'Indirect Rule and African Self-Government.' (Although my first chapter has proved that the English progressed through unifying the country and getting rid of tribal governments), Africans should not hanker after British forms of democracy: they should be content to improve their tribal organisations. 'It is natural that Africans, like Indians, should desire the full British form of representative Parliamentary democracy. So did the Italians, Germans, Russians and many other people who have now found that it is quite unsuited to their traditions and character' (p.76).

Chapter VII: 'The Problems of White Colonisation.' Do try to understand why the colour bar is maintained. Here are a few civilised people surrounded by a sea of barbarism. They feel they simply cannot allow themselves to be dragged down; their ranks must be kept pure. 'Most important, if almost unconscious, is the average white colonist's determination not to allow a mixture of races. The colour, the facial appearance and the smell of Africans in themselves give a sense of wide racial difference' (p.80).

Chapter VIII: 'Education and the Future.' The real hope for the future lies in education. Do not worry so much about your subject status. 'One thing is certain: that you must have foreign rulers, and for a long time to come. Indeed, I believe if it could all be calculated up coolly, and without the usual strong feelings on both sides, it would appear that today you have more need for the British Nation than we have of you' (p.92).[9]

There is no record of a reply from Margery Perham to this attack, though it certainly appears to have embittered subsequent personal relations with Arthur Lewis. Nevertheless, some of the shafts must have gone home. She had in her Introduction written of her links with the League of Coloured Peoples and the West African Students' Union, as well as of her acquaintance with the work of African political writers – Padmore, Azikiwe, Mockerie, Kenyatta, Kayamba and Jabavu among them. But she had also dwelt upon her own Oxford background, on the distinguished African students there, on the hope that Oxford might assist and inspire Makerere College in Uganda. No wonder that Lewis concluded by commenting that 'from the prosperous seclusion of Oxford it is easy to ride the high horse of cultural superiority, to belittle the wrongs of a people, and magnify their faults'. The book was basically 'propaganda for the British cause' and an ill-mannered 'apology for imperialism'.

Lewis blamed the cultural backwardness of Africa on its economic backwardness, and called for proper development of its resources. Yet, he said, governors who attempted this were too often labelled as difficult. 'Who makes the best Colonial governor? The man who makes the least trouble for the Colonial Office: he lets the settlers have their way, so that they do not write disturbing letters to *The Times*, and he keeps the natives quiet with a circus or two so that they do not revolt.'[10] And this was to prove during the next few months what was perhaps the most wounding element in his attack.

For it is not surprising that the 'ill-mannered apology for imperialism' evoked a very different response in the most vociferous of Britain's

African settler communities. Margery Perham had for some years been on record as an outspoken opponent of the claims of the European settlers to material hegemony in Kenya, and even the cautious endorsement of the principle of African political advance in the concluding chapters of *Africans and British Rule* was enough to incur their hostility. But she believed that on the whole the British government, in Whitehall and Nairobi, could be trusted to keep settler aspirations in check. In November 1941 she wrote to the Labour MP Arthur Creech Jones that the new governor Sir Henry Moore, whom she knew personally, was 'too sane and intelligent to be hoodwinked'.[11] So it was with considerable indignation that in June 1942 she heard from Oxford University Press that her book had been banned in Kenya. Now she wrote very differently to Creech Jones:

> A pretty lurid light is thrown on the present atmosphere in Kenya if a book which some Africans and friends of Africans find all too moderate is regarded as dangerous in Kenya. It also raises the whole question of banning books in the Colonies. I feel like trying to raise a fight over it and I wonder whether – if the Egyptian crisis is not going to be too bad and swamp all minor considerations for some time – if you would think out who would be the best person to ask a question in the House ... I suggest 'to what persons has the responsibility for banning books been delegated in Kenya? Upon exactly what grounds was this book banned? ... Could a list of other books banned in Kenya be supplied?'[12]

Creech Jones agreed to ask a parliamentary question. However, before doing so, he spoke privately about the banning of *Africans and British Rule* to a junior minister at the Colonial Office who also happened to belong to a family of publishers: Harold Macmillan. Margery Perham immediately realized that this had probably saved Sir Henry Moore's face: 'I think it is a pity to let the Kenya government off as I fear the CO will damp us down or get Kenya to withdraw'. But she persisted in pressing for a parliamentary airing nonetheless, saying 'It really worries me to think of the background against which this is possible. I do hope we can get a list of the other banned books'.[13] Creech Jones asked the question on 15 July 1942:

> Does my right hon. Friend appreciate that this raises an important question of principle? Does he agree that it means the banning of moderate statements and that the book is in no sense seditious but that it has received a warm recommendation from authorities ... in this country and in America?

Harold Macmillan responded by remarking that 'the first thing I want to find out is whether the book has been banned, which we do not know. My hon. Friend can rest assured that I have a kind of hereditary bias against censorship.'[14] What Macmillan did not tell the House of Commons was that two days before, following Creech Jones's earlier conversation with him about the banning of *Africans and British Rule*, one of the permanent officials at the Colonial Office had written to 'My dear Moore':

> We have just heard that Miss Perham's book 'Africans and British Rule' has been banned in Kenya. I should be grateful if you could let me know whether there is any truth in this. It is possible that we may get questions in the House about it.
>
> I have just learned that the book was distributed last year by the Ministry of Information to Information Officers in the Colonies.[15]

On 20 July the *East African Standard* reported the substance of Creech Jones's parliamentary question about the banning of the book, and the Director of Education in Kenya confirmed to the Chief Secretary at Nairobi that, yes, 50 copies had slipped through censorship into the hands of 'European Principals of Government and Mission schools for Africans' earlier in the year.[16] On 10 July 1942, R.G. Turnbull, writing on behalf of the Kenyan CID, had written to the Kenyan Missionary Council independently confirming earlier suggestions from the local British security forces that *Africans and British Rule* should be withdrawn from sale to Africans in Kenya pending further enquiries. Governor Moore now decided that he had better read the offending book himself. This he did, after which he drafted a demi-official letter to London:

> An unprejudiced mind regards the book as a whole as moderate in tone and reasonable, but Kenya contains many people whose minds are not unprejudiced, and it is easy for them to read into particular sections in the book an anti-settler bias which the general tone of the book does not bear out. The entry of a book of this kind into Kenya is therefore likely to stir up racial feelings to an extent that does no one any good, and I would therefore suggest that the CO might be consulted in future before any book of a similar type is sent out by the MOI for distribution in future.

Meanwhile, the book was unbanned.[18] Harold Macmillan was therefore able to write to Creech Jones on 4 September 1942 that

> I have now had a report from the Governor, and it is clear that no

ban has been imposed at any time on this book in the Colony. The book was first received in Kenya by the Education Department early this year, and copies were sent by the Education Department to the principals of various schools for Africans, and without any special instructions. Some months later, the Governor received a letter from one of the members of the Legislature, protesting against the distribution of this book, and on enquiry he ascertained that the same gentleman had lodged a formal complaint with the Police, and that the Police, in accordance with the usual procedure in such cases, had arranged for sales of the book to be temporarily withheld pending investigation. The Governor immediately called for the book and read it at once and, having done so, gave instructions that no impediment was to be placed in the way of sales.[19]

When Creech Jones passed the substance of Macmillan's letter on to her, Margery Perham thought it 'a little odd that any MP questioning a book can have it held up until the Governor can read it; still, it is better than one feared';[20] and she moved quickly on to other things – amongst them the continuance of her correspondence with Elspeth Huxley which led to the publication of *Race and Politics in Kenya* (1944). Nonetheless, the question remains – why was Margery Perham's *Africans and British Rule* banned in Kenya in 1942?

Part of the answer is provided by David Throup's comment in his account of Kenya during the 1940s and 1950s (not to mention Arthur Lewis's earlier implicit prophecy) about Governor Moore desiring a quiet life: 'Moore never got over the experience of serving as Byrne's Colonial Secretary [in Kenya during the 1930s] when he bore the [brunt] of settler criticism during the depression. When he returned as governor he wanted a quiet life, and allowed the [white] settlers to make considerable political gains during the [Second World] war.'[21] But there were other forces at work besides gubernatorial time-serving. As C.G. Richards, OUP's agent in Nairobi, related to Margery Perham subsequently:

> I run the CMS bookshop in Nairobi . . . For some time I was looking forward to this addition to the Welfare Series, but was away when the first copies arrived. It seems that other copies arrived by other means and were bought by members of the European community who at once started complaints about it. When I arrived home I was told that the copies we had must not be sold. I therefore informed the publishers. It was my duty to do so, as I am Oxford University Press agent for this sort of book. I received a cable from OUP asking for explanations and to this I replied after asking the CID the

position. They told me that the book could only be sold to people of whose bona fides I was assured. I could not be in the position of making such invidious distinctions and so said no more copies should be sent. Then the storm broke. Quotations from House of Commons speeches – with headlines and all – appeared in the [*East African*] *Standard*, & there was a lot of talk. After a bit the ban was released – of course I cabled that too.

The book is selling quite well & is I think a very valuable piece of work as it calls on the Africans to play their part in the higher development.[22]

Of course, what OUP's Nairobi agent did not know was that the OUP personnel in Britain assisted the unbanning of *Africans and British Rule* by telling Margery Perham that the Ministry of Information had purchased substantial quantities of this particular title for distribution in Africa before its banning in Kenya; though OUP in Britain wished to make sure that, when suitable political use was eventually made of this information by Creech Jones, its source would not be identified.[23] But Richards's most interesting comments about the banning were that:

Kenya is a funny place nowadays, troops & controllers of all kinds have completely altered Nairobi.

The CMS bookshop is a very busy spot, because of the growth of literacy & the consequent demand for books, plus the extra cash that most Africans have now, all these have come at a time when it is difficult to get books. However, we have been very lucky in shipments from home & we have printed a lot of books here.

It was indeed a critical time in Kenyan colonial history. Pearl Harbor had been bombed by the Japanese in December 1941, and February 1942 saw the fall of Singapore. East and Central Africa now acquired enormous importance for Britain's war effort. White settlers in Kenya were enabled thereby to entrench their powers considerably. African members of what has also been characterized as a proto-bourgeoisie enriched themselves too, through a black market that expanded massively during the 1940s as well as through the more formal encouragement of African production for Britain's war effort.[25] All this doubtless made *Africans and British Rule* a more urgent 'read' for Africans as well as a greater irritant to white settlers visibly appalled by the 'phobias and isms' of its supposedly 'fanatically theoretical' author.[26]

It has already been noted that Margery Perham's concern extended beyond the case of her own pamphlet to a more general pressure against rigid colonial censorship. Sadly, however, the unbanning of her book in 1942 did not discourage subsequent bannings of comparable discussions of Africans and British rule in East Africa by both African and non-African authors during the latter part of the Second World War. Indeed, Robert Kakembo's manuscript, provisionally entitled *An African Soldier Speaks*, was denied publication in any language by the British colonial authorities in 1945 principally because of fears regarding 'the probable reaction in East Africa'; and this despite strong arguments made in favour of publication from within the Colonial Office by Sydney Caine, Raymond Firth, and Kenneth Robinson.[27] Furthermore, this continuing censorship of 'sensitive' manuscripts by British colonial officials throughout East and Central Africa during the 1940s also serves to underline the persuasiveness, with these officials as well as with most of those in London, of the parts of Sir Henry Moore's demi-official letter about Margery Perham's *Africans and British Rule* that Harold Macmillan did *not* pass on to Arthur Creech Jones. But that is another story.

Roland Oliver has remarked upon the significance of the fall of Singapore to the Japanese in February 1942 as a catalyst for the emergence of a 'second Miss Perham' dedicated to the 'kind of rapid, indiscriminate westernization' of Africans, 'to which hitherto she had been so much opposed'.[28] Andrew Porter, too, stresses the importance of the Second World War, as well as the influence of the missionary spokesman J.H. Oldham during the 1930s, in prompting Margery Perham to become more critical of indirect rule and more aware of the positive role of Christian missions in the political advancement of educated Africans.[29] In her Introduction to *Africans and British Rule*, she had asked for African reactions; and she received them, not only from the white settler community, secretariat and CID in Kenya but from a vociferous variety of West Indians and Africans living in other parts of Africa, and these must have played at least some part too in the transformation of the first Miss Perham into the second.

Two examples of such reactions may perhaps be quoted. A West Indian reader wrote to Margery Perham regretting her assumption that West Indians were less interested in African traditions than were Africans.[30] An African Muslim teacher in Tanganyika objected to the observation on page 44 that 'it is not for Europeans, so lately guilty of profiting by similar evils, to condemn on moral grounds Arabs whose religion, unlike Christianity, did not urge them to love and pity mankind all men'. On the contrary, commented this correspondent, Islam *did* require Muslims to love and pity, and furthermore he quoted chapter and verse from the Koran in support of his view. Additionally, regarding Margery Perham's assumption of a lack of interest in politics on the part of educated Africans at the present time, he retorted that:

As an African, I think I am more qualified to talk about this experience than you are. I tell you that Africans, both educated and uneducated, are deeply interested in politics. This is largely because they do not live in a static environment. They see changes of government, of tribal institutions and now, to a large measure, they suffer loss of their natural rights. So they may conceal their grievances: knowing of course that whatever they may say, nobody will sympathise with them; and in so doing, they will be indulging in a wild goose chase.

Africans in Kenya, Southern Rhodesia and South Africa as well as other parts of Africa, have already aired their grievances against over-occupation of their land, and small salaries; and their masters have already misundertood their ideas or ignored them .... As things stand in Africa today, there is no real freedom of speech with an African.[31]

In seeking the sources of this transformation of views on the part of a publicist of such strongly moralistic and argumentative bent, it is important to identify the number and nature of her correspondents in the round as well as to analyze the arguments of the most influential amongst them in detail. It is also important to take due note of the timing of the various turning-points in the Second World War. Margery Perham might well later mark the *Africans and British Rule* file '2nd class value'; but it is in such disregarded files that evidence for the rise and fall of cultural hegemonies in colonial Africa is surely to be sought, as much as in the letters, articles and more lengthy books which passed between Margery Perham and her closest intimates.

NOTES

1. This was the start of a study of East African Asians during the last hundred years, financed in part by the Hayter and Central Research Funds of London University for whose help, needless to say, I was and remain grateful. This particular study continues now in other areas of East Africa.
2. Margery Perham to E.C. Parnwell, 6 July, and Parnwell to Perham, 11 July 1940, Perham Papers, Rhodes House Library, Oxford, Box 288, file 3.
3. Draft of the blurb sent to OUP, undated, but acknowledged by Parnwell 30 April 1941, PP 288/3.
4. Perham to Vincent Harlow, 5 July 1940, PP 329/4.
5. Parnwell to Perham, 11 Dec. 1940, PP 288/3; copy of first impression in author's possession.
6. There was discussion of making these two chapters into a separate booklet, and the historian D.C. Somervell, then teaching at Tonbridge School, was consulted as a possible collaborator.
7. 30 Aug. 1941. The reviews are collected in PP 288/5.

8. 13 Sept. 1941.
9. A copy is retained in the Perham Papers at PP 288/5.
10. Ibid.
11. Perham to Creech Jones, 11 Nov. 1941, PP 23/1.
12. Perham to Creech Jones, 30 June 1942, PP 23/1.
13. Perham to Creech Jones, 6 July 1942, PP 23/1.
14. *Hansard*, 15 July 1942.
15. A.J. Dawe to Moore, 13 July 1942, Kenya National Archives, CS/2/2496/WW/11441/ Box 46.
16. Director of Education, Kenya, confidential, 20 July 1942, loc. cit.
17. Turnbull to Kenya Missionary Council, 10 July 1942, loc. cit.
18. Undated draft, Moore to Dawe, loc. cit.
19. Macmillan to Creech Jones, 4 Sept. 1942, PP 288/6.
20. Perham to Creech Jones, 16 Sept. PP 23/1.
21. D.W. Throup, *Economic and Social Origins of Mau Mau* (London, 1987), pp. 278–9.
22. C.G. Richards to Perham, 17 Nov. 1942, PP 288/4.
23. Perham to Creech Jones, 6 July 1942, PP 23/1.
24. Richards to Perham, 17 Nov. 1942, PP 288/4.
25. Besides Throup, *Economic and Social Origins*, see J. Lonsdale, 'The Depression and the Second World War in the Transformation of Kenya', in D. Killingray and R. Rathbone (eds.), *Africa and the Second World War* (London, 1986), pp. 97–142; D. Anderson and D. Throup, 'Africans and agricultural production in colonial Kenya: the myth of the war as a watershed', *Journal of African History*, 26 (1985), 327–45; and, for Kenya's relations with Uganda, B.G. Thompson, 'Uganda and the Second World War: the limits of power in a colonial state', (Ph.D. thesis, Institute of Commonwealth Studies, London University, 1990).
26. *Kenya Weekly News*, 19 June 1942. See also the same newspaper for 25 Sept. 1942 and *East African Standard*, 30 April 1943, for further white settler comment on the Perham booklet.
27. The relevant minutes are in the Public Record Office, CO 822/118/46776. Favouring publication of Kakembo were Caine (7/5/45), Firth (15/5/45) and Robinson (4/6/45), but Cohen vetoed their minutes on 6/6/45 saying 'My main objection is the probable reaction in East Africa'. Cohen had the recent riots in Uganda in mind as well as any white settlers' objections.
28. See above, p. 24.
29. See above pp. 92–4.
30. R. Adams to Perham, 20 Sept. 1941, PP 288/4.
31. R.H. Saidi to Perham, 6 Dec. 1945, PP 288/4.

Margery Perham's *The Government of Ethiopia*

Edward Ullendorff

[Patricia Pugh has contributed an introductory note to this reminiscence, using the Foreign Office records as well as the Perham archive,[1] explaining how this book came to be written:

Early in 1941 officials of the Foreign Office realized that, as advisers to the Emperor during the period of British military control and the subsequent rehabilitation of Ethiopia, they would have to make policy decisions which would require knowledge of how the country had been governed before the Italian occupation. They consulted the Royal Institute of International Affairs, whose Foreign Research and Press Service had been evacuated from London to Oxford. Margery Perham, Lucy Mair and one or two others in Oxford wrote a paper for it on 'Some Problems in Ethiopia', and the Foreign Office enlisted their help to prepare 'a work which would be of use to government departments and help educate those outside who were interested but not too well informed about conditions in Ethiopia'. The Office arranged for one of its former field officers in the Horn of Africa, Frank de Halpert, to be seconded as an assistant to the project to read the annual and consular reports in the department's restricted records. While collaborating with Margery, who, in the event, practically monopolized the project, he became devoted to her and remained a life-long friend and correspondent.

In July 1942 the completed text was duly sent to the Foreign Office for inspection before publication, but was rejected because the authors had stopped short at the Italian annexation. Margery thereupon pressed that the Foreign Office should send her out to Ethiopia, with assurances to the Emperor that she had the support of the British government. The Institute accordingly suggested this to the Foreign Office, whose officials had meanwhile lost their enthusiasm for a book which they had not intended to be monopolized by Miss Perham. They declared they had nothing to gain from 'Miss Perham ... airing her views', and told her that though there would be no objection raised to her visiting Ethiopia, she would do so without government support. She was eventually persuaded to postpone

112

her journey for a year; further delays ensued and she never did visit the country. The Institute was anxious to get the work published and suggested that Lucy Mair might write a further section on the Italian occupation; this the Foreign Office rejected because she had only enemy propaganda as a source. Permission was granted for publication of the text as it stood, provided a section on the Emperor's foreign relations, largely taken from official records, was excised.

When Margery began revising the text in the Easter vacation of 1943 she met a further obstruction. Frank de Halpert's secondment had ended and when the Institute applied for permission for her to consult more recent records, to bring the account of Anglo-Ethiopian relations up to date, the Foreign Office refused, 'largely because of Miss Perham's personal outlook and opinions and her friendship with Sir P[hilip] Mitchell'. Those opinions had certainly not been kept to herself. As usual she had been writing to the The Times *and she had been engaged by the Ministry of Information and other bodies to lecture on the state of the war in North Africa. The book on Ethiopia was thereupon shelved until the end of the war. In 1945, even though by then she had some backing within the Foreign Office, she could still obtain no privileged access to its records. Despite all the arguments she put forward, and despite the support of her friends in the government, including Creech Jones, the department remained adamant.* The Government of Ethiopia *was therefore eventually published in 1948, with less documentation than she could have wished, and years after the Foreign Office and the members of the Diplomatic Service could have exploited it to defend the reputation of the British administration. Both the administration and the book were bitterly attacked by Sylvia Pankhurst in her paper,* The New Times and Ethiopia News – *the cuttings are carefully preserved in the archive – and Margery was convinced that Pankhurst's influence upon the Emperor made it impossible for her to visit Ethiopia thereafter. A second edition of* The Government of Ethiopia, *with a section by Christopher Clapham to bring it up to date, was published in 1968. Nevertheless, Margery always considered it the least satisfactory of her books because it lacked the personal experience of the country that she felt to be vital for such a work; she had not 'proved it upon the pulse'.]*

On 5 October 1935, when I was a schoolboy in Geneva interested in Ethiopia, I happened to read in our school library a copy of *The Times*, and found a letter on the Italian-Abyssinian war written by Margery Perham; and a wonderful letter it was, which even today must seem up to date and full of the ideals to which every right-minded person would subscribe. She said that 'mistakes in imperial policy in the past were no justification for complacency on the part of Britain, and certainly no justification for Italy to annex the only independent African nation in this enlightened age of the League of Nations'. I of course had no idea who Margery Perham was; subsequently I saw more of her letters in *The Times* on the subject of Ethiopia. On 30 June 1936 I stood in the vast multitude outside the League of Nations' building at Geneva to see Haile Selassie arriving and leaving after his famous speech to the League. I had always thought that Margery had written a letter to *The Times* in praise of the Emperor's speech, but I have not been able to confirm this.

It was not until January 1944 that I came to know more, much more, about Margery Perham. Her niece Margery Mumford had arrived with her husband in Eritrea, where I was then serving in the British Military Administration, and two months later I was appointed editor of the Ministry of Information's vernacular publications in Eritrea-Ethiopia. From Margery junior I learnt a great deal about Margery senior, who then sent me a very long and detailed article she had published in *Agenda* in 1942. It seemed to me a masterpiece in its analysis of the situation in Ethiopia and of Eden's recent policy statement on the Horn of Africa.

This statement had dealt with five points: the re-establishment of Ethiopian independence; the restoration of Haile Selassie to his throne; the absence of British territorial ambitions in Ethiopia; temporary British military guidance; and economic and political assistance by Britain. Margery had recognized at once that aims one, two, and three were bound to come into conflict with four and five, and she foresaw in great detail what did in fact happen. The rest of her article dealt with Ethiopian history, the Church, thoughts about the post-war era, and similar matters. It was, in fact, a sort of trailer for her great book on Ethiopia then in preparation. My enthusiastic response to this article induced her to send me large numbers of questions connected with her forthcoming book, which I tried to answer over the next four years.

In 1945, at a reception at Asmara, with most of the senior officers of the British administration present, a servant brought in on a silver tray a telegram addressed to me from Margery Perham and offering me the post of research officer and librarian at her Institute of Colonial Studies in Oxford. I was amazed by the enthusiasm, indeed the awe, that this telegram evoked in most of my colleagues, who were professional Colonial Service officers; they all wanted such a job. I had to postpone my acceptance until after the end of the British Mandate in Palestine, but I did take up the post in March/April 1948. Margery's importance and influence were demonstrated when she took me to an interview which would have done honour to a professorial appointment. Besides the Vice-Chancellor, W.T.S. Stallybrass, there were present Sir Douglas Veale, the Registrar; Sir Reginald Coupland, the Beit Professor; and Sir

Richard Livingstone, the President of Corpus – all for a very junior appointment.

Barely six months later, Margery resigned the directorship of the Institute of Colonial Studies to start writing the Lugard book. She and I remained in close contact, however, as I stayed on in Oxford. This was the time when her book, *The Government of Ethiopia*, was about to appear. She was at that time full of trepidation, probably more so than in the case of any other of her books, for she always feared that she lacked real expertise in the field of Ethiopian studies. Yet while studies of Ethiopian languages and literature, and of the Church, were well advanced (perhaps the Church was the only weak part in her book, because she saw it in the occidental Christian sense, and not the oriental Christian ambience, where the Church is much closer to, say, Judaism or Islam in its general ethos and customs than it is to its western counterpart), very little indeed had been written on the government or institutions of Ethiopia during the past century or so. The preface to the book sets out in great detail her misgivings about writing a book of this nature, and acknowledges extremely fully all the help she had received from so many quarters, especially from Frank de Halpert who had been adviser to the Minister of the Interior in Ethiopia. He was not in the narrow sense an expert on Ethiopia, but he had much experience of the workings of the Ethiopian government.

Margery was then, and always remained, anxious about the fact that she had never been inside Ethiopia, although she had been along its borders in Somaliland, Kenya, and of course the Sudan. *The Government of Ethiopia* was, nevertheless, a model of detached, impartial and careful analysis. It was beautifully crafted and, I would claim, was essentially correct in broad outline. It has gained in stature with every year that has passed. By the mid-1960s, when a second edition was called for and was being prepared, the book had become the generally acknowledged principal study in the area of Ethiopian governmental institutions, and indeed of the Ethiopian polity as a whole. She had asked me, when it was first published, to annotate her own copy along the margins for the eventuality of a second edition, and I had done so with quite unnecessary pedantry. Now, when working with Margery on the revised edition – we sat together for about a month then – I was constantly surprised at the knowledge she had amassed during the writing of the first edition in the 1940s. While helpers like Dr Zewde Gabre-Sellassie, or Christopher Clapham, or myself, may have added some useful details, and may have corrected some very minor errors, the quality of writing and empathy in the first edition have remained unsurpassed. Margery concluded her preface by saying: 'To Ethiopians who may read this book, and to the most eminent of them all, if his many cares should allow him to look at it, I would say that, whatever my detachment as a student, as a citizen of this contemporary and troubled world, with all my heart I wish that country well.'

I know of only one book that has subsequently been written on the government of Ethiopia, before the revolution of 1974, which can compare with Margery's work, and that is John Markakis' *Ethiopia: the Anatomy of a Traditional Polity*, published in 1974, but he had incomparable advantages by virtue of the considerable literature on the subject which had accrued in the meantime. Margery Perham's *Government of Ethiopia* will remain a pioneering achievement of rare quality. She herself, however, despite my assurances and those of others, had always remained somewhat dissatisfied with the book.

As a footnote to this, it might be interesting to mention that someone appears to have said to her in the late 1940s that with such a book she would never receive a visa to visit Ethiopia. No amount of persuasion and contrary evidence – not even a personal visit from the Ethiopian ambassador – could shift her from that belief. In the end I brought an assurance from him whom she had termed 'the most eminent Ethiopian of them all' that she would be an honoured visitor to his country. And incidentally, whenever I went to Ethiopia and saw the Emperor, there were three people he would routinely, almost as a ritual, enquire about. They were Cerulli, the greatest of all Ethiopian scholars, who had been Vice-Governor-General of Ethiopia, but was entirely accepted by the Emperor; second, Margery Perham; and third, as the Emperor put it, 'my sister, Queen Elizabeth'. I could tell him about Cerulli and Margery, but less about his 'sister'. As far as Margery Perham was concerned, it was now too late for a visit to Ethiopia. Like Moses, she would never see the promised land herself. And I think she preferred to stay at some distance from a country which she had described so well, yet with constant anxiety as to whether she had done justice, scholarly as well as political, to an enterprise on which she had set out as a duty rather than a labour of love. I am not sure now whether in the end the book was loved by her, but it certainly was respected by nearly everybody else.

NOTE

1. Public Record Office, FO 371/46100 and 53462; Perham Papers 7/3, 292, 599–604.

Writing the Biography of Lord Lugard

Mary Bull

'Lugard died on April 11th', wrote Margery Perham in 1945, ... 'and before long I shall write the record of his long life.'[1] She went on to write several pages of her opinions of his character and achievements in order, it would seem, to have something on paper of her immediate judgement of him, based on the memories of their work together, before she plunged into the immense task that lay before her. It was a task that would take her fifteen years to complete.

Margery Perham first met Lord Lugard in 1929, although she had seen him earlier when she had visited, for the purpose of her studies, the Mandates Commission of the League of Nations in Geneva, on which Lugard was the British representative. He was then 71, the elder states-man of British African affairs, and she, at 33, still a young lecturer developing an interest in colonial administration. The meeting, in the uncomfortable atmosphere of the Ladies' Annexe of the Athenaeum Club, had been arranged for her to gain background knowledge for the world tour on which she was about to set out. She thought of him initially as the Mandates expert; she wrote in her diary, when questions of the Australian Mandate in New Guinea arose: 'I am going to take it upon myself to write to Lord Lugard on the subject.'[2] After her return to England their friendship developed rapidly, and he provided her with much advice for her next African tour, to Nigeria, the territory in which he had spent so many years as governor. In 1932, Margery made her home with her sister and brother-in-law at Shere, in Surrey, seven miles from Lugard at Abinger on Leith Hill, and they were able to meet regularly. They also corresponded frequently, and by 1932 were address-ing each other as 'My dear Margery' and 'My dear Fred', and ending letters with 'Yours affectionately'.[3] During her travels, Margery had developed her knowledge of, and her admiration for, the form of colonial administration which came to be known as 'indirect rule', and she respected Lugard as its originator. Discussions of the subject came into their correspondence concerning their books – Lugard commented on the drafts of Margery's *Native Administration in Nigeria*, and Margery on Lugard's revision of his *Dual Mandate* – but the usual matters of their talks and correspondence were the current problems and crises – for example, opposition to the increase of settler power in Kenya, and the protests at the Italian invasion of Ethiopia. Lugard wrote often from Geneva, discussing matters that were concerning the Mandates Commission. Through him she met the influential men in Britain concerned with African administration, and learnt the techniques of influencing government action either by personal contact with those about to take the decisions, or by creating a climate of opinion among the informed by letters and articles in *The Times*. While most of their correspondence was on practical matters, occasionally they expressed in writing what was too difficult to say aloud. In 1935, Lugard accompanied his gift to Margery of his first book, *The Rise of Our East African Empire* (published in 1894), with a note to say that its value now lay in its views on slavery, on which 'no credit is due to me. I was the mouthpiece of Sir J. Kirk ... the ablest and most far-sighted man I have known in my life. He used to say that I of the younger generation would carry on the work for Africa, and though of course there can be no comparison I have tried to keep the torch alight to the best of my abilities and I pass it on to you ...' To which Margery replied: 'Not for a moment that I am worthy of the trust you impose upon me. In the days when you took up the torch from Sir John Kirk there were few who could work for the best for Africa. Now, thanks in part to your achievements, both in action and in counsel, there are many, and I am glad if I can count myself one of that many.'[4]

Undertaking the Biography

It was Flora Lugard who had first been concerned with a biography of her husband. In 1926 she wrote to Professor Coupland asking him to undertake the task, and was very disappointed when he declined. He considered that he would not have the inspiration, when he had completed his work on Kirk, to do justice to another major life. But he changed his mind: in 1929, after Flora's death, he wrote to Lugard to obtain his acquiescence to a biography. Apparently the matter rested there for some years, but in 1935 Lugard wrote a note doubting if Coupland's book would ever be written. He had agreed to a biography only so that Flora's wishes might be carried out, and if it were to be a full account of his life, 'there is I think no-one who could approach it from the point of view *she* desired except Margery Perham.' But he still had reservations:

> She has only seen the working side of my life, she knows nothing of the madness of my earlier years, or of the contempt I often feel for myself when I lay bare to myself the meanness and pettiness of my own thoughts and character. ... I would pass on leaving the good

and the bad unrecorded. Biographies are and *must* be a tissue of misrepresentations of attributed motives coloured by the lens of the biographer.[5]

Lugard's brother Edward, who was as anxious as Flora had been that Lugard's life should be properly commemorated, was also concerned that Coupland's many commitments meant that he would not undertake the biography, and suggested to Coupland that Margery Perham should be asked to take over the work – or rather, the privilege. Lugard wrote to Margery in 1938 saying that Ned had told him what had been discussed: 'It touches me *deeply* that you should have wished to undertake it, but I feel strongly that you have much more urgent and important work to do, now and in the future – even though it were postponed till after I have passed on.' In her reply Margery said: 'The main reason why I cannot bring myself to discuss it with you, or even to contemplate the task, is that I do not believe that biographies should appear in the lifetime of the subject.' Edward reported to his brother:

> I feel she is far away the best I can secure, and she is *very* keen to do it ... I am not sure *at present* she fully realizes what a noble task she has secured – but she will realize it before I have finished. It will be the best work of her life. Long after her books on 'Native Administration' etc. are out of date and forgotten, the Biography will remain *a classic*. You, of course, will laugh at what I say, but it is a *unique* opportunity and a great privilege for *anyone* to write the 'Life' of one of the most outstanding men of his age. ... I think Margery Perham will do it justice – it won't be *my* fault if she doesn't.[6]

Edward Lugard certainly fulfilled this pledge. He was disappointed by Margery's refusal to contemplate the task while Lugard was still alive, and more by her suggestions that she might not have the time to work on it until her retirement. But they corresponded about his work of sorting the papers which, after Lugard's death in April 1945, he began sending to Margery at Oxford. It must have been because of Ned's promptings that the papers included an account by Lugard, written in 1941, of 'the madness of my earlier years' – the betrayal of his love by the woman whom Margery Perham was to call Celia, which drove him, in 1887, to abandon his army career in India, and seek death by fighting slave-raiders in Africa. But Lugard's most private records – his 'secret diary' of 1888, and the letters he exchanged with his wife from 1902 onwards – had been left with the strict instructions that they were to be read only by Ned, who might extract what he might think useful for Margery Perham (and no-one else), and then must be burnt. When Margery, starting in 1949 to write on the second half of Lugard's life, begged for anything Ned could send her, he embarked on the tremendous task of reading the letters. In sending her the last extracts of the governor-general period, about twenty-five per cent of the whole he estimated, he wrote 'On this two-year tour alone, I have glanced through 4,129 pages.'[7]

The two volumes of the Lugard biography were written during fifteen of the busiest years of Margery's life. Not only were there her teaching and administrative commitments in Oxford, her attendance at many committees in the Colonial Office and elsewhere, and her travels in Africa, but they were the years of anguish over many developments in different parts of Africa and the decisions that had to be made by Britain, leading to private consultations and public writings which she felt she must undertake. In 1948 she attempted to reorganize her life by resigning as Director of the Institute of Colonial Studies, and as University Reader in Colonial Administration, and became Fellow in Imperial Government at Nuffield College, a post created to give her the maximum freedom in her work. The college provided her with a research assistant, as well as with all the secretarial help she needed. But the work on outside bodies did not decrease, particularly for the Inter-University Council for Higher Education in the Colonies. In College there were the vast quantities of Lugard Papers surrounding her, the letters to and talks with those who had known Lugard, and the wide background reading required before she could even begin to organize her material. The Lugard biography was written either during occasional brief holidays from Oxford, or during the nights – or early hours of the mornings – at her Oxford home.

The progress of the biography can be followed from Margery's correspondence with Edward Lugard. She proposed at first that she should write a 'Short Life' to satisfy Ned's desire for an immediate tribute to his brother's career, and for one which would be published within his own lifetime, while postponing the full biography until she had dealt with more immediate commitments – primarily the completion of her book on Ethiopia, and the projected work on the administration of the Sudan. However, she assured Ned that the biography was of the greatest importance to her: 'I not only want to write this book more than I want to do any other piece of work, but I also feel it is a clearly indicated duty.'[8] And when Elspeth Huxley wrote to her in June 1946, asking for plans for the biography, as her (Huxley's) publishers had suggested to her that she should write a short life of Lugard while Miss Perham was working on the full version, Margery replied that she was at that moment packing up her documents to go off to a vacation cottage in Wales to do just that.[9]

Margery Perham found, however, that to write a short life was not easy. As she followed Lugard's excursions into East Africa, she was led into the politics of the partition of Africa. She reported: 'I have had a fascinating afternoon at the Bodleian, reading up all the [parliamentary] debates 1892–93 [on Uganda] ... It is essential to read up the general political background, but it is a large job.' And 'I have now drafted in the rough seven full chapters on Uganda, which will be the basis for the long book as well as the short.'[10] Again, for Lugard's first expedition to West Africa, to Borgu, she stated she had to read not only his detailed diary, 'But in order to understand the meaning of Borgu I had to study also volumes of diplomatic stuff, most of which I had to read by special permission at the Foreign Office' as she had done for Uganda. 'I find that – especially as I have such a bad memory – it was best to write down at once *in the rough* at length all my impressions and important quotations. This, of course, meant a change of technique from what I had planned in writing the short book, and will delay the production of that, but it will be an immense help toward the main book.'[11]

In 1947 she abandoned the short life – or rather postponed it, for she intended for many years to condense the published biography into a shorter, popular work, which she hoped would be more widely read, and more profitable. But it was not until 1952 that she agreed to Edward Lugard's proposal, first made in 1946, that the work be published in two separate volumes, so that he could assist with the first, and, he hoped, see it published before his death. Earlier, in 1949, she had been impelled to defend herself against his concern at the delays. First, there had been 'the tremendous pressure of colonial affairs involving me as one of the experts. This coming on top of a full time job, with the attempt to write the book at the same time, has made the last two or three years some of the most miserable I have ever experienced.' But she should now have more time for research and writing:

One of my main reasons for resigning work which meant a great deal to me was in order to carry out my obligation to you. ... I had no wish until I got well into the work on this book, that it was a much larger task that I had ever imagined. ... [it] cannot be written out of the immense amount of material you handed to me alone. There is a vast mass of background stuff to be read and reflected upon if Fred is to be seen in his historical setting and signficance. This is not a process that can be carried out when one is being goaded to hurry. This book is partly the history of imperialism over a period of sixty years. ... I have made very great sacrifices in order to write this book because I want to do it. [But] I should not have drafted my chapters so quickly if it had not been to get your opinion and to give you satisfaction ... I do appreciate your impatience, but writing a book of this character is more important in a way than your or my personal interests and it is in that spirit that I have tried to do this work.[12]

Edward Lugard's scrutiny of all she wrote was helpful, for the information he provided, but must have been inhibiting, both in writing of Lugard's infatuation with 'Celia', and in any criticism she might make of him. Yet Margery was equally restrained by her loyalty to the man she had known, and had no desire to expose more of his private life than she considered neccesary to understand the events of his life. Edward died in January 1957, aged 92, a few months after the publication of the first volume; but he had been able to express his satisfaction: 'it is a *wonderful* book – an amazing story, *wonderfully* told', he wrote to Ethel Rayne – Margery's sister and also a great friend of Lugard, and to whom both volumes are dedicated.[13]

Considering the Task

'No man's life is interesting in itself except to him and his nearest connections – it is only in so far as it reflects something of universal interest. And the task of the biographer is to be able to disentangle from the welter of chronological detail, that interest and interpret it', noted Margery Perham in 1951.[14] Her aim was not only to illuminate the life and character of one man, but to use this exceptional life to illustrate the whole period of British rule in tropical Africa, to show how policy was made and executed, and, in the final section, how the British establishment viewed the nature of colonial responsibilities in the last phase of imperial confidence. She had listed five major problems in writing the biography.

(1) Compression or selection. There was enough material for five volumes, and interesting ones; her guiding line was that this was 'the story of a *man*, not of a movement (or movements), or an age, or of this or that region. And yet it is a man *in* his age and has no meaning without it. The events of his life are like a main road which I follow. The country through which it goes is the background to his life. How much of this must you put in to make the road interesting. This is the most difficult problem.'

(2) The weaving of strands. She listed at least five strands to be woven into the story – the day-to-day activities; the intimate private life; the Colonial Office and its policy; the background of political and international affairs; the significance to Africa – the peoples and regions conquered or governed, then and since.

(3) The sharp divisions in his life. The period of his retirement was the most difficult, assessing his influence in the many areas in which he was engaged.

(4) The question of standards. 'This is perhaps the hardest problem of all. I wonder if we realize how much every act of selection, or presentation, and not only of comment and judgment depends upon our standards. Once you start probing into them you quickly reach down into fundamentals, not only political but moral and religious – or unreligious as the case may be. Apply this to Lugard. Here was a man who drew his own standards from a background of religion, of military honour and national pride that he learnt in the sixties of the last century – a soldier and gentleman of that period. And a great imperialist. He lived into an age that condemned imperialism, that shudders almost by reflex action at any account of force and bloodshed in the imposition of imperial power.'

(5) The subjective factor. 'I do not approach Lugard as a scientist, nor even as a historian, but as a friend.' She must avoid, on the one hand, the dangers of hagiography and, on the other, of too great a reaction against this, of being overcritical, demanding too much of Lugard.[15]

How did she manage to deal with these problems? The question of compression or selection from the sources was bound up with the decision on the length of the book; it was not only that Lugard's long and distinguished life and the many areas in which he was involved suggested two large volumes, but that the tremendous quantity of material made it possible. There was the great volume of Lugard's private papers; he had kept all his diaries, letters, reports, memoranda, drafts. There were his published works – books, articles, lectures; and his official correspondence and reports, published and unpublished. Margery Perham was allowed access to the Foreign and Colonial Office records then closed to the public, and to the private papers of a number of relevant societies and individuals. There was the contemporary public debate of the issues in which Lugard was involved, in *Hansard*, in newspapers, and in journal articles, and there were the subsequent works of historians and biographers. She also corresponded with men, most already friends, who had worked with Lugard in Nigeria, and she had many replies to her published appeals for letters or information about him. She wished to keep the work as one book, but it was the pressure from Edward Lugard, as we have seen, combined with the acquiescence of her publisher, that led her to publish the two volumes separately.

Two separate volumes meant that the major division in Lugard's life was emphasized, for his career fell quite clearly into two parts, divided in 1898. In the first volume, subtitled *The Years of Adventure*, his youth, his soldiering in India, his expeditions for companies to Lake Nyasa,

Uganda, Borgu in West Africa, the Kalahari, and his creation of the West African Frontier Force are described. The second volume, *The Years of Authority*, is primarily concerned with his career as a colonial governor, in Northern Nigeria, Hong Kong, and the united Nigeria, and finally with his retirement years.

The problem of standards was always a major one for Margery throughout the book. She was writing in the 1950s, when the Second World War had brought a total change in the standpoint from which colonial government was judged. The question had changed since the 1930s, from 'How should Britain administer colonies?' to 'What right had Britain to administer colonies?' In the final pages of the first volume, having described the settlement between Britain and France in 1898 over the boundaries of Nigeria, she referred to the changes in the views of empire that had taken place in the ensuing fifty years:

> From this new historical perspective many of those who constitute themselves judges of their forerunners will, when presented with this record, condemn the British government and especially the mainspring of its policy, Chamberlain, for his readiness to go to war to ensure that a certain slice of African territory should belong to us rather than to France. ... The historian ... must do what he can to assist the judgments which will be made, by helping his contemporaries to enter into the minds of the men of the past so that their evaluation of their problems can be understood as well as our own.[16]

Finally, what she termed the 'subjective factor', her friendship with Lugard, was always before her. She wrote in the seminar notes:

> He and I were very close friends with a deep intimacy possible between two of our disparity in age and the closeness of our interests. For the last ten years of his life we lived close together – some seven miles apart – and I used to ride or motor over, sometimes two or three times a week, often staying the night or weekend and working far into the night. I had, and have, a deep admiration for him, especially as he was in his old age. Very gentle, very humble, very generous and unselfish – as near perfection as any person I have known.[17]

In the first volume she was able to be more detached. The young Lugard was a very different person from the man she had known, and she could draw a convincing portrait. However, she felt the need to investigate, in what most readers would consider unnecessary detail, those episodes when Lugard could be accused of failing to live up to her standards. One such is his dispute with Sir Francis de Winton in 1890 arising from

Lugard's determination to be in sole command of the expedition to Uganda – an incident illustrating one of Lugard's main characteristics to be displayed so frequently in the years to come.[18] A little later, she devoted a whole chapter to the official investigation and subsequent critical report of Captain Macdonald into Lugard's activities in Uganda, ending the account with eight pages introduced by the words:

> Up to this point the incident has been described with the minimum of comment, leaving the reader to judge its tangled issues. Some would say the biographer should stop there. But surely it is better for one who has read the evidence, made some study of the country and the scenes of the event, and also discussed it with some of the actual participants, including the chief actor and some aged Baganda, to offer, not indeed a judgment, but an opinion.[19]

The Completed Book

The first volume, *Lugard: The Years of Adventure* is, whatever its claims as biography or history, a great adventure story, dramatically narrated, of the young Lugard, ambitious, self-confident, patriotic, strong in mind and body, pushing into a largely unknown Africa, woven into the account of British and international politics that determined the 'scramble for Africa'. Margery Perham's knowledge of and love for the African scenes are revealed in the descriptions she gives of the country and people through which he travelled, and the background of British and international politics is so clearly related that it conveys an understanding of the men and the forces at work in this period of imperial expansion.

She succeeded in weaving the strands of public and private life into a highly readable account. However, the style, with her detailed, often personal descriptions of people and places, and her constant concern with the judgement of men, women and ideas, seemed old-fasioned in 1956, and appears, thirty-five years later, to belong to another age. She also used expressions which we would find offensive today. Describing Lugard's excursions from his base at Karonga, when on his first African expedition to the Lake Nyasa region, she wrote: 'He noted the happiness of these naked savages . . .'[20] Lugard had put down so much of his private thoughts in his diary that she could, she commented, have written in a romantic style such as: 'Lugard was sitting one night by the dying camp-fire. Drums beat softly in the distance. As he gazed into the embers . . .'[21] But her actual style is not so very different. She uses long quotations from Lugard's diaries, and his book, *The Rise of our East African Empire*, based upon those diaries, to convey his descriptions of his thoughts, his actions, and his surroundings. She could also summarize, or even rewrite, the diaries herself. For example, describing Lugard's return to Kampala after recruiting the Sudanese soldiers and their dependents left by Emin Pasha at the north of Lake Albert: 'There were times when, standing upon some high point and watching the endless file of humanity snaking after him for miles, his conscience wounded him not only with the thought of their misery but of what he was bringing upon the country.'[22] The diary from which this is taken, however, does not express these thoughts so explicitly.[23] There is even less justification for the passage in which she describes Lugard's first voyage up the Niger River:

> But though he was both interested and impressed he had so far found nothing to appeal deeply to him in his first view of West Africa. Certainly, to most people coming from East Africa, there is – or there was – something menacing about the Niger coast at first contact. The frequent heavy rain from dull skies; the contorted mangrove trees with their fantastic roots writhing out of the mud of the delta; the dark forests; the vague sense of their hiding a brooding witchcraft and cannibal practices; the vast numbers of people at once blacker, more negroid, assertive and strident than the easterners; all these create a nostalgia for the contrasting conditions of the east. Lugard certainly felt this and it chilled his spirits long before he reached his base.[24]

There is nothing in his diary covering this voyage up the Niger expressing these thoughts;[25] the suspicion arises that it is the reactions of Perham, rather than Lugard, that are described.[26] She was certainly more of a romantic than he ever was.

The second volume, Lugard's *Years of Authority*, presented Margery with much greater problems. Most of the book, twenty-five of the thirty-three chapters, deals with his governorship of Nigeria, and the account is not of dramatic expeditions but of administrative concerns. A major interest is to see how far the twenty-three years that had passed since the publication of *Native Administration in Nigeria* had affected Margery's views on the development of Nigeria. Of course, the objects of the two books are different; the biography, as she so frequently wrote in her letters and talks as well as in the book, is the story of a man, not the history of a country. Of the thirteen chapters describing Lugard as High Commissioner of Northern Nigeria, from 1900 to 1906, most are largely narrative, describing Lugard's activities in establishing his protectorate and creating an administration, his marriage to Flora Shaw, his conquest of the northern emirates, his suppression of the Satiru revolt, and his relations with the government and the Colonial Office at home – including the Lugards' scheme for continuous administration of tropical colonies. But two chapters are entirely thematic: 'Indirect Rule: the Idea' and 'Indirect Rule: the Structure', while that entitled 'The High Commissioner' describes his methods of work. Indirect rule had been the subject on which Margery had made herself the authority in the 1930s; but by the time she wrote the biography it had been largely discarded as colonies prepared for independence. This was her opportunity to describe the origin of Lugard's system in Northern Nigeria which could 'claim to be the most comprehensive, coherent and renowned system of administration in our colonial history.'[27] And she goes on to show that while the principle of 'indirect' administration was not new, Lugard's detailed working out of the chain of authority, and the instructions that he sent to his officers in the form of 'political memoranda', were new in the creation of a form of rule for Africans in contrast to earlier views of regarding them as inhabitants of an ill-defined 'protectorate'. Her description of his administrative achievements, however, is not wholly consistent. Referring to the outline which Lugard had jotted down before he arrived to take over the territory in 1900, she wrote: 'the word instinct must not be misused, but at least he had such an aptitude for administration that he hardly seemed to need the processes of reasoning or discussion, whether with himself or with others, or even of experiment.'[28] Yet she herself had already shown that Lugard's deep interest in the administration of the inhabitants of Africa had developed from his first encounters with the continent, including those with his new Protectorate in 1894–5 and 1897–8; and that he had discussed the problems in England, especially with Kirk, Goldie, and Joseph Chamberlain. The *Political Memoranda*, Lugard always insisted, were the outcome of discussions with his senior staff, and always provisional, subject to change.[29] Margery also catalogued his serious faults as the head of a government administration: his need for personal devotion from his staff, distrusting those who disagreed with his policy in any way; and his inability to delegate or to develop an efficient secretariat, insisting on deciding on every matter himself.[30] There were also the problems in his relations with the Colonial Office, above all his battle with the officials for the adoption of the 'Scheme' for continuous administration – a scheme of which she endorsed the Colonial Office criticism and which, for the few years in which it was in operation, did lead to administrative chaos.

It was when she came to describe the period of Lugard as Governor-General of Nigeria that Margery Perham appears to have had more serious doubts of Lugard's achievements – as, indeed, have all other students. With the material for this section, there are some typewritten sheets of her thoughts on Lugard and of how to judge his work. 'The main danger is that of being too comprehensive, and trying to write a history of Nigeria as well as the story of Lugard as Governor. The two are hard to distinguish and it is almost a handicap that I know so much about Nigeria and am interested in it for its own sake.' Her first sentence under the heading of general impressions of Lugard as Governor-General was that he was an authoritarian, who considered that 'the whole country should be as closely as possible under his authority'. From this principle came most of the conflicts that arose during the period – with the Colonial Office, with his staff in Nigeria, and with the Nigerian people. The western educated in the coastal towns of Nigeria were not yet demanding independence, or even self-government, but they had absorbed western principles of civil liberties and justice.

Margery assembled the arguments against Lugard, criticizing his personal faults under four heads. First, his limitation of vision; he could not conceive of Nigerians ruling themselves. Second, his lack of any real liberalism, especially in his prejudice against the Lagosians; he did not see that the class of westernized Africans would expand and be the people to whom power would be transferred. Third, he was not always humane; in his earlier career, he was humane to the individual Africans with whom he came in contact, but at a distance, he showed no regret or pity for those who perished in the suppression of the Satiru or Abeokuta risings, nor did he show, in letters to his wife, a warmth towards the individual Africans – in this she contrasted him with Newbold in the Sudan. Fourth, his unsociability; he was shy and disliked social occasions and small talk, but he carried to excess his preference for communication by paper, and had far too little human contact either with his officials or with the people he ruled. These points are made in the book, but they are softened by all possible excuses and arguments in Lugard's favour, while his positive achievements in creating an administration for Nigeria are emphasized.

Margery was also concerned in these notes about the standards by which to measure success in administration. 'Success in what? Can we answer "In giving Nigeria good government?"' But what, beyond the maintenance of law and order, and impartial, efficient justice, is good government? For not only were the African societies changing rapidly, but also Britain's purposes in ruling African colonies were themselves subject to change.[31]

In the light of these concerns, how did Margery Perham discuss Lugard's administration of Nigeria? Lugard had three governments to administer: the new central government that he was developing, and the existing Northern and Southern administrations. Margery shows how his minimal central government, with central departments of finance and communications only, were designed to enable him to spend half of each year administering Nigeria from London under his scheme for continuous administration, leaving the lieutenant-governors of the North and the South to deal separately with most governmental concerns.

In her discussion of the northern system, and of Lugard's attempt to exercise control over the Residents who, during his absence from the territory, had sought to preserve and extend the powers of the emirs and protect the territory from outside influence, Margery could whole-heartedly endorse Lugard's policy. She had discussed the problem with him when planning her first trip to Nigeria in 1931; and he had written to her there: 'Your view that there was a danger of stereotyping traditions in the North coincides with my own fears' and: 'it is a very natural tendency to aggrandise the Emirs, and I have constantly warned the Lieutenant-Governors about it.'[32] Study of the Lugard letters and the Colonial Office records reinforced the view that Lugard had had to struggle, with little success, against the conservatism of the northern administrators – mainly over the question of central control of the native treasuries, but also over education and Christian missions. Here she did not hesitate to give a judgement from the perspective of the 1950s:

> In the writer's view Lugard's policy was at least well worth attempt-ing since, if the new direction he tried to give to policy had been steadily followed by his successors, the Northern Region today might have been more uniform in its administration, more centralized, with more fully developed central services. Secondly, it would have presented today rather less of a political contrast with the Southern Regions. Thirdly, as the system which many British governments in Africa and elsewhere soon came to regard as the archetype of native administration, it would have been a little less remote both in spirit and form from the more modest realities of these other colonies.[33]

However, she found Lugard's attempts to extend the northern system to the south less easy to endorse. On the whole, she attempted to confine herself to demonstrating Lugard's view of the administration, so fully explained in his letters, and she felt he did have considerable justification for his assessment of native administration in the south 'with a rather haphazard economic development outrunning administrative control, and with no clear system or objective in its government.'[34] However, while she tried to explain Lugard's aims, she could not but be critical of such attempts as to 'make an emir out of the Alafin' of Oyo, and to place the town of Ibadan under his control;[35] of the manner of the abrogation of the treaty with Abeokuta which had recognized its autonomy; and of the events leading to, and the suppression of, the 1918 rising in Abeokuta. The measures which caused the most opposition in the south – the restriction of the Supreme Court and the Legislative Council to Lagos Colony, and the introduction of direct taxation – are dealt with fully, not only to attempt to explain Lugard's policy, but to explain the opposition. For what she had always regarded as the most difficult area for indirect rule policies, the Ibo and related peoples of south-eastern Nigeria with their small chiefless societies, she wrote: 'he was neither overconfident, nor unsympathetic nor doctrinaire. And yet ... he could not escape from the association of his system with its recurring central figure of the chief. Nor are his instructions wholly consistent.'[36] Whereas she had ended her account of the eastern region in *Native Administration in Nigeria* by stressing the need for further study of the nature of the Ibo and other societies, as a prelude to devising a satisfactory method of administration,[37] in the biography she concluded with a statement the the self-governing region had abandoned attempts to base administration on 'the complex indigenous pattern' and had chosen instead a British model of local government based mainly upon straight election.[38] However, there is no general assessment of indirect rule as a system; she clearly did not feel that this was the place for it. By the mid-fifties the future that had seemed so distant twenty years earlier had arrived.

Margery was able, from Lugard's letters to his wife, to describe sympathetically the strain on him personally of the 1914–18 war. The war also dominates her economic chapter 'Colonial housekeeping'. Apart from Lugard's concern with the Nigerian budget, and his desire to end the dependence of the revenue on the customs duties on imported gin, it is largely an account of his resistance to British attempts to exploit Nigeria in the desperate wartime need to secure supplies of tropical products, mainly palm oil. There is little on economic life in Nigeria, whether the indigenous or the export economies.

Perhaps the area which caused Margery the most surprise in her investigation of new material was that of Lugard's relations with the Colonial Office. She was given privileged access to the Office files, and in them she encountered constant criticism of Lugard and his proposals. Since most of these files were read, in fact, by her research assistant, not by Margery herself, it is possible that she saw in the notes a disproprotionate emphasis on the criticisms.[39] However, those minutes were there, and she could support the hostile attitude of the Colonial Office from outside references[40] as well as from the obviously one-sided accounts of the Lugard letters. She had to balance her account between defending, or at least understanding, Lugard's point of view, and concluding that on most issues the Office was right. With her own experience of the Colonial Office in mind, she wrote: 'the ultimate source of continuity must be in the Whitehall department and not in the sequence of governors working under it.'[41]

Margery Perham was right to think she could not view Lugard impersonally. Her desire was to justify him; her integrity demanded that she have real grounds for justification. It is clear that she did not wish to give a comprehensive judgement on his work as governor-general: she discussed the matters on which he could be criticized, but did not go on to consider thoroughly how these measures affected the future of the country. She tried to concentrate on developing the picture of the man. One description in the book compares him with Charles Temple, the Acting Governor of Northern Nigeria when Lugard arrived back in 1912. 'Temple, for all his streak of fanaticism, could be detached and speculative, his mind could range both widely and forward into the future. By contrast, Lugard was practical, concentrated, with hardly a moment when he could laugh at himself or his work; his mind reached a certain distance out into the future and stopped where such exploration seemed to be a mental indulgence.'[42]

While Margery used all the sources available to her for the biography, they are still British sources, whether originating from Lugard, the Colonial Office, or independent observers. There is very little of the African view of Lugard and his administrative measures. To some extent Margery is conscious of this; in dealing with Lugard as High Commissioner, she wrote:

> In our generation, which has seen a development towards colonial, and certainly, Nigerian, self-government of a kind never imagined by Lugard and his colleagues in the first decade of this century, interest has shifted to the native side and indeed the native view of the imperial association. Already, among the millions of Africans, the first few hundreds, if not more, are studying the beginnings through foreign conquest of a modern state in their country. Their first question must be 'What of us, and what of our fathers? How were *they* treated and how regarded?'[43]

But it is typical of Margery Perham's outlook that this last question is in the passive mood: Africans are seen as the objects of regard, not as subjects regarding Lugard and his staff. She does, of course, try to take African reactions into account, whether of peasants in revolt (as recorded in official reports), or of the educated inhabitants of Lagos expressing their views in the local newspaper; and she had the very legitimate excuse of the lack of sources available to her at that period. She extrolled the value of anthropological study, but the twentieth-century African, adapting to the new world, finding a new way to earn his living, impinged upon by government in its local roles, is missing – though it must be conceded that in Lugard's time this was a very small group. At the beginning of the chapter 'The Lagos Opposition' she inserted a footnote to say that as she was completing her work she had seen James Coleman's book *Nigeria: Background to Nationalism*,[44] and had been able to insert some references to this valuable contribution to the subject.[45] Coleman's work was one of the first major attempts to see African political life from the viewpoint of this new class in Africa – the businessmen, teachers, clerks, urban workers – amongst whom nationalist feeling was developing and political parties, demanding independence, were being organized. Margery recognized the existence of this new world, but she never entered it.

The other two sections of the second volume presented Margery with different problems. The Hong Kong interlude was a diversion for Margery as well as for Lugard; she worked hard in learning of the colony in his time, and of Lugard's attempts to cope with role of governor there. When she came to write about him in the twenty-six hard-working years of his retirement, Margery Perham was returning to the man she knew personally. In her 1945 diary account she had tried to sum up her thoughts of his retirement work, the many activities that seemed at first disjointed:

> In fact they were marked by two main characteristics. They were scientific and international. The man of action had become the scholar and the promoter of studies in colonial affairs: the once reputed nationalist buccaneer and annexer had become the apostle of international collaboration in the interests of native betterment.[46]

These three chapters give only a brief outline of his activities, since she was intending to write a book on colonial policy between the wars – later altered to a book on Kenya, and finally abandoned – in which Lugard would take his place among the other actors. Working from personal knowledge and unqualified admiration for the man, she was able, however, to give a vivid picture of him as a person.

The two volumes were both published, fortuitously, in years in which there was much interest in West Africa – Volume I in 1956, on the eve of the independence of Ghana, the first of the new states to develop from the British tropical African colonies; Volume II in 1960, the year of Nigerian independence. They met with much praise, though the length was criticized by some reviewers.

Later writers have certainly considered Margery Perham's judgements of Lugard too favourable. D. H. Muffet, in *Concerning Brave Captains*

(1965), criticizes Lugard's conduct in relation to his campaign against Kano and Sokoto; and I. F. Nicolson, in *The Administration of Nigeria 1900–1960: men, methods and myths* (1969), condemns everything that Lugard did, attributing his fame to the successful propagation of the 'Lugard myth' by the writings of Lugard and his wife. John Flint gives a more balanced assessment of Lugard; but he is certainly critical of the governor-general period, and the method of amalgamating the two colonies.

> It was doubly unfortunate that these decisions were taken on the eve of the first world war, which unleashed new forces of nationalism that Lugard's measure were expressly designed not to accommodate ... Through his policies and in his writing, he did more than any other individual to fix the concept of indirect rule firmly in British policy as a conservative philosophy, hostile to the ambitions of educated Africans and those influenced by Christian missionaries, to urban growth, to the spread of the money economy, and to the vision that new African nations were in the making.[47]

Assessments of Lugard will vary through the years, but none can be made without reference to Margery Perham's biography, and its richness of detail will provide the basic material for many different views. In her concluding paragraphs she was more concerned to assess him as a man than to judge his achievements:

> This record of his life has been full and all those qualities which sound so trite when listed – courage, endurance, industry, the capacity to love – have been shown in action. But the whole was held together within a quality for which it is not easy to find a word. 'Order', 'constancy' come to mind ... I have known no one else who walked so closely along the line of a sustained purpose. He was all of a piece, sincere in the real meaning of the word, solid marble with no faking mixture of wax.[48]

In her diary passage of 1945, she described the scene familiar from the many meetings she had attended, where, among the educational and sociological experts inclined to question all fundamentals, 'that small figure of Lugard with his leonine head seemed to stand rock-like amongst the variegated company based upon his absolute allegiance to Britain and his belief in a few simple ideals for which he believed he stood. In such a spirit men can handle creatively the practical affairs of life.'[49]

Writing the biography had become a great burden to Margery Perham during the fifteen years, as the task conflicted with all the immediate pressures upon her. Yet she always wanted to do it, both as a tribute to the memory of the man to whom she owed so much, and as her major essay in writing history, rather than comment and recommendations on current affairs. In reply to her friend Arthur Creech Jones' congratulations on the publication of the first volume, she said: '[Your letter] comes as the most joyful reward after all the years, on and off; of slugging away night after night with all the avalanche of facts and notes which had to be fitted into some sort of coherent pattern.'[50] We can regret the loss of the other books that she might have written in this period, yet would they have been a greater achievement, or contributed more to her, as well as our, understanding of Africa? The biography provided her with the opportunity not only to write on the history of British colonial policy, but also to study the latest work on the history of the pre-colonial societies with which Lugard came into contact. A biography also gave her greater opportunities for creative writing. There is a letter in the Perham Papers which must have encouraged Margery. Graham Greene, with whom she was not personally acquainted, wrote: 'I find it impossible not to write you a "fan" letter. Your life of Lugard has made the first of a three-day railway journey from Montreal to Calgary go more quickly that I wanted. I have read criticisms that your biography is too detailed: I can only say that I find every detail of extreme interest, and the flow of the narrative magnificent and, to a novelist like myself, enviable.'[51] Reviewers wrote of the literary qualities: 'Miss Perham has even been able to retrieve a remarkable background of that social intercourse between human beings which is the despair of most historians',[52] 'Miss Perham knows the man, the problems, the territory, all from the heart as well as the head; all are compellingly alive'.[53] 'biography in the grand style – vast, leisurely, packed with detail – in the construction of which Miss Perham has combined the arts of a nineteenthcentury novelist and a twentieth-century scholar'.[54]

In assessing the two volumes as historical biography, the main question that arises is whether the portrait of the man has become obscured by the wealth of historical discussion, and whether the history is distorted from being centred on the life of one man. These are problems posed by all such biographies; different readers will judge differently the degree of success achieved by an author, but most, surely, will regard these volumes as among the best in this tradition. The life of Frederick Lugard is of great interest to all concerned with Africa, and with colonial rule; his long career spanned almost the whole period of European rule in the interior of tropical Africa, as he was in turn explorer, administrator and international expert. Margery Perham has brought not only the man and the country, but also the changing climate of thought in which he worked, alive for us; she has succeeded in the task of the historian of, in her own words, 'helping his contemporaries to enter into the minds of the men of the past so that their evaluation of their problems can be understood as well as our own.'

NOTES

1. Private Diary, 20 April 1945, Perham Papers (hereafter PP), Rhodes House Library, Box 33, file 4.
2. Margery Perham, *Pacific Prelude*, ed. A.H.M.Kirk-Greene (London, 1988), p. 195.
3. Their correspondence is in PP 22. Perham wrote in the 1945 diary entry that she found it difficult to think of Lugard as 'Fred'; and she used that name only in direct address or in referring to him when writing to his brother.
4. Lugard to Perham, undated, and Perham to Lugard, 1 April 1935, PP 22/2.
5. PP 312/2.
6. Lugard to Perham, 19 May, Perham to Lugard 22 May, E. Lugard to Lugard, 27 May 1938, PP 293/1.
7. E. Lugard to Perham, 28 Oct. 1949, PP 293/5; E. Lugard to Perham 19 Aug. 1951, PP 293/6. Perham managed to persuade Edward and his son that the diary and letters should not be burnt, but placed under restriction in Rhodes House Library until 1995.
8. Notes on discussion with E. Lugard, 28 April, and Perham to E. Lugard, 29 April 1945, PP 293/3.
9. Huxley to Perham, 29 June, and Perham to Huxley, 1 July 1946, PP 314/1.
10. Perham to E. Lugard, 15 and 30 Aug. 1946, PP 293/4.
11. Ibid., 19 Sept. 1946.
12. Perham to E. Lugard, 19 Feb. 1949, PP 293/5.
13. 10 Aug. 1956, PP 315/1.
14. Notes for talk to Nuffield College research seminar, 31 Oct. 1951, PP 236/16.
15. Notes for talk to Professor Harlow's seminar, 1950, PP 236/12.
16. Margery Perham, *Lugard: The Years of Adventure* (London, 1956) (hereafter *Lugard I*), pp. 711–12.
17. PP 236/12.
18. *Lugard I*, pp. 182–9.
19. Ibid., p. 378.
20. Ibid., p. 136.
21. PP 236/12.
22. *Lugard I*, p. 281.
23. Margery Perham (ed.), *The Diaries of Lord Lugard*, vol. 2 (London, 1959), p. 373.
24. *Lugard I*, p. 500.
25. Margery Perham and Mary Bull (eds.), *The Diaries of Lord Lugard*, vol.4 (London, 1963), pp. 84–6.
26. See Margery Perham, *West African Passage*, ed. A.H.M.Kirk-Greene (London, 1983), pp. 24–5, describing her first view of Nigeria.
27. Margery Perham, *Lugard: The Years of Authority* (London, 1960) (hereafter *Lugard II*), p. 138.
28. Ibid., p. 140. This sentence is taken by I.F.Nicolson, in *The Administration of Nigeria* (London, 1969), p. 127, to lead to the conclusion that since Lugard did not feel a need for reason or discussion, his decisions were irrational and militaristic.
29. *Political Memoranda: revision of instructions to political officers on subjects chiefly political and administrative, 1913–18* (HMSO, London, 1919).
30. *Lugard II*, pp. 180–7.

31. These notes are undated, but refer to the first volume as already published; PP 304/1.
32. Lugard to Perham, 22 Feb. and 12 March 1932, PP 22/1.
33. *Lugard II*, pp. 487–8.
34. PP 304/1.
    Lugard II, p. 446.
36. Ibid., p. 466.
37. Margery Perham, *Native Administration in Nigeria* (London, 1937), pp. 221–2, 253–4.
38. *Lugard II*, p. 465.
39. Since the notes on the C.O. records in her papers are typed, it is not clear who made the
    notes on any particular file. It is only possible to say, from personal knowledge, that
    Margery Perham read and noted some of the files, but that the bulk of the notes were
    made by her research assistant from 1948 to 1952, Hilary Chadwick-Brooks, later Mrs
    Giles Bullard.
40. *Lugard II*, p. 636.
41. Ibid., p. 632.
42. Ibid., p. 476.
43. Ibid., p. 197.
44. California, 1958.
45. *Lugard II*, p. 581.
46. Private Diary, 20 April 1945, PP 33/4.
47. John E. Flint, 'Frederick Lugard: the making of an autocrat' in L.H. Gann and Peter
    Duignan (eds.) *African Proconsuls: European Governors in Africa* (Stanford, 1978),
    pp. 290–309.
48. *Lugard II*, p. 709.
49. Private Diary, 20 April 1945, PP 33/4.
50. Perham to Creech Jones, 24 Oct. 1956, PP 23/1.
51. Greene to Perham, 19 Dec. 1956, PP 315/2.
52. Roland Oliver, *Times Literary Supplement*, 12 Oct. 1956, PP 315/2.
53. John Fage, *Observer*, 25 Sept. 1960, PP 316/2.
54. Thomas Hodgkin, *New Statesman*, 22 Oct. 1960, PP 316/2.

The Coming of Independence in the Sudan

Wm. Roger Louis

'After Uganda and Kenya it is a drop into an abysm of backwardness.'[1] Margery Perham thus recorded her dominant impression of the southern Sudan during her first visit in February 1937. Like an Edwardian travelogue, her diary records her thoughts with unguarded candour and reveals a romantic and enquiring mind. To those accustomed to think of her as the wise and committed defender of African causes in the 1960s, some of her early reactions to black Africans in the Sudan might appear out of character. She wrote about the mountains of Jebel Mara in Darfur:

> We are in a great wide basin, ringed by peaks of pointed or domed rock. It all seems so un-African that I was quite surprised, and perhaps almost disgusted, to meet negroes in this Paradise. For whatever I may feel about negroes, they are not romantic. Their appearance and their generally servile character must always from this point of view, put them in a category apart from Red Indians, Polynesians or Arabs.[2]

Certainly her diary entries do demonstrate how far she travelled from the age of Lugard and Hailey to the time of Oliver and Fage when she was elected the first President of the African Studies Association a quarter of a century later in 1963. Yet it is also true that she never wholly lost the intense preoccupation with 'racial' differences, an interpretation that is a striking feature of her first encounters with Africa. There is also an irrepressible element of fun in her diaries of the 1930s, a sense of the absurd which must have confounded some of her more proper British hosts in the Sudan and elsewhere. There is, she once pronounced, 'something difficult as well as unaesthetic about swimming in a helmet.'[3]

From the outset she distinguished the Sudan from all other African dependencies. On her first visit she landed at night on a flight from Uganda at Torit in Equatorial Province. She recorded as one of her first impressions 'the two flags flying in the light of the flares, one on each side of the bonnet, the Union Jack for England, and a green flag with a crescent for Egypt.'[4] Though the administration of the Sudan was British, its status was half Egyptian. The Agreement of 1899 between Britain and Egypt established the Sudan as a Condominium but conferred on Britain administrative control. 'The two flags, which can be seen today flying on all public buildings in the Sudan', she wrote later, suggested 'equal status', but the Governor-General's 'almost unfettered power' was the principal element of British administration.[5] Britain ruled the Sudan, in one of her phrases, as a benevolent autocracy. It was an autocracy, however, that did not come under the Colonial Office but the Foreign Office. This bureaucratic arrangement contributed to the distinctive nature of the Sudan Political Service, the corps of officers who presided over the country's administration. The Foreign Office was acutely sensitive to Egyptian influence, which catapulted the Sudan into independence at a far earlier date than Margery Perham believed to be desirable. The Sudanese were able to play off the British against the Egyptians.

On her second visit to the Sudan, at the end of 1937, she travelled through Egypt. She was conscious that as a woman she placed Egyptian politicians and officials in an uncomfortable position. After a talk with the head of the Egyptian Agricultural Society in Cairo, she noted that 'he was making a great effort to do something almost as difficult and ludicrous as standing on his head in having a serious political talk with a woman.'[6] She spent Christmas Day 1937 in Luxor. Her descriptions of Egyptians, again, were not flattering. At the Office of Antiquities she encountered 'a fat official in a tarbush', which led her to generalize that 'all Egyptian "effendies" are fat with a triangular extension of the paunch and the face.' After trudging through 'filthy crowded streets', she summed up her overall reaction by stating that 'everything run by Egyptians was dirty and disorderly'.[7] These disparaging remarks would not be noteworthy were it not for the lasting contrast with the Sudan. She travelled with American companions as she crossed the frontier:

> I was thankful to leave this [Egypt], with its sordidness, dirt, unspeakable lavatories, and dishevelled and indifferent officials, and to enter the atmosphere of efficiency, intelligent paternalism and cleanliness which marks the Sudan.[8]
>
> I bade the Americans note the order and comeliness that reigned under British rule, and the sudden end of that long chorus of 'bakshish' ['tips'], and the clean and soignés uniforms of all officials, white and coloured.[9]

The injunction to the Americans is significant. She was never hypersensitive to American criticism; but, especially in the case of the Sudan, she took what she believed to be a justifiable pride in sound colonial administration.

First impressions are sometimes lasting impressions. Throughout her writings, the seat of government in the Sudan, the Palace at Khartoum, acquires an almost symbolic significance as a stabilizing and civilizing influence, in marked contrast to the average Government House elsewhere in British Africa. She similarly regarded the Sudan Political Service as distinctly a cut above the Colonial Service. She recorded her first reactions to the colour and vivacity of the Palace on her arrival in Khartoum:

> It stands right over the Nile on the four mile river-front along which most of Khartoum's large solid buildings are placed. ... I must confess ... that I was never in a Government House where things were done so efficiently and impressively.
>
> The women here exhibit a high standard of looks and dress. ... The whole social tone is upon a higher level than the Colonial Service. The Black Watch officers, with their striking dress uniforms, contribute another mass of colour to the parties.[10]

Before the Second World War, she believed that the Palace would last as a centre of benevolent British authority for the indefinite future. Ten years later, however, she reflected on the same landscape along the Nile:

> I felt suddenly an intense regret for what was passing or at least beginning to pass. This solid building, these statues of the man the Sudanese murdered [Gordon] and the man who conquered them [Kitchener] – the men *we* honour – all these great buildings, the banks, the smart police, this structure of efficient, honest government – these are the outward signs of British rule set up in the years of our high confidence in our own power, the priority of our interest, our certainty of the justice and welfare we had to bring. In 5, 10, 15 years what will remain?[11]

It was a perceptive foreboding. British authority began to collapse only five years later in 1953.

Her attachment to the Sudan, of course, went much deeper than her aesthetic appreciation of the buildings along the Nile. She developed loyalties and lasting friendships, above all with Sir Douglas Newbold. When she first met him in 1938 he was Governor of Kordofan. He later became Civil Secretary, the highest post in the Sudan Political Service. He grew into a legendary figure, in part through her own efforts after his early death in 1945. In 1952 she wrote an introduction to a book publishing his letters and memoranda.[12] Her analysis of his method of colonial government demonstrates her own command of local detail and administrative procedure, above all at the district level but extending through general financial, legal, defence, and educational policies. It is clear from her papers that Newbold gave her unrivalled and complete access to the records of the Sudan government. At one time she hoped to write a major work on the Sudan, but she got only as far as outlines and a few draft chapters. One can only lament that the book was never finished.

Wartime circumstances caused the Foreign Office and Colonial Office to believe that Britain might become involved in a long-term administration of Ethiopia. Margery Perham was thus requested to write a book examining the problems in historical perspective. In 1948 she published *The Government of Ethiopia*, which analyses the history and institutions of the country from a western vantage point. There can be no doubt that the book on the Sudan would have been a far more significant work.

She once wrote that two men had a marked influence on her life, Lugard and Newbold. Her friendship with the latter gave her description of his work a warmth and insight that raises her comment to a level of historical significance. In a broad political context, the Sudan becomes a microcosm of the British colonial experience, with its past errors, present problems, and future hopes. Newbold is the protagonist, the archetypal colonial administrator as District Commissioner, Provincial Governor, and Civil Secretary. He faces problems resembling those of an earlier age in India and, more recently, in Nigeria:

> We can see him [Newbold] dealing, in the very special and rather isolated situation of the Sudan, with the same main problems which had confronted Britain in India and were still demanding solution in nearly all the colonies.
>
> Following the establishment of law and order ... had come the construction of a system of local government for both tribal and urban groups; and the juxtaposition, if not the harmonization, of two systems of law and of law-courts; the delicate tasks of fitting Western education upon societies formed in a wholly different physical and mental environment; and the introduction of Western economic principles into communities of peasant farmers or semi-nomadic pastoralists.[13]

The universal problems of colonial administration thus manifest themselves in Sudanese circumstances.

One problem had become especially pressing. Newbold had to deal with the dual culture, Arab and black African, the long-term relationship of an Arab and Muslim north with a black African pagan and partly

Christianized south. Under the direction of Sir Harold MacMichael, the Civil Secretary from 1926 to 33, a 'southern policy' had developed that attempted to exclude northern Sudanese and Arab influence from the south. In the Perham Papers, Newbold can be seen hesitantly trying to develop a more harmonious and constructive policy. The fate of the south became a cause of anguish to Margery Perham 'as the political pace quickened and as the Sudan administration attempted to adjust, in her words, 'the future relationship of an Arab and Moslem north with a Negro and pagan south'.[14]

In the 1930s she came to grips with the issue of 'Indirect Rule', which MacMichael had implemented in the Sudan (with the Nigerian model in mind). Newbold began to adjust the principle to circumstances of local government. It was Newbold's work in the district and the province that stirred her imagination. She believed him to be 'the ideal District Commissioner', who, despite an exasperating fault of procrastination, did an admirable job in difficult circumstances. He brought humour, balance, and common sense to his work. Despite her use of the word 'ideal' she did not idealize him, but she did regard him as a person of such integrity and humanity that his attitudes became a touchstone of her own judgement.

Newbold himself adopted a mildly sceptical and teasing attitude towards the phenomenon of an Oxford female don with boundless energy coming his way by chance at El Obeid (the provincial capital of Kordofan), but he obviously enjoyed her company and found her intellectually engaging. He wrote the following 'Ode' to her in 1938 after witnessing her prodigious research in his files on the problem of 'Native Administration', or administrative units of indirect rule. He used her family nickname, 'Pro'. Newbold described the circumstances of his authorship: 'Written in sweat & agony while buried in files on town lands, witchcraft, aerodromes, bloodmoney, & soap factories.'

> ODE to the 'PRO'
> Margery P. lives on weak tea,
> Refuses to eat pies or red meat.
> But *she'd* travel miles, to devour old files.
> Like Oliver Twist, to her mill all is grist,
> And shouts Hip! Hooray! when she tastes some N.A.[15]

For her, Newbold was a lasting source of inspiration. She wrote of her joy in his companionship in 1938: 'We played tennis in the afternoon and talked until late at night. Newbold is marvellous. He ... was acute and humorous and as idealistic as ever. It renews my faith and my hopes for Africa to stay with him. We could not stop talking.'[16]

The Post-war Sudan

Both Lugard and Newbold died in 1945, making the year a landmark not only as ending the war but also in her personal life. During the war years she had not been able to follow the affairs of the Sudan as closely as she might have liked, and now she had the task of Lugard's biography thrust upon her.[17] It became obvious that her book on the Sudan would have to be a long-term rather than an immediate project. In any case the time for the kind of book she had originally planned was already past. Though the country continued to be one of her principal interests, she knew that the post-war Sudan would be radically different from the benevolent autocracy of her pre-war visits. Perhaps the most lucid example of the combination of her old and new ideas can be found in a letter written in 1946 to one of the officers in the Sudan Political Service. She restated the theme that the Sudan represented a microcosm of the British Empire and that the Condominium would be in the vanguard of colonial change. But now the time had come to cease ruling and begin yielding power:

> I think the Sudan Service has got a hard task in front of it for the next few years, but if you will forgive me for being platitudinous, this phase is a great test of all that has gone before, not only in the Sudan, but elsewhere in the Empire.
> It is clear we have got to switch over from ruling to helping and advising, and if the British can manage the transition, it will be a most wonderful achievement.[18]

The idea that the Sudanese would be managing their own affairs in 'the next few years' was a fundamental departure from her pre-war views.

The change in outlook can be traced to her stock-taking after the fall of Singapore in February 1942, when she saw more clearly than most other contemporary observers that the old British Empire was a thing of the past, and that the British would have to adjust rapidly to a new order.[19] After the war she was still optimistic about the Sudan and generally about the future of the other British dependencies in Africa. The handling of the question of Sudanese independence, however, caused her to have grave misgivings. I shall argue that the management of the transfer of power in the Sudan failed, from her point of view, to take into account some of the lessons she had drawn as early as the fall of Singapore.

The storm clouds were already on the Egyptian horizon in 1946. In October of that year the Foreign Secretary, Ernest Bevin, attempted to negotiate an agreement with the Egyptian Prime Minister, Sidky Pasha, that would revise the Anglo-Egyptian Treaty of 1936 and would end the

dispute over the British military presence in Canal Zone. To find common ground with the Egyptians, Bevin yielded to Sidky's insistence that
Egypt and the Sudan shared, and would share, the same sovereignty. In
essence this meant that Egypt and the Sudan would be as two states under
a 'common crown' – that is to say, under an 'Egyptian' crown. Bevin
believed that this theoretical or juridical concession to the Egyptians
would not interfere with the Sudan's right to self-determination, but
there were riots in Khartoum. The discontent was not restricted to the
Sudanese. The British officers in the Sudan Political Service believed that
they had been betrayed by the Foreign Office. All of this is common
historical knowledge. What is new, on the basis of the Margery Perham
papers, is the way in which Newbold's successor as Civil Secretary, James
Robertson, turned to her for help in mobilizing public sentiment in
Britain against the proposed agreement with the Egyptians.

'It is extremely improper', Robertson wrote to her in November 1946,
'for me as one of the senior officials of the Sudan Government to write to
you in this way but the gravity of the situation ... make[s] it imperative
that people at home should know what the danger is.' They had previously met only over 'a very hurried and uncomfortable lunch'. But he
now divulged his inner thoughts on the crisis in the Sudan. He described
the way in which the protest against the proposed agreement with Egypt
had nearly led, in Khartoum, to a 'serious breakdown of public security'.
Should the future of the Sudan be decided without consulting the
Sudanese? This appeared to him to be a violation of the principle on
which British rule rested. Robertson was obviously nervous about writing
to her in this manner. But he did so in the hope 'that you [and] .. your
many influential friends' would not wish to see the 'betrayal' of British
pledges that the Sudanese would determine their own future.[20]

He need not have worried about his plea falling on unsympathetic ears.
'[Y]our letter', she responded, 'gave me sufficient confidence and information.' She was inspired to write a letter to *The Times* which was
published on 10 December 1946.[21] In it she cogently pointed out the
contradiction between the premise that people should determine their
own fate and the assumption of the projected Anglo-Egyptian accord,
whereby Britain 'has signed away her share of sovereignty and given it
solely to Egypt'. There were some things that she thought were best left
unsaid in public. She had always believed that the officials in the Sudan
underestimated the danger of the British and Egyptian governments
undermining the colonial order in the Condominium. Now the reality had
to be faced. The Foreign Office might sacrifice the Sudan for security in
the Canal Zone. 'At the moment', she wrote to Robertson, 'I fear that
you must all have an overwhelming sense of bitterness and disillusion-

ment.'[22] In the event, the plan for common sovereignty was scrapped because of the protest by the Sudanese.

She became a comrade-in-arms with Robertson. Such was the extent of his trust that each month he sent her secret intelligence reports. In his judgement, she could be relied upon to put forward sympathetically the point of view of the Sudan Political Service. 'I shudder to think what might have happened if it had not been for the influence of people like you', he wrote to her in 1952.[23] Sometimes he flattered her. One can also detect strains of tension in the correspondence. An official point of view does not necessarily coincide with the outlook of a scholar, even though in this case she believed the Sudan administration to be almost beyond reproach. 'It is probably the most considerate and honest foreign govern-ment that history has ever seen', she declared in early 1947.[24] That judgement on the past must strike one as romantic, if not naïve. From it derived idealism about the future: 'What is needed is the building up of a new vision, a new positive task of friendly cultural co-operation in which we give freely what they want in a way which allows them to accept it.'[25] Her thought can also be translated into the language of *realpolitik*: nationalists should be given power, not given the opportunity to seize it.

Robertson from time to time tried to restrain her enthusiasm. She was a worthy ally, but he and others in the Sudan Political Service thought that her zeal sometimes exceeded her knowledge. She was herself aware of the limitations on her expertise imposed by other commitments. The Sudan was only a part, though a vital one, of her African concerns. The pace of Oxford life, the research on the Lugard biography, and the press of committee work gave her a sense of frustration in coming to grips with the problems of the Sudan. 'I do wish we could meet', she wrote to a Sudan official. 'It is this eternal pressure of overwork plus all the little worries and extras of life to-day that leave no margin for friendship or other things that matter. I am generally. . . so exhausted at the week-end that I want to crawl into a corner and hide. Unfortunately everyone descends on Oxford at week-ends, eager for official business, so that the week's work simply goes on into the week-end.'[26] Yet she always found time to meet Robertson's requests to provide information, for example, on colonial constitutions.

After the breakdown of the 1946 negotiations with Egypt, the devising of the future constitution became her principal Sudanese preoccupation. From the vantage point of the 1990s it is not easy to recall or understand why people forty years ago devoted such time and energy to drafting African constitutions. For Margery Perham it was a time for the planning of Africa's future. It was an age in which she, for one, hoped that the British could ensure a stable and durable order in the post-colonial era by giving the Sudan, and other British African territories, the benefit of Britain's own political tradition. In retrospect it appears clear that it was rather Anglocentric to believe that the 'Westminster model' would provide a pattern along which ex-colonial states would or should develop. But it would be a mistake to underestimate the importance that she and others attached to constitutional development as the key element in colonial planning. Here was her basic idea:

> People cannot be fundamentally changed in 50 years. But if we can keep a vital relationship with these people we may continue to be able to help them in many ways, especially if they maintain a constitution based on our model.[27]

With the benefit of hindsight, again, it is clear that she attached too much significance to the Sudanese adopting British parliamentary ceremony, and that she was too optimistic about their 'natural dignity and courtesy' prevailing indefinitely after they had learned 'House of Commons procedure'.[28] Nevertheless her constitutional instincts were sound. 'It seems to me', she wrote to Robertson in March 1947, 'that when a backward country makes a sudden [constitutional] advance like this, it is very important that the executive should be as strong and independent as possible. ... The danger surely in a country like the Sudan is a weak administration following the firm administration of the former regime, and the fear of an utter collapse of good government.'[29] The problem was that the pace of events seemed to be moving too rapidly to allow time for the constitution to be accepted as the supreme law of the land. Political ambition seemed to be outstripping prudent planning. She had written a year earlier that she was reduced 'almost to tears by the the utter unreasonableness of young coloured nationalism'.[30]

During the war she had briefly had as a student in Oxford a young Sudanese official who gave her considerable intellectual pleasure but who also caused her anguish about Sudanese nationalism. This was Mekki Effendi Abbas, one of the most outstanding of her African students. He had an incisive mind, buoyant vitality, and an infectious laugh. After his return to the Sudan in 1940 both she and Newbold kept in touch with him. He became in turn a member of the Local Government Advisory Board, the Advisory Council for the Northern Sudan, and various conferences set up to advise on Sudanization. But in 1947 he resigned from his official post to espouse 'radical' political views and began editing what she described as a 'pro-Egyptian' weekly newspaper (*El Raid*). This was undoubtedly one of her most painful experiences with a student, but he helped her to develop a perceptive understanding of Sudanese politics during a two-month visit which she paid to the Sudan from February to

April 1948. It was her longest visit to the Sudan. Two months may not seem a long time, but she was able to compress interviews and research with a remarkable intensity. This journey certainly left the most lasting impression on her and in some ways was traumatic because of her meetings with Mekki Abbas.

Mekki gave her insight into the religious and historical traditions behind the two leaders in Sudanese politics, the Sayed Ali Mirghani and the Sayed Abdel Rahman el Mahdi, the latter the son of the Mahdi who, in British imperial history, is indelibly associated with the death of Gordon. The Sayed Ali Mirghani, or 'S.A.M.', was associated with the Ashigga, or pro-Egyptian party. The Sayed Abdel Rahman el Mahdi, or 'S.A.R.', was the force behind the Umma or independence party which, in her view, might lead the Sudan into a new Mahdist dictatorship. She described the two Sayeds as religious figures who divided the allegiance of Muslims and infused politics with the religious zeal of the sects in the northern Sudan. She later distilled her thoughts in formal political analysis, of which the following extract is useful because of its insight into the two figures dominating Sudanese politics at the time.

> Sayed Sir Ali Mirghani [was] pious, aging, delicate and retiring in disposition ... [and] he had neither desire nor capacity to lead a political party, but as a rival to the other outstanding religious leader, he became, inevitably, the symbol round which opposition was grouped.
>
> On the other side stood Sir Abdel Rahman el Mahdi, the Mahdi's son, who had by this time become a great public figure, winning his way by his moderate and astute political leadership and the great wealth he had amassed from growing irrigated cotton.[31]

Those two descriptions help to make comprehensible some of the salient issues in her conversations with Mekki. He challenged the good faith of the British government. He believed that the British did not wish to grant independence to the Sudan, at least in the immediate future:

> We talked for over 2 hours and it was even more painful than I expected. ... The whole mind of the most intelligent, sensitive and liberal Sudanese [Mekki] who has yet been developed, torn between his admiration and respect for the British and his sense of having been deceived by them.
>
> He sees with a dreadful clarity the danger of his country between the Egyptian menace on the one side and the threat of a new Mahdia from S.A.R. and his family, who would establish something like an

Egyptian pashadom in the Sudan. The people remember the hor-
rors of the Mahdia, whereas the Egyptian oppression is becoming a
matter of history.[32]

She acknowledged that Mekki helped her to understand the Ashigga, 'the
so-called Egyptian party', better than she had before. 'I gather', she
wrote, .. 'that Egypt means no harm to the Sudan and that ... they [the
Sudanese] can have a status like that of a British dominion.'[33] She had a
frank discussion with him over the range of Sudanese politics. But there
were some issues on which she could not be candid. Even though he had
been her student in Oxford, certain subjects were still taboo or too
sensitive to debate. She could not discuss with him, for example, the
question of religion and the saving of 'Southern negroes ... from Islam
and female circumcision'. Mekki told her that political issues could never
'affect his friendship for me, and his trust, and once or twice his grand
laugh rang out.' But she came away 'deeply depressed'.[34]

Yet she still refused to lose faith in Mekki or in the hope of winning him
back to the cause of gradualism. On her return to England she helped him
to obtain one of the first studentships at Nuffield College and a grant from
the Rhodes Trust. 'I am playing Lord Elton here', she wrote of the Trust's
chairman, 'but have not yet landed him ... he is very Right wing and is
worried about Mekki's political views.'[35] Under her supervision Mekki
eventually completed his B.Litt. thesis on 'the Sudan question' and later
she went to great lengths to secure its publication, contributing a
generous introduction of her own.[36]

The main object of Margery Perham's 1948 visit was to respond to the
invitation of the Civil Secretary, Robertson, and the Principal of Gordon
College (which became in 1951 the University of Khartoum) to advise on
the future training of Sudanese administrative officers and the development of the School of Administration of the College. Her wartime
correspondence with Newbold shows that they had both come to accept
the principle that Sudanese officials should replace the British administrative officers.[37] She had abandoned her earlier support of the 'scaffolding theory' which argued that the administrative service established by
the British should dissolve on their departure. The functions would be
transferred to local government and judicial officials, on a British domestic model.[38] She was not only concerned about the initial courses for
administrative officers. The British, she hoped, would leave a system of
administrative training for officials of all departments, who would continue throughout their careers to take refresher courses. She had always
been impressed by

the spirit of cooperation and friendship between British and

Sudanese in the partnership in administration [but] it is inevitable that this partnership should feel the strain of that most testing of all political operations, the transfer of power. ... But at least these conceptions of conscious and continuous training 'on the job' will, far more than any attempt to turn lectures on government into sermons on social obligations, make it possible for the British officials to communicate to their Sudanese colleagues the high qualities which a non-official may be permitted to recognise in their own service to the Sudan.[39]

She was also beginning to address herself intensely to the wider aspects of 'the problems of the *transfer of power*'.[40] In the year following the independence of India and Pakistan, the phrase came naturally enough. What is remarkable is the clarity of her vision in seeing that the end of British rule would come quickly and that the Sudanese would have to be granted independence, in her view, before they were actually ready for it. There is a paradox here. She pressed the Sudan officials to move forward rapidly but she was haunted with fear about the consequences of 'premature' independence. Yet unless the British moved quickly the initiative would pass to the 'extremists'. She explained her contradictory impulses in a way that went to the heart of the matter:

I have a dreadful feeling that we are missing the psychological moment in this country's history by being, as we nearly always are, just too late and too grudging in our constitutional concessions.

If we lose the last moment when we have some good will left among the moderate elements we shall be forced into much larger surrenders of power in an embittered atmosphere when they will do little good.[41]

The resolution of the paradox thus becomes the yielding of power quickly in order to preserve as much good will and influence as possible among the moderates – but not so quickly as to throw them into disarray. She debated this proposition with everyone she encountered: Robertson, the Sayed Abdel Rahman el Mahdi, Mekki Abbas. She was impressed with the relentless logic with which Mekki pursued the same point. 'As Mekki said to me bitterly,' she recorded in her diary, 'it is no good the British waiting until the Sudan is a Utopia before they hand over.'[42]

There are two especially poignant passages in her 1948 diary, one about a church service, the other describing a dinner. In the atmosphere of the church she believed she witnessed the spirit of a vanishing age. She experienced the exuberance of the Sunday service attended by the British community in Khartoum. She noted that eighty per cent of the congregation consisted of British troops. 'They seemed very young and clean in their newly ironed biscuit coloured linen shorts & tunics and their very red faces and legs.' They sang the old hymns 'with enormous zest'. She thought it was probably nostalgia for home that caused most of them to attend.[43] For her, on the other hand, the church in Khartoum on more than one occasion became a place to reflect on the meaning of the British presence in the Sudan.

> Whatever may come, the age of confidence and power has passed, and it has been very brief as the history of Empires goes – too brief to have affected the hearts and minds of these people [the Sudanese] deeply. ...
>
> [W]hat a difficult and delicate act of judgment is asked of the men in this secretariat! The yielding of power and the timing of that yielding, and by men formed in a tradition of authority whose only reason for their presence here is confidence in what they are doing.[44]

'The glory', as she reiterated on another occasion, 'the glory of absolute confidence not only in our beneficent autocracy but in its indefinite duration, is departing.'[45]

The transience of the British era was also a theme when she wrote about less sombre things than churches and soldiers. On the eve of her departure she attended a dinner at the Palace. It was held out of doors because of the heat. It is probably fair to say that she only half lamented the passing of the British era. The part of her that resisted the new era relished the entertainment characteristic of an earlier age. She had an eye for pomp and imperial circumstance. Her diary would probably have been read with interest by critics of British imperialism at home and abroad who believed that the end of the British Empire would come none too soon. In any case her comments would have provided good ammunition for Evelyn Waugh.

> Lamps in silver candle-sticks lit the long table and lamps hung on the palm trees and flowering shrubs. Everything was of the highest English standard – the standard of 20 years ago – beautiful silver, glass and flowers, luxurious food in many courses, perfect service, wines, liqueurs, bon-bons.
>
> The women were, of course, in full evening dress, a little pale and tired with the heat, but responding to the growing coolness of the evening and the wine. I felt like a watcher at a well produced play – admiring the scenery, the dresses, the actors – and wondering how long the run would last.[46]

On her last day she accepted an invitation to sail up the Nile and swim. 'I knew I ought not to do it', she wrote. 'But on this whole tour I have hardly had one hour of recreation and this was the last day.'

The Crisis of Sudanese Independence

'I have followed constitutional events in the Sudan with almost breathless interest', she wrote to Robertson about the developments in the year following her visit in 1948.[47] Within the next few years the creation of the superstructure of what she described as 'Western democratic institutions' seemed to be complete. She wrote that the British had helped to create in the Sudan 'an elective two-chamber legislature, a Cabinet system, Westminster parliamentary procedure, and an independent judiciary and Civil Service.'[48] Had the British in the Sudan Political Service and the Sudanese then been left to themselves to develop those institutions, the result, in her view, would have been far more satisfactory than what actually transpired. In the event, the question of the Sudan's future, as she had feared, became entangled once more with the problem of the Canal Zone.

I shall not attempt to describe the sequence of events leading to the Sudanese declaration of independence in late 1955. There are, however, two landmarks that are important to recognize in order to make the problem of the transfer of power comprehensible from her vantage point. The first is the unilateral denunciation of the 1899 Agreement by the Egyptian government in late 1951 and the proclamation of King Farouk as King of Egypt and the Sudan. The second is the Egyptian revolution of 1952. These were momentous external events. In 1951 the Egyptians aimed at breaking the British grip over the Sudan by repudiating the legal foundation of the Condominium. After the revolution in July 1952, the military officers who had ousted Farouk now abandoned the ancient slogan of 'unity of the Nile Valley' and proclaimed that the Sudanese would be free to determine their own future. She wrote about General Mohammed Neguib, the prominent leader of the revolution, and the problems of the Sudan in 1952:

> General Neguib, by the refreshing contrast between his personality and methods and those of his predecessors [of King Farouk's regime], seems to have so captured the good opinion of the British Press and public that neither seems in the mood to scrutinize his recent [proposals] ... on the Sudan with the care that our responsibilities for that country require.[49]

The faint praise of Neguib was in fact a veiled warning. She feared a Foreign Office sell-out to Egypt.

Her suspicions of the Foreign Office were deep-seated. She had no doubt at all that the Sudan would be sacrificed to Egypt if the strategic needs of the British Empire demanded it. She wrote in 1951 about the plans to bring Egypt into a 'Middle East Defence Organisation' that would complement NATO: 'Let us hope that the fate of the Sudan is not going to be the pawn in North Atlantic strategic interests.'[50] Unlike the Colonial Office, the Foreign Office, in her view, had no tradition of protecting indigenous inhabitants from external predators, Egyptian or other. 'I don't trust the Foreign Office in these matters', she once wrote to Robertson. 'Their tradition is all against what I should regard [as] a properly open and democratic way of handling these situations.'[51]

The mistrust was reciprocated. Willie Morris, the head of the Sudan Department of the Foreign Office, diligently read her letters to *The Times*. He was not one of her admirers. Morris was later Ambassador in Cairo. He was one of the ablest Foreign Office officials of his generation. His annoyance at her gratuitous advice to the Foreign Office boiled over in response to her letter to *The Times* about Neguib and the implication that the Foreign Office did not take seriously the commitment in the Sudan. He commented sarcastically about her suggestion that there might be a premature transfer of power:

> It is entirely appropriate that she should do it [make the suggestion], since no one has done more to foster the illusion that if only we never contradict the politically ambitious amongst African peoples when they claim to be ready for the highest responsibility, if only we show unlimited sympathy, and never remind them of harsh practical facts which might offend, then they will somehow rise to the occasion and show an equivalent sense of responsibility.[52]

If she had been able to read the Foreign Office minutes, her fears would have been confirmed. 'I think this price is worth paying', the Permanent Under-Secretary, Sir William Strang, wrote about yielding to the Egyptians on the Sudan to resolve the problem of the Canal Zone.[53]

She did not know, of course, of the secret Foreign Office calculations. Nevertheless she had, in her own phrase, 'a great suspicion' that the business about the Canal Zone might throw out of step the already rapid yet measured stride towards a transfer of power in the Sudan. One of the remarkable features in her correspondence with Robertson was the comparison with India:

> The experience of India seemed to show that the act of transfer is not one that can be easily performed, but takes a tremendous

amount of energy, determination and good will, on the side of the transferring power. ... I cannot help thinking that the more quickly we act, the greater the likelihood of our retaining the good will of the moderates.[54]

She hoped that the Sudan, like India and Pakistan, would become a member of the Commonwealth, or at least would be treated more or less the same as other members through a treaty of alliance. She wrote to Robertson: 'If there is still any chance of bringing the Sudan, if not into the Commonwealth, into a kind of alliance with us, it would allow us to go on helping them.'[55] There was in fact never any prospect that the Sudan might be encouraged to join the Commonwealth. The Foreign Office officials, among other things, were wary of complications with Egypt.[56] Robertson knew of the Foreign Office's reasons, but in his letters to Margery Perham he preferred to emphasize the Sudanese rather than the British motives not to press for Commonwealth membership: 'These [Sudanese] chaps are all so ignorant and hidebound, mention of member-ship of the Commonwealth means to many of them continued British domination – and the phrase "dominion status" seems to prove that.'[57]

The Indian example appealed to her in part because of the skill of Mountbatten and the pageantry of the transfer of power in 1947. Was not the Sudan worthy of similar attention and ceremony? Mountbatten had captured her imagination, though not entirely positively. She wrote again to Robertson:

> Do you not think it might be a good idea if some big political figure came over to Cairo and Khartoum to carry through the hand-over? Don't for a moment imagine that this means that I have not got 100% confidence in you personally but I feel that these terribly difficult transfers have to be carried through with a certain amount of drama.
>
> Would not a Mountbatten help, especially if he were a little less ruthless and tempestuous in his methods?[58]

Her choice of the person to 'do a Mountbatten' in the Sudan was her friend Arthur Creech Jones, the former Secretary of State for the Colonies in the Labour Government. She believed that Creech Jones had the stature, the sympathy with Africans, and the sense of timing that would allow him to rise to the occasion. As Colonial Secretary, he had taken the measure of African nationalism and had become convinced that it was better to take the risk of moving forward too quickly rather than yielding, as she once put it, 'too little and too late'.[59] In her judgement he had handled the nationalist movement in the Gold Coast in a manner that inspired confidence for the Sudan. She pointed out to Robertson the importance of drawing lessons from the Gold Coast experience:

> In almost all our dealings with the development of self-government (coloured people) we tend to underrate the psychological factors. I am following Gold Coast affairs very closely and I really think that we owe it to the Labour Government that we took the plunge there at the right moment.

> The immense good will that we have gained and the sense of responsibility that has been shown by Nkrumah have made me realise that if we give away gracefully in time what we have to give away we gain something quite new and of immense importance.[60]

Again, Robertson felt it necessary to damp down her enthusiasm. The lessons of India and the Gold Coast did not inspire the Foreign Office, which made no effort to find someone to do for the Sudan what Mountbatten had achieved at the time of Indian independence. Nor was the Sudan administration at first responsive, though Robertson did eventually arrive at a similar conclusion.[61] It must be said that, if her suggestions had been followed, the events of Sudanese independence might have been more satisfactory from both the British and the Sudanese vantage points.

Instead, the Anglo-Egyptian Agreement on the Sudan of February 1953 came as a terrrible blow to her. To pave the way towards agreement on the Canal Zone, the Foreign Office made concessions in the Sudan. These included a speeding up of the Sudanization of the administration, an international commission (including Egyptian representatives) to supervise the process of self-determination no later than the end of 1955, and a target date set for independence shortly thereafter. These were terms, of course, that the Sudan political parties accepted wholeheartedly. As Robertson wrote in his diary, 'There seems little point in struggling, if all the [Sudanese] political parties are with Egypt.'[62] The Sudanese would be given the choice to decide on independence or union with Egypt (the option to join the Commonwealth was added to placate the British public but was not seriously pursued).

The agreement of February 1953 was a turning point. Then and forever after it signified to her the negative lessons to be learned about the management of African independence. One is reminded of her sober assessment at the time of the fall of Singapore, when she stated that experience was a rough teacher. For her personally the calamity in the Sudan caused a comparable amount of soul searching. At Singapore the Japanese had been a recognizable enemy. The military collapse precipitated a moral crisis within the British Empire. In the Sudan the real enemy, as she had suspected, turned out to be the Foreign Office. The diplomatic collapse, as she viewed it, demoralized the Sudan Political Service and called into question the capacity of the British government to deal with the general problem of the transfer of power in Africa. At one stroke the Foreign Office nullified, in her judgement, the good work of half a century.

The charge is serious and the issues are complex, but essentially what happened was the dismantling of the colonial administration *before* independence. Here was her own description of the agreement as she analysed it in a letter to *The Times*:

> Under the terms of the agreement of February 1953, which the Foreign Office made with Egypt in the vain hope of easing the Suez Canal dispute, the British in the administration, the Defence Force and the police are to leave *before* the date set for self-determination. ... The terms of the agreement are unfortunate: they leave men tied to posts which are becoming difficult to hold, and entrust the initiative to discharge and the arrangements for cancellation and compensation to a Sudanese Ministry which has hitherto shown more complaisance towards Egypt than towards Britain.[63]

The last sentence is slightly cryptic but critical. She referred to the officers of the Sudan Political Service whose contracts could be cancelled. They now faced an abrupt termination of their careers. In her view this was no less than a feckless abdication of responsibility by the imperial government by leaving the civil servants of the Sudan Political Service to fend for themselves. There was also one regional problem to which she was especially sensitive. A British exodus would 'spell misery to the primitive south, where the tribes need expert and sympathetic handling'. She referred generally to 'a bitter conclusion to our partnership with a fine people'.

She visited the Sudan for a week in the month following the conclusion of the February 1953 agreement. Her diary is filled with words of bitterness, remorse, and despair. She immediately went to see Robertson:

> We went to the bone of our subject, and saw it in all its horrible shape. The end of one of the finest chapters in humane and efficient administration by one people of another that the world has ever seen.
>
> Everything crumbling – everything threatened with more or less ruin. If the F.O. had gone ahead [with the plans for elections without Egyptian interference] ... they would have had a Sudanese Parliament and could have laughed at Neguib.

But now the way was open for Egyptian interference and she [Egypt] was going to see the administrative service, the keystone of the arch, knocked out in 3 years.

Now how could they [the officers in the S.P.S.] hold on for so long? Why should they? The service was full of bitterness – soon it would not be a service at all.

Their misery, personal and professional and, deeper still, their love of the country and people, chimed in with my realization of all that may happen of collapse and bitterness and I went wretchedly to bed.[64]

She found nothing to be optimistic about. But she admired the fortitude of the officers of the Sudan Political Service. 'These people are the salt of the earth – or at least of our imperial world.'[65]

If her thoughts appeared to be morose or melodramatic, they were no more so than those of the officers who felt that they had been betrayed. A Sudan official wrote to her in 1954:

You have struck the nail right on the head when you lay the Agreement or the blame for the authorship of the Agreement solely on the Foreign Office ... the work of fifty years in the Sudan was thrown away in the hope that Egypt might toe the line over the Suez Canal issue.[66]

There is of course another side to the story. Willie Morris and others in the Foreign Office would have warmly denied her interpretation of scuttle. The British withdrew from the Sudan, rather as they would from a Middle Eastern than from an African country, and remained on good terms with the Sudanese. But from her point of view it was a calamitous example to set for the rest of Africa. She watched with distaste the approach to independence and the way in which the men of the Sudan Political Service were forced to wrangle over the severance of their salaries. 'Certainly the way our administration is running out slowly and rather sordidly, with all these arguments about pay and so on, is very disheartening.'[67]

'The Sudan has declared its independence', she wrote to The Times in December 1955. She earnestly wished the Sudanese well in the future. The birth of the new state had not been auspicious because of the serious revolt in the south, where unrest has persisted in one form or another to the present day. At the time she lamented 'an appalling personal and professional loss' of British officers in the Sudan Political Service who might have reduced the killing.[68] About the insurgency itself, she believed that it might have been prevented only by a radically different policy towards the south begun much earlier. On the other hand there were some things that she was certain could have been prevented, above all the Foreign Office's treating the Sudan as 'the pawn in our Egyptian policy'.[69] To her the high politics of the British government seemed to have reverted to the days of the Scramble for Africa. Yet it is worth recalling the confidence she had expressed a few years earlier that the British effort would not have been in vain. She had written in 1946 to Robertson:

> I feel sure that none of the good work that the British have put into the Sudan will be wasted. You have trained some good men and true among the Sudanese, and you have established standards of administration, and though they will certainly decline under Sudanese or Egyptian rule, the situation will never be as though they had not been established. I am certain these things enter into the fabric of society and are not lost.[70]

This fundamental optimism was characteristic. By 1952, however, there was one new note of disillusion that tempered her future outlook. The Sudanese had shrewdly manipulated the Egyptian and British governments to achieve their own independence. They had received Egyptian support, but it was the Sudanese themselves who had kicked out the Sudan Political Service. Gratitude was not a characteristic of colonial nationalism. That she already knew, but the point was now driven home with a vengeance. It was a sadder and a wiser Margery who wrote: 'Strange, that nothing short of the final act of transfer ever satisfies the nationalist.'[71]

NOTES

1. Uganda–Sudan Diary, 24 Feb. 1937, Perham Papers (hereafter PP), Rhodes House, Oxford, Box 49, file 7.
2. 21 Feb. 1938 Diary.
3. Ibid.
4. Ibid., 19 Feb. 1937.
5. Margery Perham, 'The Sudan Emerges into Nationhood', *Foreign Affairs* (July 1949); reprinted in *Colonial Sequence 1949–1969* (London, 1970) (hereafter *Col. Seq. II*), p. 3.
6. Sudan Diary, 22 Dec. 1937, PP 50/3.
7. Ibid., Christmas Day 1937.
8. Ibid., 26 Dec. 1937.
9. Ibid., 28 Dec. 1937.
10. Ibid., 29 Dec.1937–9 Jan. 1938.
11. Sudan Diary, 22 Feb. 1948, PP 53/2.
12. K.D.D. Henderson, *The Making of the Modern Sudan* (London, 1953). Margery Perham's Introduction is reprinted in *Col. Seq. II*, pp.47–67.
13. Ibid., pp. 53–4.

14. Letter to the *Manchester Guardian*, 22 Dec. 1955; *Col. Seq. II*, p. 129.
15. Dated 22 March 1938, PP 536/6.
16. Sudan Diary, 7 March 1938, PP 50/7.
17. She wrote in 1945 about her decision not to carry on with the Sudan book: 'Lord Lugard died, and very strong pressure was brought upon me from the highest quarters to start work on his Life.' Presumably she referred to Lugard's brother, Major Edward Lugard. Perham to Robertson, 1 June 1946, PP 536/7. See Chapter 8 above.
18. Perham to K.D.D. Henderson, 29 July 1946, PP 536/1.
19. Letters to *The Times* of 13 and 14 March 1942; *Colonial Sequence 1930–1949* (London, 1967) (hereafter *Col. Seq. I*) , pp. 225–31. See W. R. Louis, *Imperialism at Bay* (Oxford, 1977), pp. 135–9.
20. Robertson to Perham, 25 Nov. 1946, PP 538/2.
21. 'The Anglo-Egyptian Treaty'; *Col. Seq. I*, pp. 292–3.
22. Perham to Robertson, 10 Dec. 1946, PP 538/2.
23. Robertson to Perham, 7 May 1952, PP 536/7.
24. Perham to John Monro, 1 Jan. 1947, PP 538/2.
25. Sudan Diary, 22 Feb. 1948, PP 53/2. See above p. 25 for her 1954 views.
26. Perham to R. Davies, 14 Dec. 1946, PP 538/2.
27. Perham to W.H.T. Luce, 24 May 1954, PP 536/1.
28. 'Parliamentary Government in the Sudan'; *Col. Seq. I*, pp. 329–32.
29. Perham to Robertson, 19 March1947, PP 536/7.
30. Perham to Henderson, 29 July 1946, PP 536/1.
31. 'The Sudan Emerges into Nationhood', *Foreign Affairs* (July, 1949); *Col. Seq. II*, p. 7.
32. Sudan Diary, 27 Feb. 1948, PP 53/2.
33. Sudan Diary, 28 March 1948, PP 53/3.
34. Ibid.
35. Perham to V.N. Griffiths, 13 May 1948, PP 537/3.
36. See M. Abbas, *The Sudan Question* (London, 1952).
37. See, for example, Newbold to Perham, 18 May 1940, and extracts from Newbold's reports, in Henderson, *Making of the Modern Sudan*, pp. 139 and 512.
38. Margery Perham, *Native Administration in Nigeria* (London, 1937), p. 361. See above Chapter 4.
39. Notes for discussion on report, Khartoum, 9 March 1948, PP 583/3.
40. Sudan Diary, 27 Feb. 1948, PP 53/2. Emphasis added.
41. Sudan Diary, 5 March 1948, PP 53/3.
42. Ibid., 29 March 1948.
43. Ibid.
44. Ibid., 22 Feb. 1948.
45. Ibid., 10 March 1948.
46. Ibid., 21 April 1948.
47. Perham to Robertson, 15 Feb. 1949, PP 536/7.
48. 'Delicate Transfer of Rule in the Sudan', *The Times*, 16 June 1954; *Col. Seq. II*, p. 90.
49. 'The Choice before the Sudan', *The Times*, 17 Nov. 1952; *Col. Seq. II*, p. 72.
50. Perham to Creech Jones, 11 Oct. 1951, PP 23/1.
51. Perham to Robertson, n.d. but Jan. 1952, PP 536/7.
52. Minute by Morris, 18 Nov. 1952, FO 371/96912 (Public Record Office, London).
53. Minute by Strang, 4 Dec. 1952, FO 371/96915.
54. Perham to Robertson, 6 Dec. 1951, PP 536/7.
55. Ibid.
56. See, for example, FO 371/96852.
57. Robertson to Perham, 28 Jan. 1952, PP 536/7.
58. Perham to Robertson, 27 Nov. 1952, PP 536/7.
59. Sudan Diary, 4 March 1948, PP 53/3.
60. Perham to Robertson, n.d. but Jan. 1952, PP 536/7.
61. Robertson eventually wrote: 'Someone like Lord Mountbatten, General Templer or Mr Eden himself is what I have in mind.' (Memorandum by Robertson, 1 July 1954, FO

371/108324). He failed to persuade the Foreign Office.

62. Sir James Robertson, *Transition in Africa* (London, 1974), p. 151. In Robertson's view the real villains in the piece were the Americans, who had pressed the British to settle with the Egyptians, thereby 'selling the Sudan' (p. 150).
63. 'Delicate Transfer of Rule in the Sudan', *The Times*, 16 June 1954; *Col. Seq. II*, p. 91.
64. Sudan, Kenya, Uganda Diary 1953, 6 March 1953, PP 54/2.
65. Ibid., 8 March 1953.
66. R.C. Mayall to Perham, 16 June 1954, PP 536/5.
67. Perham to Mayall, 30 June 1954, PP 536/5.
68. Letter to *The Times; Col. Seq. II*, pp. 128–9.
69. Perham to Mayall, 23 June 1953, PP 536/5.
70. Perham to Robertson, 10 Dec. 1946, PP 538/2.
71. Sudan, Kenya, Uganda Diary 1953, 11 March 1953, PP 54/2.

'Dear Mr Mboya':
correspondence with a Kenya nationalist

Alison Smith

> Kenya is one of the ... parts of Africa which seem to have reached
> my heart as well as my head ... because, I suppose, I find both
> nature and man of absorbing interest. And man in Kenya is a rather
> comprehensive term; it covers a lot of types nearly all interesting in
> themselves and even more interesting when thrown together in that
> superb scenery of mountains, hills, lakes, and vast dry plains.[1]

So Margery Perham wrote, in a self-revealing passage, to the young Luo
politician Tom Mboya at the outset of an exchange of letters which was to
extend intermittently over two and a half years. Her concern with Kenya
went back to 1930, almost to the beginning of her African involvement. In
a prophetic passage in her travel diary in that year she had described the
crowds of intent, silent, Kikuyu attending one of the earliest African
political trials. 'So they will go on watching, with ever-growing appreciation of the issues, and the Kangethes will multiply as they have in South
Africa, and the Kikuyu, nearly a million of them, sit at Nairobi's
backdoor.'[2] She soon became active in the controversial issues of the
1930s over settler and African interests in Kenya. But while her central
preoccupation was with the obstacle presented to African advancement
by the European settlers, she was also quick to condemn bureaucratic
myopia and inefficiency, as shown in the Mombasa dock strike of 1937.[3]
At that point she was regarded as a formidable critic of British administration, considerably in advance of the 'official mind'. Twenty years later
she found herself left behind by the landslide to independence in East
Africa, when British politicians were scrambling – in the words of the
settler leader Michael Blundell – 'to discard the robes of empire', and
when she described herself in a later letter to Mboya as 'just panting after
you in your hurried progress towards this undiluted democracy of yours'.[4]
Although it was never published as intended, her correspondence with
the young labour leader and aspiring politician, running from mid-1957 to

159

the end of 1959, gives a vivid picture of the seasoned liberal imperialist striving to adjust to the pace of African nationalism and imperial disengagement.

It was in the 1940s that Margery Perham was most closely in tune with Westminster and Whitehall, and can be judged to have had some direct influence on colonial policies.[5] Partly no doubt this was due to the atmosphere of wartime dedication, transcending party divisions. Although this atmosphere generated a great acceleration of thinking on African administration, away from the cramping (as they proved) concepts of indirect rule, the emphasis was still essentially on 'good government' – on laying the administrative, economic and educational foundations on which political advance could be patiently and securely built. Margery's particular friend and ally in this thinking was Arthur Creech Jones, the middle-of-the-road Labour politician who in 1946 became Colonial Secretary in the Attlee post-war government. Creech Jones' plan for preparing Africans for power at the centre was to transfer control of local government responsibilities. By the devolution of such power to elected local authorities, educated Africans would be incorporated into the political process and the influence of 'extremists' undermined. In the Kenyan context all this accorded well with Margery's lasting concern with the difficulties and frustrations of the poor and the unprotected, the tenant labourers on European farms, the migrant workers in the slums of Nairobi and Mombasa.

In 1944 Margery also welcomed the appointment as governor of Kenya of her old friend Sir Philip Mitchell. But already there were jarring notes. Overstocking and erosion in the crowded reserves, together with housing shortages and unemployment in the mushrooming towns, confronted Mitchell with the need for drastic action. The agricultural policies designed to meet this provoked strong local opposition. At the same time both Mitchell in Nairobi and Creech Jones in London found themselves – irresistibly as it seemed – drawn into a measure of cooperation with the European settlers. In contributing to wartime needs these had strengthened their economic and political position; their support was felt necessary in case Kenya should be needed as a major military base on the Indian Ocean after Middle Eastern footholds were relinquished; their productivity seemed essential to attract the capital without which agrarian reforms could not be sustained. Yet every advance in settler power added to African and especially Kikuyu discontents. It was against this background that the Mau Mau Kikuyu rising erupted in 1952, leading to a state of emergency which was to remain in force for seven years, and which – temporarily at least – would still further distort the course of Kenya's political development.

Mau Mau was far from being the crude 'peasants' revolt' which Mitchell had predicted in the densely populated Kikuyu and Kamba reserves if agrarian reforms were delayed. Nor was it intelligible in terms of the pressures discussed by Margery Perham and Elspeth Huxley in their correspondence of 1942/43 entitled *Race and Politics in Kenya*. Not until the 1960s and 1970s was there any idea – certainly not in government circles – of the full extent to which the changes set in motion by the Second World War, and culminating in the 'second colonial occupation', had undermined the authority of the incorporated élite around the chiefs, especially among the Kikuyu. Kenya during the 1940s, in the pre-Mau Mau era, was thus a tinder box of conflicting interests.[6] But if Margery Perham failed – as did others – to realize the real nature of the conflicts convulsing Kikuyu society, she did recognize Mau Mau as embodying a core of genuine though distorted nationalism; a nationalism, moreover, which would no longer be confined to the Kikuyu, but which would soon gather force throughout African Kenya.[7] She became increasingly conscious of her own difficulty in comprehending this growing force on the Kenya political scene. Ten years earlier she had been surprised and hurt by the way in which, in the Sudan, her pupil and protégé Mekki Abbas had been caught up in the currents of Arab nationalism, and more recently she had confessed herself perplexed by the facility with which her Oxford contemporary Africanist Thomas Hodgkin tuned in to the variegated political movements of West Africa.[8]

To her, therefore, the arrival in Oxford in late 1956 of the young Luo trade unionist Tom Mboya for a year's study seemed a golden opportunity to build a bridge to this new world. He was just twenty-five years old, but already had proved his political mettle by establishing a strong foothold in the Kenya trade union movement – the only viable political forum not proscribed under the Emergency regulations. In August 1953 he had become General Secretary of the Local Government Workers' Union, and had quickly taken it into the larger Kenya Federation of Registered Trade Unions, thus securing channels of communication not only with the British Labour Movement, but with the International Confederation of Free Trade Unions, based in Brussels. Within two months he had become general secretary of the larger body, and over the next two years had skilfully built it up into a vehicle of general political, social and economic protest, while meticulously cooperating with the administration on labour matters. He had also survived threats to his position from within the movement, which in May 1955 was consolidated into the Kenya Federation of Labour.[9]

Mboya, however, was anxious to make good some of his lack of formal education, as a foundation for his political career. He secured Labour support for a year's study at Ruskin College, Oxford, and the Kenya government contributed a supplementary allowance. In London the Colonial Office wrote to Margery Perham and other senior academics in Oxford commending him;[10] it was the official hope that some sound academic grounding for him would help to keep the Kenya labour movement under control.

Mboya's stay in Oxford and return to Kenya politics

Tom Mboya's year overseas was highly successful, not only by his own reckoning but in the estimation of his sponsors and teachers. He did not spend all of it in Oxford; he was busy consolidating in all directions his lines of political communication. He renewed his links with the Commonwealth Office of the Labour Party, with the Fabian Society and with the TUC; and he established others, for instance with the Africa Bureau and the Movement for Colonial Freedom. He was invited to address the West German Social Democratic Party in Hamburg, to hold a press conference at Transport House, and to be one of the speakers at a special Kenya conference convened by the Africa Bureau and attended also by such established figures as Arthur Gaitskell, Margery Perham and the Kenya Finance Minister Ernest Vasey.[11] Before returning to Africa he made his first fund-raising and lecturing tour of America.

He did nevertheless give serious attention to his studies, and earned praise not only from the staff at Ruskin College, where he made stimulating friendships among the West Indian students, but also in wider university circles. He was particularly at home at Nuffield College, with its contacts with the worlds of politics and journalism, under the friendly patronage of Margery Perham and Kenneth Robinson. At Nuffield, too, there were graduate students working on African politics, who, with the encouragement of Margery and her research assistant, Isabel Ferguson, formed a circle of friends of his own age. Altogether they were perhaps the most happily unconstrained twelve months in his career.

Margery regarded Mboya as one of the most impressive minds she had ever met – a clear, logical intellect combined with great strength of purpose.[12] It was she who encouraged him, before he left Oxford, in the publication of his first political pamphlet, *The Kenya Question: an African answer*, to which she contributed a foreword. It was published by the Fabian Society, and outlined his own view of Kenya's history and the roots of Mau Mau, together with his ideas on how Kenya should make a peaceful transition from European domination to non-racial democracy. Margery's foreword, at once praising and criticizing, was of the kind she had already contributed to two other comparable works by African politicians, Awolowo's *Path to Nigerian Freedom* and Mekki Abbas' *The Sudan Question*.[13] She seems to have been somewhat taken aback by its instant success – it was sold out in seven months and long continued in demand. She also wished to keep the pamphlet clear of the patronage of British Labour Party politicians.[14]

Within the wider spectrum of attitudes on the Kenya question, the gap between Perham and Mboya in political outlook was never, in constitutional terms, impossibly wide. Margery had no doubts about the inevitability of eventual African majority rule, and in looking towards it she was highly critical not only of the settler stance but of government tendencies both in Nairobi and Whitehall to make concessions to it. The way to cover the transition period until Africans were sufficiently advanced to be trusted with full democracy was for the British government to hold essential power in its own hands, resisting further moves towards self-government. But that transition period, as she saw it, was going to last a long time: she believed that Kenya Africans in general were still far too backward and divided to take charge of their own government. She also held that the immigrant communities needed, and deserved, some constitutional safeguards during this interim.[15]

Tom Mboya returned to Nairobi at the outset of a new phase in Kenya's constitutional development. The country was still run under the 'Lyttelton Constitution' imposed in 1954 at the height of the Emergency.[16] Elections to the European and Asian seats in the legislature had been held in September 1956, and now in a few weeks' time the first elections were to be held for eight African seats. The newly-devised franchise was narrow and complicated, and the electorate was further reduced by the fact that the Emergency still debarred the Central Province from taking part. Despite having condemned the 'fancy franchise', Mboya decided to stand as a candidate, and flung himself into a well-organized electioneering campaign, contesting the Nairobi seat against C. Argwings-Kodhek, a fellow Luo and one of the two Kenya African lawyers. On 10 March he was returned with a clear majority, and before the end of the month took his seat as a Member of the Legislative Council, along with seven other elected African members all pledged to oppose the Lyttelton Constitution.

Margery immediately wrote to congratulate him. As a postscript to the letter she suggested cautiously that in his new position of influence, he might care to join her in an exchange of correspondence on the lines of that which she and Elspeth Huxley had published in 1944 as *Race and Politics in Kenya*. Mboya readily agreed,[17] and by May they were settling the ground rules for the letters: that the dating need not correspond precisely with reality, that they would also exchange political documents, that not too many topics should be discussed in a single letter. Margery further urged that the letters should be as far as possible spontaneous and human – 'just dash off whatever comes first into your head'.[18]

The project almost foundered before it was fairly launched. On 21 May the *Manchester Guardian* published an article reporting an incautious speech by Mboya at Kisumu which could be construed as an incitement to violence and the forcible dispossession of settler farmers. This confirmed the European view of him as a dangerous firebrand (the governor, Sir Evelyn Baring, had already described him privately as 'intensely arrogant, a lapsed RC with the morals of a monkey')[19] and prompted a sharp note from Margery expressing dismay and demanding to know what had actually been said; at the same time she wrote to Ernest Vasey in Nairobi indicating that she would probably have to 'cut out' of her proposed exchange of correspondence. Mboya had hitherto been careful to eschew violence and now was quick to recognize that he had over-reached himself. He immediately despatched reassuring letters to *The Times* and the *Manchester Guardian,* and hastened to convince Margery that he had been misunderstood, and that he was still eager to start on the correspondence.[20] Thus it was not until June 1957 that the first letters were exchanged.

The collaboration between the middle-aged establishment figure in an Oxford college and the hard-headed young Luo populist in a Nairobi location was an unlikely one. While it would be cynical to discount, on either side, a genuine element of mutual warmth and respect, it is worth considering what each of them expected from it in more practical terms.[21]

To both the idea was an extension of their collaboration over Mboya's *Kenya Question* pamphlet of the previous year – Mboya had written expressing the hope that 'this is not the last work we do together'.[22] For Margery Perham there were several incentives. She was, as we have seen, intensely anxious to have a window on to the African side of the political turbulence in Kenya. She also hoped to act as a bridge between Mboya and the established order; when he left Oxford she wrote warmly of him to the Colonial Secretary, Alan Lennox-Boyd, to the Governor, Sir Evelyn Baring, and to the leader of the European Elected Members in the Legislative Council, Michael Blundell.[23] To Baring she described him as

> rather a remarkable young man and by the time he returns to Kenya ... he will have accumulated a great deal of experience here in Oxford, at the headquarters of the International Confederation of Labour in Brussels, and in the United States. ... He is coming to see me today before leaving for Kenya and I intend to have a very serious talk with him – for what that is worth – in the hope that he

may see the need for using his experience in a constructive rather than destructive direction.

She urged Blundell that he should not be met 'the moment he sets foot in Kenya, with ready-made hostility'. Personal contacts, she pointed out, 'may not be able to breach deep political differences but they may take some of the bitterness out of them. So much of African psychology is made up of a sense of being personally despised or underrated.' Underlying this advice was her conviction that only through the African élite, and the acceptance of this élite into Western political institutions, could the general mass of the African peoples be reached and influenced. In Kenya she looked upon her old pupil of fifteen years earlier, Eliud Mathu, now one of the nominated Africans on the Legislative Council, as such a key character. She wrote to him too, on the eve of Mboya's return:

> I have noticed with much interest your very moderate and courageous statements and do hope you will be able to maintain your leadership and co-operate at the same time with some of the younger men who are coming on. I have seen a good deal of Tom Mboya and I hope that you and he will be able to work together.[24]

All these letters had envisaged for Mboya a sedate rate of personal advancement. Now, with her protégé forcing his way so abruptly into the political limelight, she felt a great responsibility for exerting restraint upon the quality of his political maturing.

For Mboya the exchange was, as he often reiterated, a valuable way of clearing his mind and testing his theories. In writing *The Kenya Question* he had learnt 'that ideas put on paper revealed so many things to the writer, that more than often one could even by himself discover flaws which would otherwise be completely hidden'.[25] In short, it was indeed a mode of extending the Oxford ambience of controversy tempered by friendship and of sharpening his political armoury. But for him, too, it was a way of building bridges; not directly with his settler opponents or with the authorities in Kenya, but with a variety of influential potential supporters on the wider political scene. Margery Perham was unrivalled as a publicist on African affairs, and the arguments and the political manifestos that he showered across her desk stood a good chance of being fed into public debate in Britain. Conversely, she could be a sounding board for the broad body of British liberal opinion; she was directly in touch with some of his friends in the Fabian Society, the Africa Bureau, and the Commonwealth Office of the Labour Party. More distantly, he probably foresaw that this was a useful means of preserving material for his political autobiography.

The First Exchanges: the 1957 elections and after (June–July 1957)

Margery Perham had agreed to Mboya's suggestion that the letters should start with the run up to the elections that had taken place in March – which of course meant that they were mainly retrospective and were headed with fictitious dates. Nevertheless her first contributions probably faithfully reflect her sentiments at the beginning of the year and her mixed feelings about the rapidity of Mboya's success. She imagines him transforming himself back 'from the Oxford student into the labour leader and the politician – rather more of the second than the first, I suppose':

> The big unknown factor now is what the Africans as a whole will want when they are able to think and act as a whole or find leaders who will help them to define their hopes and plans. As I feel pretty sure that you will be among those who will help in this process of definition I should greatly value a letter from you. ... [26]

Her next letter, supposedly written on the eve of the elections, warned Mboya against setting too much store by success. He was after all still very young:

> If your character and experience qualify you to be of use in Kenya ... then even defeat in this election will not disqualify you. Indeed, we have often seen in English political life that a man has emerged stronger from defeat if that defeat came because he would not abandon his principles and make some doubtful bargain in order to gain or keep power. [27]

Mboya, however, had not been defeated, and in writing to congratulate him on his success she confessed her own surprise that his main support had come, not from those with two or three votes under the elaborately qualified franchise, but from the smaller folk – the single vote electors. She had also been surprised, and disappointed, at the defeat of all the former nominated African members of the legislature, including her old pupil Eliud Mathu who, 'as one of the best debaters in the chamber, with years of accumulated experience of public affairs, should still be able to give his people his mature service'. [28] When she next wrote she was hoping to have some reaction from Mboya to his first participation in the Legislative Council:

> It must have been a great day for you all when you took your seats in the House. I think the Chamber is a very impressive and beautiful room in a very delightful building. The architect has struck, in

colour and design, a rather light-hearted note for a legislature. I can only hope this will have some effect on the conduct of the inmates!

In fact, as she went on, the first accounts she had received of their performance were disquietingly abrasive. But the parliamentary game was a very old one, and 'it takes a new player a long time to learn the rules'. While Westminster should not be idealized, 'the object of government by debate is to exercise human reason to the full and this cannot be done in an atmosphere of heated antagonism or mental obduracy'. Among other points, she found it hard to follow the demand that the eight African members had immediately made for a further fifteen African elected seats in order to establish parity with the non-African members. Why so many all at once? 'Apart from any other considerations, to flood a small chamber like yours with so many members utterly new to parliamentary government, one carried on in a foreign language, might reduce it to utter inaction.'[29]

The opening paragraph of Tom Mboya's first reply to Margery included a few words about his lake home on Rusinga Island in Lake Victoria and his mother whom he had not found time to visit since 1953. This was virtually his only attempt to meet her hopes that he would 'be human. Tell a little story or reveal a personal feeling now and then.'[30] He did however launch into a robust description of his decision (half reluctant as he claimed) to stand for election on his return to Kenya and of his hopes for the future:

> When I remember those days in Oxford I find myself wondering how easy it is to indulge in theories and make problems look so easy and solutions so readily available. As I see things the future of Kenya is in a melting pot, and the solution will need patience and tolerance on the part of all concerned. I still have as my objective full democracy, and am still convinced that there must be a transitional period before this objective is attained. The most urgent step in my view must be one of constitutional reform of the Legislative Council.[31]

In his second letter Mboya described his election campaign – giving ample evidence of his talent for political organization; his worries over his Luo lawyer rival, Argwings-Kodhek; his choice of a cock as an election symbol.[32] In his third, notionally dated a week or two after the election, so far from being impressed with the atmosphere of the Council Chamber, he was at pains to make clear that he and his colleagues were not to be overawed by it. They had cheerfully flouted the convention that maiden speeches should be uncontroversial, regardless of resentment on the government and European unofficial benches. 'The thing is these ministers do not realize that they are for the first time listening to the people's voice.'[33] It was not the members on the floor of the House that he was wooing, but the crowded public gallery above them. The Council, wrote one observer, was 'like a theatre, charged with drama. ... When the Africans spoke, they spoke to this gallery, literally as well as metaphorically.'[34] Mboya also described with relish how they had fought, and partially won, a tussle to influence the choice of African members on the government Meat Commission.

But already in these first exchanges one of the major issues dividing them was becoming clear. Margery wrote apprehensively of the ignorant and illiterate African electorate. Did many of those who were demanding, or beginning to exercise, the vote realize how recent universal adult franchise was in Britain? Would Swahili be a suitable language for tribally mixed audiences?

> You have begun this democratic process and you will go on enlarging its scope and its power. But I do think it would be a mistake just to take this imported device for granted, as you might buy a British-made car and expect it to run perfectly from the moment you drive it away from the shop.[35]

The real danger was that the Africans, from the circumstances of their short history within the wider world, were inevitably governed by the compelling desire to obtain equality with the immigrant races. And the arguments about poverty and backwardness had so often been misused by those in power that it was not easy to grasp their basis of reality. To this argument Mboya responded briefly:

> I am particularly interested in your remarks regarding the Africans' poverty and backwardness. I hope one day we shall be able to discuss this point at some length, but I should like to point out that to me the motive power behind my political activities and I believe those of my colleagues is the desire to remove this poverty and ignorance. To achieve this we need political power.[36]

The Second Phase: the Lennox-Boyd Plan of November 1957

Mboya's fourth letter strikes a new, harder, and more resonant note. In July he and his colleague Ronald Ngala, also an African Elected Member, had come to Britain on a delegation to bring the Kenya question to the centre of political debate. Not only were meetings held with Lennox-Boyd, the Colonial Secretary, but Baring and several other key figures – including leading settlers and an Asian elected minister – converged on London. The upshot was a decision that Lennox-Boyd should go to Kenya in mid-October to preside over a discussion on the Lyttelton Constitution under which the country had been governed since 1954. This letter, written in late September or early October, is in effect a definition of the stand he proposed to take with the Colonial Secretary. A week or two earlier he had dined with Margery, who was briefly in Nairobi, at the Norfolk Hotel. 'He wants softening,' she wrote; 'his mind is too hard and logical. He ought to have more fun in life after his hard youth.'[37]

The arguments he now set out were on lines that were to become increasingly familiar. Kenya was commonly represented as a testing-ground for multi-racialism, and as a halfway house between the extremes of South Africa and Ghana. Some believed there was a stark choice between a 'black man's country' and European dominance. His own view was that all people in Kenya and Britain must accept

> that Kenya is primarily an African country and that the aim ... is ultimately to see created a government and society of individuals enjoying equal rights and opportunities regardless of race, colour, sex or creed. On this basis my policy demands that the British government immediately make a definite and clear declaration that any self-government for Kenya will only be that in which all men shall have equal and effective voice as individuals.

The ability to govern did not depend on racial origins or so-called civilized standards, nor did the record of South Africa, Southern Rhodesia or Algeria give any reason to trust in European settler trusteeship. The current Lyttelton Constitution, although claimed as multi-racial, was in fact heavily weighted in favour of the European settlers, and the only way to prevent their further entrenchment was to call a halt to experimentation and to demand constitutional reforms to ensure that Africans had effective representation in the legislative council. In the absence of this no African could feel that he was effectively represented and that the government would play an effective role in his development against the time when he would take his rightful place in government and society. 'Essentially my policy would not demand that all immigrant communities should leave Kenya. I hold that physically they can stay but that all the privileges they now enjoy must go.' Ghana, contrary to the belief of some, was not an extreme racialist state, but a country in which Europeans and others who chose to reside there were treated with respect and recognition before the law. Why should anyone expect that the presence of 45–50,000 Europeans in Kenya would alter the national aspirations of the Africans?

His policy, he wrote, did imply that with full democracy remaining the objective, a transitional period must be accepted. For the time being communal representation must continue, but the proportions must alter drastically – in the first instance to introduce parity as between Africans on the one hand and non-Africans on the other. He believed that such a reform would provide the political and economic stability needed for development; and that it would not prejudice the inflow of capital. In any case economic development without social justice was meaningless.

This letter has been cited at some length because it states with typical clarity the position from which Mboya refused to budge for the next two years; and since it diverges at certain key points from the gradualist view to which Margery had long been intellectually and emotionally committed, one might expect that the correspondence would become progressively barren and strained, and that it would be tedious to pursue it further. But the reactions of each of them to the unfolding of political events do take the controversy beyond the realm of mere rhetoric.

Margery did not make a full reply immediately.[38] In the meantime the political confrontation in Nairobi ran its predictable course. In conformity with Mboya's arguments, the African members had already rejected a limited offer of additional seats in the legislature made by the European elected members earlier in the year, and by persisting in a refusal to accept ministerial office, they had rendered the Lyttelton constitution virtually unworkable. At length the crisis came to a head with the resignation of the leading ministers; the Lyttelton Constitution was dead. Lennox-Boyd then introduced a new set of proposals which ostensibly went a considerable way to broaden the basis of the multi-racial government. But Mboya and his colleagues were adamant in sticking to their own formula of priorities. The talks broke down; and the Colonial Secretary had apparently little option but to 'impose' his own plan, with no African cooperation.

At the end of November Margery did, in the light of the breakdown of the talks, write a considered answer to the manifesto constituted by Mboya's statement.[39] It contained several familiar features: the reproof about his unyielding tactics; her conviction that there was no danger of Kenya going the way of Southern Rhodesia; and above all her belief that because of their political immaturity and gullibility,

> Kenya today stands in greater danger from a premature advancement of Africans to control over the government than from settler privilege. You may have it in your power to whip up political feeling

> ... in support of your position to an uncontrollable extent. ... The stage might be set when ... a man of emotion, a new Kenyatta, would take over from your more rational leadership.

She betrayed once more her misconceptions about current Kenya society by writing of the potential for intimidation 'in which the large number of sensible, prosperous farmers who, perhaps, play a constructive part in local affairs, are pushed aside and silenced by the minority of young discontented, the unemployed, or the townsmen'. But it is striking that a substantial part of the letter is devoted to expressing support for Mboya. 'I must admit that, generally speaking, I think you have a good case and I think your policy statement of November 13th puts the matter clearly and forcibly from your point of view.' They both favoured a declared objective from the government, and felt that a constitutional conference might be useful; moreover Margery shared several of the specific doubts about the Lennox-Boyd plan that had led to the breakdown of the talks; she agreed that some of the devices proposed to secure impartiality (such as a Council of State and a number of additional special selective seats) might well prove deceptive. And, in private, personal correspondence she was beginning to wonder whether Mboya's stonewalling might not after all have something to be said for it. Tom Mboya, she wrote, 'seems to have a very inflexible sort of mind, it is very hard to negotiate with people who cannot distinguish between negotiating and fighting: but can one be quite sure that from his point of view these are not the best tactics?' In another letter she admitted that she did not wonder that the Africans called the Lennox-Boyd plan a trap.[40] Nevertheless her letter to Mboya ended by reaffirming her plea for tolerance and flexibility towards the minorities, for refraining from tactics and speeches that alienated and alarmed them – 'they have far more to fear than the Africans, and the afraid are never reasonable':

> it is my belief that, taking a long view, the African position is so strong, so sure of the future, that you can afford to be wise and moderate. ... And I want to see you, personally, not only feared for your power as a leader to marshal the forces of African discontent, but respected as a man, for your wisdom, foresight, integrity and moral courage.[41]

Mboya's reaction to this peroration, in his next letter, was studiedly low-key: 'I hope that in my small way I may contribute to the peaceful development of Kenya.' The reply itself, however, sent early in the new year, treated her arguments seriously. It was his longest letter yet, and shows no sign that he was getting bored or impatient with the correspondence. He fastened and built upon the points of agreement in Margery's letter. The Lennox-Boyd talks had broken down, he contended, because the plan itself and the manner of its imposition were indeed seriously flawed; there was clear evidence that it had in fact been concocted by the European members well before Lennox-Boyd's arrival in Nairobi. By contrast, he emphasized the consistency of the African stance, acknowledging as it did the need for gradual change and minority safeguards. From this he went on to challenge the whole notion of good faith on the European side, and the belief that the Central African situation could not be repeated in Kenya:

> Our only assurance must lie in our ability effectively to wield power and opposition within the legislature, Council of Ministers and through effective political organization in the country. Then and only then can we be sure of our position. We can no longer rely just on the Opposition Party in the UK or the Colonial Office – both have not been very successful in the past.[42]

The reference to the Labour Party was significant. During his year in Oxford and since Mboya had had close and constructive relationships with the Labour Party, but the breakdown of the Lennox-Boyd talks had, temporarily at least, cost him this support. An editorial in *Venture* had called the Lennox-Boyd plan 'a genuine advance for Africans' and said that 'one can learn to govern only by experience, and to stay outside government is to waste opportunities'.[43] Margery Perham, therefore, was at this juncture one of his few lines of political communication in Britain, and he was determined to make the most of it by stressing the Africans' basic reliability and moderation. However, Margery's formal response to his arguments was less sympathetic than her previous letter. It defended Lennox-Boyd and reproved Mboya again for obduracy:

> I do not deny that there is an element of logic in some of your arguments, but it is a cold, inflexible logic which seems to ignore the nature of politics, that is, of human nature in politics. ... It is surely better to convince others that you can win something in a general discussion than to convince yourselves that you have won some barren procedural points to justify your not negotiating at all.[44]

The Third Phase: April to September 1958

Although there was a brief meeting in Nairobi in January, it was not until towards the end of April 1958 that the main correspondence was resumed. An extensive series of visits took Margery to West, as well as

East, Central and South Africa until mid-March; in March-April Mboya was away for several weeks for the formal celebration of Ghana's independence. From the series of letters that followed, running through to mid-July, three main themes emerge.

The first of these was the furore that arose when several African candidates proved willing to stand for the 'selected seats' provided for under the unacceptable Lennox-Boyd Constitution. These were promptly denounced by the African Elected Members as 'stooges, Quislings and "black Europeans" in our community' who 'consequently must be treated as traitors to the African cause'. The Government responded by serving summonses on the Members under the Election Offences Ordinance. The case was a highly publicized trial of political strength, and funds flowed in from all over Africa to aid the defence. When at the ensuing trial in June they were acquitted on a charge of conspiracy, although convicted and fined on one of defamation, the outcome was greeted by cheering African crowds as a resounding political victory for Mboya. Meanwhile the People's Convention Party had organized highly successful (but strictly peaceful) boycotts of drinking, smoking and buses.

The episode sharply delineated one of the basic disagreements between the two protagonists. Margery pointed out that personal denunciation of this kind offended against the whole tradition of parliamentary government: however, she did not dwell – as she might have twelve months earlier – on this issue of parliamentary practice, choosing rather to go straight to the fundamental contrast of approach which the incident exposed:

> You Africans desire to take over the European political and economic system. ... There are two ways by which you can attempt this. One, to use military metaphors, is to infiltrate into the citadel gradually and take it over little by little as a fully going concern. The other is to organize all the forces you can outside the walls, and take it by storm. You will risk destroying it in the process because, in order to rally sufficient force for the attack, you are obliged to mobilize as large a number of followers as you can. Many of these are inevitably ... mere blind supporters moved less by an intelligent appreciation of the value of the citadel and its contents than by a militant fervour which your leadership has aroused. ... To abandon the military metaphor, the option is between gradualism and co-operation on the one side and immediacy and conflict on the other.

The rest of her letter is devoted mainly to an eloquent defence of the principle of gradualism and, explicitly, to the praise of the steady, co-operative type of African who was ready to work patiently within it. She concluded by pointing out some of the immediate costs of confrontation – in this case for instance the lost opportunity to influence the African 'selective' seats.[45]

Mboya took up the general question of method in an extended letter in mid-July (see below). He was, however, wholly unrepentant about the political charges and the trial, merely reporting with satisfaction how well the boycott had succeeded: 'This was the first peaceful, positive action of its kind in the history of Kenya.'[46]

In March Mboya had gone to West Africa to take part in Ghana's independence celebrations. It was natural, therefore, that the relevance of the Ghana model for Kenya should come to the fore. He came back from Ghana deeply impressed; he had been hugely feted, and had established warm personal relations with Kwame Nkrumah. The foreign press, he thought, and particularly the Kenya press, had done a lot of harm in interpreting Ghana's situation to the world. Some of Kenya's European settler leaders could well do with a trip there to see for themselves. He also returned convinced of the need 'to organize the African community into a well-disciplined political force' if violence was to be avoided.[47]

Margery was anxious not to seem grudging in her admiration of Ghana's achievements – she had great hopes, she wrote, for the country's future. But she still did not agree that 'what Ghana Africans have achieved today Kenya Africans can achieve tomorrow, by which I mean during the next five or ten years'. Moreover, she disliked Nkrumah's style; he could not 'have added to his reputation in responsible quarters by setting up a vast statue of himself not only in his own lifetime but when he has had only a few years of leadership'. He should not be supporting his minister Edusei in a violent personal attack on a respected opposition leader such as her friend Professor Kofi Busia – a distinguished Ghanaian scholar. And he might have waited a few years to find his feet before launching his ambitious pan-African conference 'with the aim of settling the affairs of the rest of the continent'.[48]

Mboya admitted to some difficulty in understanding the personality cult represented by the Nkrumah statue; and he agreed that the lack of an effective opposition was, temporarily, a cause for concern – though he had felt on his visit that this was partly because the opposition was too intellectual 'to speak the language of the people'. But on the main issues he was quite clear. On the pace of advance:

> I agree with you that the Ghanaian people are more developed and advanced than we are today. I feel however that in so far as our

aspirations, desires and aims are concerned there is little if any difference. The presence here of the European settlers does not alter this position apart from the fact that we have to acknowledge their existence and right to equal democratic rights.

And, on Nkrumah's pan-African initiative:

> You have ... suggested that he might have waited. I cannot accept this view. I feel that Nkrumah has acted according to what would be expected of any African state and in a manner consistent with the general trends of world affairs today. We in the dependent territories feel that his action will fill a vacuum that would otherwise have been filled by other forces whose interests may have been completely foreign to Africans.[49]

In fact, he had already been quick to act on this basis. He maintained the impetus of the pan-African initiative by going to Makerere College in early July to deliver a stirring address to the first pan-African student gathering being held there, and he enclosed a copy of the speech with his letter. Before the end of the year he was to find himself once more at Accra, as the unopposed president of the first pan-African Conference to be held on African soil, addressing the delegates of twenty-five African countries and observers from all over the world.

The third theme of argument in these mid-1958 exchanges arose from Margery's comments on a key speech he had made in February in a 'no confidence' debate. Her criticisms opened on characteristic lines: the speech was too long – more than two-and-a-half hours; and it was too negative and querulous, failing to recognize undeniable government achievements or to attempt to enlist government sympathy. Yet she did for the first time concede, if only as a point of argument, that the speech, and indeed the attitude of the African members generally, could be defended as politically expedient:

> By quite another standard it may well be that you succeeded. If your aim was to convince your constituents and, indeed, Africans as a whole, that you are an uncompromising critic of the Government and to define for them their often inchoate grievances, sharpen still further their sense of frustration and teach them to find all its causes in the errors of government, then your speech would go far to succeed in its aim.

She herself could not easily judge the wisdom or even the effectiveness of day-by-day actions on either side: 'My position on the bank is not an easy one from which to expound to you who are swimming in the fast current of immediate political events, amidst pretty choppy waves which must often obscure the distant view and sweep your feet off the fundamentals of solid ground.' [50] Similar questionings are evident in other letters she wrote at this time. Discussing Mboya's use of the defamation trial as a political platform, she commented that from his point of view he did not seem to be making many mistakes. She wished she could understand what 'ordinary tribesmen' felt. Elsewhere she reflected that in the light of Nkrumah's successes it was not to be wondered at that Mboya and others were pressing hard for the goal that lay so close to their grasp. [51]

Nevertheless, in addressing Mboya himself she returned firmly to the attack, summarizing the main heads of her general contentions. She challenged him to set out clearly his methods, which she found questionable, his aims, which seemed obscure, and his timing, which was crucial. On methods, she herself felt his mode of constitutional disagreement to be needlessly offensive and likely to debase still further the standards of social relationships. Surely it was better to cooperate with the many wise and moderate settlers who did want to see the country 'go forward peacefully in the interests of all the inhabitants'? 'Should it not be for your group, who has all to gain, you who are challenging the established situation, to show more patience and moderation, more courtesy and understanding?'

On aims, while agreeing on the goal of 'unlimited democracy', did this not imply – since he did accept that it could not be attained immediately – that interim constitutional barriers would be needed? And if the answer was to fall back upon the 'control of the Secretary of State acting through the Governor', then it was unreasonable to reject that control when it was exercised, as through Lennox-Boyd's imposed constitution. What constitutional barriers *would* Mboya accept? As to timing, she still believed that the 'unreadiness' of the Kenya Africans must be faced and weighed. Ghana, with its long history of cultural homogeneity, political organization and overseas contacts, was not an appropriate guide. Moreover, whereas 'there was no room in Ghana for the European colonist, in Kenya he came in to fill a vacuum, both of empty lands and economic and political competence.' [52]

Mboya readily took up the challenge. He wrote back in the middle of July at a length of 14 pages - a far cry from the short, spontaneous letters which Margery at least had envisaged at the outset of the exchange. [53] He took the opportunity to elaborate and sharpen his familiar arguments in the light of recent developments and of the headings that Margery had proposed.

On method, he argued that her plea for cooperation presupposed agreement on what it was meant to achieve. In the absence of any statement from the British government or the European settlers, it could only be inferred that they did not agree with the Africans' stated objective of full democracy. It was therefore unreasonable, with the Europeans still in a position of power, to suggest that all the giving should be on the African side. 'We stand for co-operation, but believe in co-operating when all the parties are agreed as to where we are going and secondly when we feel confident that we have a similarly effective part to play in the team work.'

Recent happenings in Southern Rhodesia, particularly the eclipse of Prime Minister Garfield Todd, had served as a timely warning. He had faith that Kenya *would* become a democracy, but not unless he and his colleagues acted continuously to steer it away from a South or Central African path. At the same time, he emphasized, he was firmly opposed to the use of violence: 'I have condemned this from time to time and my record during various strikes speaks for itself. I believe in non-violent positive action and this I have been expounding in the last few months.'

On aims, he reiterated those which he had proclaimed ever since his *Kenya Question* pamphlet – to create a government and society of individuals enjoying equal rights and opportunities. There was no question of seeking to establish a black racialist state or of seeking the expropriation of land or other property. The land question remained one of the most sensitive, but it was not insoluble. And once the minorities demanded safeguards they must accept the principle of majority rule.

The third question, that of timing, was the one which went to the heart of Margery's gradualist approach – how to deal with the 'unreadiness' of the Kenya Africans for full democracy. Distinguishing between the movement to defeat or remove the existing European settler dominance in the legislature, the cabinet and generally in the social and economic life of the country, and the movement from colonial to independent and self-governing status, he insisted that the second should not be permitted until the African was in a position effectively to defend his interests:

> I agree that as at present we have secured a position which makes it almost impossible for anyone to create a Southern Rhodesia here but I feel that most of our advance, especially in the last year, has not been the direct result of British Government impartial guardianship but rather our ability to exert a certain amount of pressure. . . . I hold the view that whereas we must acknowledge the Africans' handicaps, the most important thing is to find a constitution that will permit for the Africans' rapid development.

This required that Africans should have an effective position in the legislature. Only then could there be a dynamic education policy, more positive Africanization in the civil service, and more widespread professional training.

Six weeks later Margery replied in a letter which really signals both the climax and the close of the effective exchange of views between them – although the correspondence was to continue sporadically for another eighteen months. She recognized (as indeed she had for months realized in her private correspondence) that arguments based on history and liberal political principle limped behind the practical test of political action. She began by writing of the competing demands on her attention and energies – above all the completing of the second volume of her biography of Lord Lugard:

> But I think my hesitation springs from something deeper than this effort to find time and, literally, to orientate my thoughts. I have a doubt whether a student of history and government, such as I try to be, can usefully say anything to a young revolutionary – in a peaceful revolution, we hope – who is engaged to the hilt in his day-to-day struggle, one aimed at nothing less than to destroy the power of the European oligarchy at home and the European autocracy from abroad. I feel rather like the voice in a Greek chorus standing at the side of the stage, making a running commentary on events and often exclaiming at the violence and unreason displayed by all the chief figures in the drama, without having the slightest influence upon their action. It is therefore in a somewhat hesitant and self-depreciatory frame of mind that I sit down to answer you.

Nevertheless, characteristically, she did proceed to make her answer. Some of it made practical points on issues where they had common ground: she endorsed the importance of his attempt to build up a Kenya-wide party and hoped the government would encourage it; she hoped he would support the criticisms made by his Central Province elected colleagues of more localized and therefore divisive movements. She shared his view that a clear government declaration of objective was required. She took as her main text, however, the speech Mboya had made two months earlier at the pan-African students' conference at Makerere – and the tone is indeed somewhat reminiscent of a Greek tragic chorus.

To an audience of university students at least, she asked, should it not have been possible to appeal to reason and not rely upon sweeping emotional concepts? There might be political value in exhorting his audience to look to the future and not at the past of the 'Dark Continent'. But should it not be acknowledged that 'the Africa of today, its government, economy, and much of its education and religion, and certainly all its ideas of modern democracy, are the creation of Europe?' And if Africa still needed cooperation and aid from the West, why was it necessary to play this down, to talk in terms of freedom from oppression, of the evils of colonialism and the rest? Ghana's independence might be claimed, she contended, not as 'exploding once and for all the myth of European superiority', but as proving the good work and the goodwill of the European power which happened to be in control. The speech had sought to persuade the young students that there was something in common between all African colonial grievances: but an intelligent audience should be taught to distinguish between the factors which were common and those which were not, to recall the British successes in, for instance, Nigeria and Sierra Leone.

> You may say, Do these things matter? I am creating a movement, breaking the old bonds of servility in African minds, not teaching history or political science. I think it does matter that politics and truth should not be too far separated. The habit of distortion, the indulgence in facile emotion, the cultivation of hostility and self-satisfaction, are demoralizing and will leave you in the end to build up your new nation out of citizens with lazy, rigid minds, who project all the real difficulties of the colonial situation, and their own weaknesses, upon the wickedness of the other party. It does matter, in other words, because everything you do now is not only destroying the old but constructing the new.[54]

She went on to argue that the achievement of freedom did not preclude misgovernment or bloody disorders – witness events in India, Burma, Indonesia, Indo-China. For some of the difficulties of the transfer of power the British *were* responsible – but was not this a reason to seek to learn from the past? In Kenya, she believed, to achieve self-government with the minimum of suffering and loss required three things: the building up of leadership experience and of professional training; the goodwill of the present rulers to ensure their practical cooperation; and in order to gain this, leaders who could rise to statesmanship and reject temptations to demagogy. 'Could we not ... get away from at least some of the old conventions of colonial assertion: the whipping up of indignation; the clichés about colonialism; the damning of almost everything the west or the colonial government has done in the past?'

And so back to the old theme of cooperation. She reminded Mboya that if he did rise to high responsibility it would have to be as a leader of *all* races. For the minorities, if they were not frightened away altogether, had services to give out of all proportion to their numbers:

> I wish I could persuade you that the settlers are not to be feared. ...

> They are like a besieged garrison who shout defiance and are
> prepared to die in defence of their position because they dare not
> trust either the word or the wisdom of the besieging force. . . . Why
> not do something to reassure them – to make some of them say 'Do
> you know, after all, I believe these African leaders would not be so
> utterly impossible to work with?' And in time 'to work with' would
> even change into 'to work under'.

Margery concluded with an appeal to the natural responsiveness of the
'African personality' – which she found so hard to evoke in Mboya and his
fellow African members of the legislature.

> In private relations the great quality of the Africans . . . is that they
> are the most quick to respond to kindness and consideration . . . to
> smile and laugh or to grieve in sympathy with another. . . . And in
> our strained world of today it may be that the great African contri-
> bution will be these qualities of joy and sympathy . . . cannot this
> precious side of the African personality begin to show itself a little
> more in public life?

Conclusion

The correspondence that follows these two monumental letters is not
without interest but it adds little of substance to the arguments. One gets
glimpses of Mboya involved even more energetically in politics, both in
Kenya and abroad; the Kenyatta controversy; visits to Dar es Salaam,
Portuguese East Africa, Ethiopia and America.[55] His international status
was increasing, and with it his sources of support. For Margery, some of
the more revealing hints of her thinking are in her correspondence with
other informants: her sympathy with African suspicions – 'this multi-
racialism is a kind of hoax and I fully sympathise with Africans in refusing
to have white colonists built into the constitution in a dominant status. . . .
Tom's game . . . is I suppose quite a good one from his point of view';[56] her
(correct) forecast that when Mboya returned (this was in May 1959) from
a visit to America, the moderation which had begun to thaw the Kenya
political scene would evaporate. 'From the point of view of a man who
would rather be minister at the head of his people in two years' time than
in ten, one can understand the intransigence.'[57] In September 1959 she
made one more serious effort to re-activate the formal exchange, but at
this point it was overtaken by the acceleration of 'wind of change' politics,
particularly when in October Iain Macleod took over the Colonial Office
from Alan Lennox-Boyd. Margery indicated that she herself had been
drawn into this – she had had interesting talks, she wrote, with Macleod

and Douglas Home.[58] But in general, the pace of events had swept past both her own gradualism and Mboya's stonewalling, to the point when the British government was seeking simply to identify a political body to which power could credibly be transferred, not in five or ten years' time but immediately; while Mboya and his colleagues were concentrating their energies on party manoeuvring. Over the next few months Margery realized that further replies were unlikely, though it was not until September 1960 that Mboya finally agreed that the correspondence should cease.[59]

What is remarkable up to this point is that it was Tom Mboya who, despite his unremitting political programme, despite the moral assaults to which Margery subjected him, and above all despite the diminishing practical usefulness of her good offices, appeared the more anxious to keep the correspondence going. In late 1959 he was still writing of taking time off to go through the book with her, and in March 1960 there was even talk that he might find time after the Lancaster House Conference to visit Oxford for this purpose.[60] The fact that in 1960 both of them were looking forward to publication does suggest that they had found the exchange a worth-while exercise. But this only partially answers the questions posed earlier in this paper about their aims in entering into it.

It may be safely surmised that on the personal side it had proved to Margery something of a disappointment. There are hints of this throughout the correspondence, perhaps most plainly in her heartfelt appeal to the natural responsiveness, the qualities of joy and sympathy, which were her perception of the African personality. Nor does there appear (hardly surprisingly) to have been any overt response to the various letters she sent expressing solicitude for Tom's moral and domestic welfare – his debts on leaving Oxford, a quarrel with a taxi-driver, and in particular, the progress of his relationship with Pamela Odede, his future wife.[61] And it needed more that an occasional meeting at the Norfolk Hotel to take her out of the establishment milieu to which she had long grown accustomed and into any real feeling for the politics of the African locations.

Moreover, Margery had been singularly unsuccessful in her aspiration to build bridges between the African politicians and the representatives of the establishment. Whether in Kenya or Britain, such bridges were not what the Africans desired. 'I don't flatter myself that I have much influence with him', she wrote of Mboya to Lennox-Boyd in 1959.[62] In another letter she lamented the total contrast between his private reasonableness and his public intransigence.[63] On the other hand she did learn a great deal about the hard practicalities of political action in the Kenya context; this is clear from the changing tone of the main correspondence, and, more vividly, from other letters that she exchanged. Already in December 1958, for instance, she was writing to Lennox-Boyd:

> I can't resist saying that my own general conclusion is that I can't see that the presence of settlers in Kenya makes it a wholly different situation from neighbouring countries where the Africans are told they are living in a primarily African state. I am so afraid that the moderates in Kenya, among whom I number Mboya, will be out-flanked.[64]

Despite all her jeremiads about the political immaturity of Kenya Africans she had moved a long way in her insight into the dynamics of decolonization.

What of Tom Mboya? It certainly seems, from the patience and thoroughness with which he drafted his letters, that they did afford him a valued opportunity to sharpen his political thinking – even where the main message remained obstinately unyielding, its impact on specific issues had to be examined and spelt out. They did also give him a channel of communication with liberal thinking in Britain, although with the intensifying imperatives of decolonization this became less important. Finally, it is perhaps not fanciful to conjecture that his genuine respect for the elderly Oxford don with her demanding code of political be-haviour – together with his Oxford associations – did indeed have at least a marginal effect; that it aided Mboya in his efforts, as he described it, in his small way 'to contribute to the peaceful development of Kenya'.

Margery Perham was well aware that Tom Mboya was indeed a moderate, both by temperament and from the fragility of his Luo power base. For her part she had been consistent and outspoken in her support of the most central of the African claims. At the same time she had steadily endorsed Mboya's opposition to the use of violence; and cer-tainly, among all the settler territories of Africa, Kenya was remarkable for the peacefulness of its initial transfer of power. Perhaps one reason why the correspondence lapsed is that there was so little real disagree-ment between them.[65]

NOTES

1. Perham to Mboya, 1 June (but dated Jan./Feb.) 1957, Perham Papers (hereafter PP) Rhodes House Library, Oxford, Box 343, file 2, f 187.
2. Margery Perham, *East African Journey* (London 1976), p.36.
3. See, for example, Elspeth Huxley and Margery Perham, *Race and Politics in Kenya* (London, 1944), pp. 96, 111–12.

4. Perham to Mboya, Aug. or Sept. 1959, PP 343/2, f 7. Blundell describes his own part during these months in *So Rough a Wind* (London, 1964), pp. 261–82.
5. The following paragraphs, summarizing the political background to the correspondence, owe much to the paper presented by David Throup at the Margery Perham seminar in July 1989.
6. There is an extensive literature on the political and social analysis of Mau Mau. See especially D.W. Throup, *Economic and Social Origins of Mau Mau* (London, 1987).
7. For some indication of her views, see 'The Struggle against Mau Mau', *The Times*, 22, 23 April 1953, and 'Kenya after Mau Mau', *The Times*, 18 March 1957, reprinted in Margery Perham, *Colonial Sequence 1949–1969* (London, 1970), (hereafter *Col. Seq. II*), pp. 108–14, 146–9.
8. See below, p. 195.
9. The background facts of Mboya's career throughout this article are based mainly on the political biography by David Goldsworthy, *Tom Mboya: the man Kenya wanted to forget* (London, 1982).
10. Gorrell Barnes to Perham, Harlow, K. Robinson, 14 Oct. 1955, PP 457/1, f 1.
11. Africa Bureau, *Report of Conference on Questions affecting Kenya and Britain*, 12 May 1956. Press Release (mimeo).
12. Goldsworthy, *Mboya*, p.51.
13. O. Awolowo, *Path to Nigerian Freedom* (London, 1947); Mekki Abbar, *The Sudan Question: the dispute over the Anglo-Egyptian Condominium* (London, 1952)
14. Perham to Mboya, 16 June 1956, PP 434/2, f 105.
15. Perham, Foreword to *The Kenya Question: an African answer* by Tom Mboya (Fabian Society, 1956); reprinted in *Col. Seq. II*, pp.130–42.
16. *Cmd 9103*, HMSO, 1954.
17. Perham to Mboya, 11 March 1957; Mboya to Perham, 17 April 1957, PP 343/2, ff 200, 199.
18. Perham to Mboya, 14 May, 1 June 1957, PP 343/2, ff 184, 187; Mboya to Perham, 8 May, 22 May 1957, PP 343/2, ff 198, 183.
19. Goldsworthy, op.cit., pp.77–9; Perham to Mboya, 22 May, 6 June, 14 June, 1 July 1957, PP 343/2, ff 182, 174, 173, 162.
20. Mboya to Perham, 28 May, 14 June, 19 June 1957, PP 343/2, ff 181, 166, 165.
21. Isabel Ferguson (Roberts), who was Margery Perham's research assistant at this time, feels that she (Perham) did not warm to him personally as readily as to her Uganda friends or her Nigerian students. 'He was really a bit awe-inspiring, even frightening, because he was so single-minded. She carried on the relationship in spite of herself.' Personal communication, March 1991.
22. Mboya to Perham, 25 July 1956, PP 457/2, f 3.
23. Perham to Lennox-Boyd, to Baring, to Blundell, all 18 Oct. 1956, PP 457/1.
24. Perham to Mathu, 18 Oct. 1956, PP 434/2, f 9.
25. Mboya to Perham, early Oct. 1957 (notionally dated 7 May, Letter IV), 343/2, f 137.
26. Perham to Mboya, 1 June (dated Jan./Feb., Letter I) 1957, PP 343/2, f 187.
27. Perham to Mboya, 1 July (dated Feb., Letter II) 1957, PP 343/2, f 163.
28. Perham to Mboya, mid-July (dated 15 March, Letter III) 1957, PP 343/2, f 152.
29. Perham to Mboya, ? Aug. (dated 3 May, Letter IV) 1957, PP 343/2, f 145.
30. Perham to Mboya, 1 July 1957, PP 343/2, f 162.
31. Mboya to Perham, 19 June (dated 14 Jan., Letter I) 1957, PP 343/2, f 168.
32. Mboya to Perham, 13 July (dated 4 March, Letter II) 1957, PP 343/2, f 155.
33. Mboya to Perham, Oct. (dated 30 April, Letter III) 1957, PP 343/2, f 148.
34. Nottingham to Perham, 25 July 1957, PP 434/2, f 142.
35. Perham to Mboya, mid-July (dated 15 March, Letter IV) 1957, PP 343/2, f 152.
36. Mboya to Perham, Oct. (dated 7 May, Letter IV) 1957, PP 343/2, f 148. The summaries and quotations from these and subsequent letters in the correspondence are necessarily highly selective. They cannot properly reflect the range of arguments deployed on both sides.
37. Perham to Nottingham, 13 Sept. 1957, PP 434/2, f 143.

38. In mid-October she did draft a letter, but it is doubtful whether it was ever sent off (Mboya claimed that he had not received it). She later noted on the draft 'rather a poor letter' and, interestingly, her difficulty seems to have been in envisaging the kind of UK direct control that might ensue if the Lennox-Boyd talks broke down. Such control 'will not be an easy part for HMG to fill. Autocratic government is against all our traditions . . . .' This may well be the point at which she first acknowledged to herself that direct government control during a period of transition was no longer politically practicable. Perham to Mboya, draft of mid-Oct. 1957 (Letter V), PP 343/2, ff 131, 114.

39. Perham to Mboya, 28 Nov. 1957, PP 343/2, f 108.

40. Perham to Nottingham, 29 Oct., 27 Nov., 1957, PP 434/2, ff 145–6.

41. Perham to Mboya, 28 Nov. 1957, PP 343/2.

42. Mboya to Perham, 7 Jan. 1958 (Letter VI), PP 343/2, ff 100–7.

43. See Goldsworthy, *Mboya*, pp. 87–8.

44. Perham to Mboya, 30 April 1958 (Letter VII), PP 343/2, f 91.

45. Perham to Mboya, 25 April 1958 (Letter VIII), PP 343/2, ff 87–9.

46. Mboya to Perham, 14 July 1958 (Letter VIII), PP 343/2, f 64.

47. Mboya to Perham, 18 April 1958 (Letter VII), PP 343/2, f 99.

48. Perham to Mboya, 25 April 1958 (Letter VIII), PP 343/2 f 87.

49. Mboya to Perham, 14 July 1958 (Letter VIII), PP 343/2, f 75.

50. Perham to Mboya, 30 April 1958 (Letter VII), PP 343/2, f 93.

51. Perham to Nottingham, 11 June, 6 Aug. 1958, PP 434/2, ff 149, 151.

52. Perham to Mboya, 30 April 1958 (Letter VII), PP 343/2, ff 94 sq.

53. Mboya to Perham, 14 July 1958, PP 343/2, ff 64 sqq. He confirmed to John Nottingham that the correspondence was still helping him enormously to clear his mind – 'she is very provocative'. Personal communication from Isabel Roberts (Ferguson), quoting a letter from Nottingham of August 1958.

54. Perham to Mboya, 1 Sept. 1958 (Letter IX), PP 343/2, ff 53 sqq.

55. Mboya to Perham, 1 Oct., 29 Oct. 1958 (Letter IX), PP 343/2, ff 47, 44.

56. Perham to McWilliam, 13 Nov. 1958, PP 434/2, f. 43.

57. Perham to Nottingham, 18 May 1959, PP 434/2, f. 157.

58. Perham to Mboya, 7 Jan. 1960, PP 457/2, f. 10.

59. Mboya to Perham, 24 Sept. 1960, PP457/2.

60. Mboya to Perham, 10 Aug. 1959, PP 343/2, f 35; Perham to Mboya, 7 Jan. 1960, PP457/2, f.10.

61. Perham to Mboya, 24 Oct. 1956, PP 457/2; 29 Oct. 1957, PP 343/2 f. 144; 24 July 1960, PP 457/2, f. 11. There is a contrast here with the unforced tone of her earlier correspondence volumes with Curtis and Huxley, who came from a background more familiar to her.

62. Perham to Lennox-Boyd, 30 April 1959, PP 457/1.

63. Perham to Nottingham, Dec. 1958, PP 434/2, f. 153.

64. Perham to Lennox-Boyd, 1 Dec. 1958, PP 457/10.

65. They did not lose touch, however; and Margery was deeply shocked by the news of Mboya's assassination in July 1969.

Margery Perham and the Colonial Office

Kenneth Robinson[1]

The title of this article is misleading: it promises much more than it could possibly provide. My intention was only to review what might emerge from her private papers about Margery Perham's contacts with ministers and officials of the Colonial Office after a necessarily summary reconnaissance with the invaluable assistance of Patricia Pugh's index to the archive. At the back of my mind when I embarked on that review was a question I was asked in Oxford forty years ago after I had given a talk on the Colonial Office: 'How far is Margery Perham Miss Mother Country?' I did not then think that she occupied any such position, and I do not now. Those who recall Charles Buller's celebrated, witty, and grossly unfair caricature of the greatest of the permanent under-secretaries of the Colonial Office, Sir James Stephen, will understand why.[2] This account lays no claim to arriving at an assessment of her overall influence on colonial policy-makers or on public opinion on such issues. For my part, I believe this to have been considerable, notably on members of the colonial services as well as governors, those members of either house of parliament who were not Colonial Office ministers, and her academic and publicist colleagues. My review addresses only a much more limited problem: how influential was she in consequence of her personal contacts with ministers and officials?

Personal relationships tend to colour our assessments of her life and work especially when the records are still not entirely available and those that are have not yet been scrutinized at all completely. For this reason, I hope I may be forgiven a brief autobiographical excursus which may help to discount the bias in what follows. My earliest recollections of Margery Perham are as a guest at the Ralegh Club[3] in the academic year 1934–5 to which I was fairly often invited by friends who were members, including her nephew Robert Rayne. Her talk to the club in 1933 on 'Trusteeship for Native Races in Africa' is recorded as the first occasion on which it had been addressed by a woman. Women were indeed expressly excluded from its membership except it seemed as 'senior members' and in October 1935 Margery Perham was so elected (when J. Melly spoke on 'Abyssinia as I saw it').[4] I remember now the vivid impact she made on me at these meetings. Strikingly handsome, elegantly dressed, a quiet but confident and masterful speaker, she conveyed a splendid impression of controlled vitality, more like an eloquent athlete than a don. She was of course already something of a public figure by virtue of her articles in *The Times* and just becoming much more of one by her public advocacy of the Ethiopian cause. I am sure that her exciting message was one, at least, of the reasons why I chose the Colonial Office when I joined the civil service in 1936, there to spend twelve strenuous but happy years until I succeeded her in 1948 as Reader in Colonial Administration, a job I sought at her suggestion. For the next nine years we were colleagues at Nuffield. In retrospect it seems to me that our paths did not cross in those years as much as might have been expected, partly because we both spent a good deal of time abroad, mostly in Africa, partly because my own research and writing were concerned rather with French than British imperialism, and mostly I suppose because we were both so busy, though I could never even begin to rival her incredible capacity for hard work. In one of her letters to Creech Jones Margery Perham once remarked that she had intended to contribute to the 'Penguin Special' *Attitudes to Africa* but had withdrawn for various reasons: 'I prefer to write alone'. She also preferred to teach alone. In the 1950s various Oxford colleagues and myself regularly collaborated in several seminars on Commonwealth and colonial government as well as on colonial public finance and African politics. I do not recall any seminar jointly directed by Margery Perham with any academic colleague. The rest of us I am sure lost much in the absence of the cross-fertilization that there might have been. I left Oxford for London University in 1957, and went to Hong Kong in 1965, so that from then on I saw much less of her than when we were together at Nuffield. This may have some bearing on my tentative suggestion that her contacts with the Colonial Office were largely concentrated in the period between 1939 and the late 1950s.

As my questioner in 1949 implied, there was a tendency for some to see her relationship with the Colonial Office staff in isolation from those of many other academics or outside experts as more special than I think was justified, certainly as more intimate and personal than it emerges, so far as I can judge, from her papers. This perception derived perhaps from the fact that her academic expertise was specifically concerned with problems of colonial, indeed African, policy and administration rather than any more general academic discipline such as political science, economics, or anthropology. It was, moreover, closely related to her teaching for the Colonial Service at Oxford and the infrastructure she was constantly developing with colonial administrators and governors, and later with African politicians. Still, such a concern with current problems of colonial administration was shared, even in the 1930s, by the anthropologist Lucy Mair, whose initial post at the London School of Economics was as Lecturer in Colonial Administration, and whose book, *Colonial Policies in Africa*, was actually published in the year before Margery Perham's *Native Administration in Nigeria*; and also by W.M. Macmillan, whose *Africa Emergent* appeared only a little later. But what made Margery Perham's position so special was not only her concentration on current problems but her ever-increasing success as a publicist of her views on these issues, notably in *The Times* and on the BBC. When she was establishing her position in the 1930s and earlier 1940s there was no competition from journalists with specialist experience of Africa, as later from Oliver Woods of *The Times*, or Colin Legum of the *Observer*. Such notable access to the formation of establishment opinion no doubt facilitated in her initial activities the application of that imperative which several of her close collaborators have stressed: 'Always go to the top.' That policy is no doubt reflected in her extensive contacts with ministers or with officials whose positions were somewhat outside the bureaucratic hierarchy like Ralph Furse and Christopher Cox, but its correlative may well have been a failure to exploit the potential help of more commonplace (or even eminent) civil servants. The names of permanent under-secretaries occupy only an inconspicuous place in the archive.

Nonetheless, her position *vis-à-vis* the Colonial Office should be seen in context. David Goldsworthy, whose study of *Colonial Issues in British Politics 1945–61* began as a doctoral thesis under her supervision, has observed:

> By no means all the Office's co-opted advisers, of course, were group representatives. Many were simply private individuals distinguished and knowledgeable in their specialized fields. What is worth noting is that a great many of these individuals did share a common profession – the academic one. The prevalence of academics in and about the Colonial Office was not fortuitous. It had been accepted since the days when Lugard, Oldham, and later Hailey made it their business to establish contacts with academics interested in colonial affairs, that trained thinkers and research workers could offer valuable contributions to policy formation. Creech Jones set the post-war pattern.[5]

Margery Perham's formal connection with the Colonial Office may be said to begin with her appointment in 1939 as a member of the Advisory Committee on Education in the Colonies, but it was rooted in her association with the teaching of administrative cadets, the two Summer Schools on colonial administration which she and Reginald Coupland had sponsored in Oxford in 1937 and 1938 and was soon to be followed by her attendance, together with Coupland, Keith Hancock, and Julian Huxley at a meeting in October 1939 with Malcolm MacDonald, then Colonial Secretary, on 'Future Policy in Africa' (Lugard, Hailey, and the Parliamentary, Permanent, and Deputy Under-Secretaries were also present). This meeting was in many ways prophetic, although it was rather coolly received by some of the permanent staff who had not been present. Hailey emphasized that any increased powers for existing colonial legislatures would be 'irretraceable' and stressed that he had 'never seen any attempt to square native administration as we now see it with the development of parliamentary institutions'. Margery argued that

> political life in Africa was moving on two planes. There was the plane of the tribes which corresponded to realities. Then there was the plane of our state system imposed artificially from above. We have never related Africans to the big state through Legislative Councils and through the Civil Service. On the tribal plane political education through indirect rule is slow. Meanwhile on the plane of the big state the intelligentsia are very rapidly acquiring political consciousness and naturally wish to capture the state system. We shall probably give in to them too soon. We ought to try to connect the two planes by setting up large regional councils of native administrations. The object of this should be to speed up the political education of the native authorities and to head off the intelligentsia from the state system.

The note of the meeting, compiled by Fred Pedler, states that Lugard, Hailey and Coupland signified their agreement, while Henry Moore (then a Deputy Under-Secretary, later Governor of Kenya) 'agreed that on the political development of Africa, we have to race against time'. It was at this meeting that Hancock pointed out that Britain was no longer a net exporter of capital and emphasized the colossal scale of capital investment that would be required to meet expectations of colonial development. His views were neither shared nor, it seems to me, understood.[6] In that same month Hailey was formally appointed a Senior Adviser in the Colonial Office and commissioned to visit Africa and report on native administration and political development.

I have quoted Margery Perham's views as recorded at this meeting not only because they seem to me to summarize succinctly much that was central to Colonial Office thinking in the 1940s, and to her own, but also because her presence at this meeting suggests – as do the minutes on her appointment to the Advisory Committee on Education – how well she was then regarded by the Office and the Secretary of State. One intriguing fragment in her archive is part of a copy of a letter of 24 March 1939 from Lugard to MacDonald recommending Margery as successor to Hailey as the British member of the Permanent Mandates Commission of the League of Nations and stating that she would accept it, if offered.[7] It would be interesting to know how this was received by the Secretary of State and his advisers. Perhaps there may be a clue in the MacDonald papers at Durham University.

She continued to develop links with the Colonial Office through the Colonial Research projects, which she initiated and directed at Nuffield, and through the planning in informal association with the Director of Recruitment at the Colonial Office (Sir Ralph Furse) and the Registrar of the University (Sir Douglas Veale) of much enlarged provision for colonial studies at Oxford as the essential prerequisite for any adequate post-war training of the Colonial Service. It was, however, her appointment in 1943 as a member of the Asquith Commission on Higher Education in the Colonies and of its West Indies Committee which marked the beginning of what was to be a long-continuing and major concern with the problems of developing university education overseas, mainly but not exclusively in Africa. The Asquith Commission recommended the creation of a new body, representing all the UK universities and independent of government, to help the development of higher education in the colonies. Margery Perham was at once made a co-opted member of the Inter-University Council, whose historian has recorded: 'Through the twenty five years of her devoted membership her profound appreciation of the political scene was invaluable'.[8] In 1944 she began another long stint as a member of the newly formed Colonial Social Science Research Council which ended only when it was abolished in 1961. Raymond Firth, who was for a time its secretary, once said to me that I was one of the few members of the Colonial Office staff who had strongly supported her appointment, and that I had done so only on the ground that she would be better on than off. If this was so, it was not from any doubt of the desirability of her appointment, but rather to persuade others who might be less sure.

There has never been any doubt of the importance of her long and close friendship with Arthur Creech Jones, especially during his tenure of the office of Secretary of State – and indeed, until his death. This was largely because, as was obvious to anyone who knew them both, their ideas of what was required in colonial policy were in many respects similar, partly, as was revealed by one occasional comment she made to me when he was first out of office (in 1950), because she was much distressed by what she thought shabby treatment by the party in failing to find him a seat. I was therefore very excited to find in the archives a substantial collection (174 folios) of her letters to him, but disappointed that those written when he was in office were for the most part hurried notes about the possibility of meeting when she had to be in London for other engagements, or the chances of a country walk, and hardly more than a very occasional comment on questions of policy – certainly very few until after he left office. An early one in June 1947 gives something of the flavour of this one side of a correspondence. 'It was really grand to have two leisured days in which to wander about the country and talk. I appreciated to the full both the pleasure of your company as a friend and the privilege of such free discussions with the Colonial Secretary. That sounds rather stilted. It is not meant to be.' There is an occasional flash of her humour: 'Oh the mechanics of life! How they get in the way of things that matter – including friendship. What a tragedy we did not live in the period of slavery – or even before 1914.'[9] Some comments seem to me astonishing in a professed student of politics: 'We have got to do a lot of rethinking in this country. This fighting over just where the knife falls in cutting the cake between groups is sordid and destructive. Let's hope your new leader will give a lead to something more up-to-date.'[10] Sadly, there are no letters from Creech Jones; it appears that Margery destroyed them all in an immediately regretted impulse, fearing that they were too politically sensitive.

It has been remarked that Margery Perham did not serve on any political or constitutional mission chiefly because she was so influential a publicist.[11] Although it was not publicly known at the time, she was in fact a member of what might have been a highly important enquiry, the Committee of Enquiry into Constitutional Developments in the Smaller Colonial Territories, appointed by Creech Jones in October 1949 as a result of sustained pressure by the Prime Minister. Attlee thought that it had been too readily assumed that the parliamentary and administrative system in large countries should be reproduced in miniature in the smallest countries and that the position should be authoritatively examined by a Royal Commission. Creech Jones feared that such an enquiry might provoke political agitation and urged that it should be 'strictly confidential'.

This reluctance on the part of the Secretary of State for such a comprehensive review perhaps explains its curious composition, especially the absence of any member with high level practical experience of government and politics. The Chairman, Sir Frederick Rees, Principal of University College Cardiff, was an economic historian who had been a member of the Commission on Constitutional Reform in Ceylon which reported in 1945, but whose other interests seem to have been in industrial rather than imperial relations. Besides the two officials initially proposed, there were two members of parliament, one Labour and one Conservative. Both had overseas administrative experience, one in Ceylon and the other in the Sudan, unlikely models, one might have thought, for smaller territories. Nor can it be said that Margery Perham's practical studies were notably relevant. The territories under consideration included only two that were not islands, British Somaliland and the Gambia (the latter of which she had not visited). Neither the Caribbean islands nor British Guiana, which she had visited in the course of her work with the Higher Education Commission in the West Indies, were within the Committee's purview.

When she received the invitation to join the Committee she commented to Creech Jones:

> This is a very interesting idea and I do feel it an honour to be invited. At the same time I am a little puzzled as to how we should set about it in the office and in camera. I have visited 6 out of your 16 territories but I don't feel that is any qualification. ... It is a very difficult constitutional problem and I have often wondered how it was going to be solved. ... Please don't put Rees Williams on this Committee.[12]

But her papers throw little light on her own contribution to its discussions. By the time the Committee reported in August 1951, Creech Jones had lost his seat in the 1950 election and had been replaced as Secretary of State by James Griffiths, a post he lost as a result of the general election later that year.

The Committee proposed the creation of a new constitutional status of City State or Island State organized on municipal lines with an elected State Council. This was to be an executive body employing the public service, except for the State Secretary, the Financial Secretary and the Attorney-General; and not subject to budgetary control so long as it remained solvent. All states would be represented in a central consultative council. The Committee also recommended that the Commonwealth Relations Office and the Colonial Office should be recombined under a Minister for Commonwealth Affairs with the advisory, research and recruitment functions of the Colonial Office available to all Commonwealth countries. The comments of the Colonial Office, the Commonwealth Relations Office and the governors of the territories concerned were, says the official historian, 'clearly mostly unfavourable'.[13] Margery can hardly have been anxious for further employment of this kind; one cannot help regretting that we shall never see what she might have written in The Times on this episode.

Of the senior officials of the Colonial Office she did of course know

Andrew Cohen well, but there is little that I have found in her papers to show this until he became Governor of Uganda in 1952 when, as it seems to me, their discussions follow a pattern not dissimilar from those with many other governors.[14] A letter of January 1955 is mostly about a possible visit to Uganda, and asks whether she should visit the Kabaka (who did not return to Uganda until later that year) before leaving England. 'I have a great hesitation in intervening when things are so difficult and the situation varies from day to day. I feel I must stick to being an observer rather than an actor, and yet if there was anything I could do to help, I would want to do it.'[15] Several letters from William Gorell-Barnes are also mostly about meetings and some private memoranda produced by him. One characteristic insight: 'I much enjoyed our talk the other day. I am not sure however that from my point of view I handled it very well since I did too much talking myself to get as much out of you as I might have.'[16]

I have said nothing of one member of the Colonial Office staff with whom she worked closely over a quarter of a century in the Inter-University Council for Higher Education Overseas on whose executive committee they both served; this was Christopher Cox, who had taken up the post of Educational Adviser in 1940 after a year or two as Director of Education in the Sudan, and whose papers are now in the Public Record Office. He was a Fellow of New College, Oxford, and retained his rooms there until his death. Their long association in the development of African universities surely merits detailed study.

Although there are a few letters to or from several of the Secretaries of State in office during the 1960s (Macleod, Maudling, and Greenwood – the last of whom was concerned with the Smaller Territories problem) they are not revealing except for one to Macleod on 13 November 1961:

> I must congratulate you with all my heart on solving what I thought was the insoluble in Uganda. I think when history is written your handling of intensely difficult problems that have come to you will record a decisiveness which is rare in our colonial history. Perhaps the most difficult and decisive act was the break you made with a long and involved past of Kenya. But how blind a series of governments have been in their dealings with the settlers. I still feel that official encouragement of the settlers up to the last moment put a heavy responsibility on the British Government to help them out of the final ruin of all their hopes.[17]

The last Secretary of State with whom any special relationship is suggested by the few letters in her papers is Alan Lennox-Boyd, though as so often these are largely concerned with possible meetings or visits to his home at Ince Castle, Saltash, rather than issues of high policy. There is no doubt however that she was in fairly close touch with him over Kenya questions in the critical months of 1957–8. In December 1958, for instance, she was trying to persuade him that the Kenya settlers did not after all constitute such a special case: 'I am so afraid that the moderates in Kenya, amongst whom I number Mboya, will be outflanked by the extremists, to whom we may have to surrender in no very long time much more in a hurry than we might now give in measured instalments.'[18] He wrote to her some months before his resignation in 1959: 'It was a joy to have you here [his house in Belgravia] ... I would welcome very much another talk with you soon' (apparently about Kenya).[19] In 1967 he sought her help in securing finance and employment for the exiled Kabaka of Buganda. 'Helen Cohen came here yesterday and we discussed the problems of the Kabaka. ... On employment: I wondered whether he could have helped with the Colonial Records scheme.' And later: 'I am delighted you feel so strongly that HMG ought to pension the Kabaka in view of our long relationship with his country and dynasty, and it would be of the greatest help if you would write yourself to the Prime Minister in those terms.'[20] She wrote a few days later to 'Dear Mr. Prime Minister' setting out the case, in terms of what Baganda cooperation had contributed to British rule in Uganda. Mr. Wilson (or his advisers) was unmoved. The government feared that any such help to the Kabaka would be interpreted by Milton Obote as evidence of British support for his opponents in Uganda.[21]

I have said nothing of her contacts with ministers and officials when she acted with a pressure group, as over Central Africa, or as almost a one-woman pressure group, as in the case of Tshekedi Khama.[22] Interesting as the latter issue is, it seems to me that she was doing something that many others did for other reasons and in other cases. There was, in short, a necessary element of formality in such manoeuvres. But these activities certainly deserve careful examination as exemplifying another dimension in her contacts with Whitehall.

Can one propose any tentative conclusions, or hypotheses to be further tested, from this review? First a truism, but one which my forays into her papers have emphasized to me more than I expected: the necessity of a substantial examination of other records, official and private, if any firm conclusions are to be drawn on many of these issues. Because the Perham archive is so extensive, it is perhaps easy to suppose it to be more complete than it is. It is astonishing that a historian who retained even her notes on books, articles and seminar papers should have destroyed the letters of a Secretary of State. Second, at the level of membership of advisory committees her role was hardly exceptional; for example, Coupland and other academics had preceded her on the Advisory Committee on Education in the Colonies. But especially before the end of the war there were few outsiders who shared her particular expertise in 'native administration' or even colonial policy; and none who already had so substantial and growing a data bank derived not only from study on the spot and in the files of colonial governments to which she was so freely given access, but also from continued, carefully cultivated and growing contacts with men in the field – administrators and governors in particular, but increasingly a small élite of African leaders and former pupils. Third – but this can hardly be said to have been established from her papers – the other major source of her early influence and one which inevitably grew as time passed and her reputation grew, was her success as a publicist. If Oxford, as she often said, was one essential 'base' for her activities, *The Times* – and increasingly the BBC – provided another, not less essential 'base'. Fourth, by the end of the inter-war years her ideas were very close to those of the Colonial Office advocates of what the historians of the wartime Colonial Office, Michael Lee and Martin Petter, have called 'the forward policy', and moved closer to them when the fall of Singapore led her to call for a 'revision of the time factor' in 'all aspects of our colonial policy' and in particular resulted in a change of emphasis in her own thinking on African participation in government.[23] Fifth, while one might have expected some evidence of a more personal relationship with Malcolm MacDonald when he was Secretary of State, I have found little to support this in her papers. Such evidence as there is to suggest that she was well regarded in the Office is to be found in her presence at the 1939 meeting on 'Future Policy in Africa' and some comments by the Under-Secretary Lord Dufferin. On the other hand, while there is ample evidence of the mutual regard and understanding between her and Creech Jones, there is a sad lack of material on the interaction of their views on policy. This will need a special effort on other material. There is, indeed, evidence of an understanding friendship with Alan Lennox-Boyd, but it mostly comes from the years after his resignation and again there is little to throw light on policy discussion. This too might repay wider investigation. Of officials, it seems that she was well regarded by Arthur Dawe (at least in his early days as head of the Africa Division);[24] she was certainly close to Andrew Cohen, though I am uncertain, from my own friendship with him, how far one would expect any clear cut evidence of her influencing his actions.

Lastly, there is one reflection which cannot be said to emerge, in any way, from this exercise. To the extent that her vast network of friends among administrators, governors, former pupils and some African leaders remained the major source of her data base, it became less and less adequate in enabling her to assess the new sources of power and political activity in post-war Africa. When Thomas Hodgkin published his series of articles in *West Africa* in 1950 entitled 'Background to Gold Coast Nationalism', Margery Perham asked a colleague: 'But how does he know so much about it?' One might have replied: 'By spending his time in Africa with Africans and in Adult Education Summer Schools, political meetings, travelling in mammy buses rather than seeing members of the Colonial Service and a small selection of African "leaders", in short doing something more like what you did in South Africa in 1929–30.' In the changed Africa of the 1950s her very eminence became a source of difficulty in learning enough about the dynamic and – let us candidly admit it – to her sometimes distasteful – elements in African societies.

NOTES

1. A reflection based on personal recollections as well as on some preliminary exploration of the Perham archive.
2. Conveniently summarized in F. Madden with D. Fieldhouse, *Imperial Reconstruction, 1763–1840: Select Documents on the Constitutional History of the British Empire and Commonwealth, Volume III* (Westport, USA, 1987), pp.57–8.
3. On the Ralegh Club and its origins see F. Madden, 'Commonwealth History and Oxford' in F. Madden and D.K Fieldhouse (eds.), *Oxford and the Idea of Commonwealth* (London, 1982), pp.11–12. Minutes of the Ralegh Club (in Rhodes House Library, consulted by kind permission of Professor K. Kirkwood), 170th meeting, 5 March 1933. F. M. Hardie, then its secretary, was President of the Oxford Union when the 'King and Country' debate took place a few weeks earlier.
4. Ralegh Club Minutes, 193rd meeting, 27 Oct. 1935.
5. D. Goldsworthy, *Colonial Issues in British Politics 1945–61* (Oxford, 1971), p.59.
6. CO 847/17/47135/39. Among the comments of those to whom the record of this meeting were circulated was that of Sir Grattan Bushe, the Legal Adviser (later Governor of Barbados): 'No matter what the old Guard may say you cannot turn Africa into Conan Doyle's "Lost World".' Margery Perham's copy of the record contains a note, typed so that it is not certain that she wrote it, which is valuable in elucidating Hancock's far-sighted and realistic assessment; PP 685/2.
7. Lugard to MacDonald, 24 March 1939, PP 8/5.
8. I.C.M. Maxwell, *Universities in Partnership* (Edinburgh, 1980), p.12. Ian Maxwell has told me that much of this advice arose from her special access to the views of colonial administrations.
9. Perham to Creech Jones, 7 June 1947, 10 Jan. 1954, PP 23/1.
10. Perham to Creech Jones, 5 Feb. 1956, PP 23/1.
11. Goldsworthy, *Colonial Issues*, p.61.
12. Perham to Creech Jones, 20 June 1949, PP 23/1. David Rees-Williams, later Lord Ogmore, war Parliamentary Under-Secretary at the Colonial Office.
13. D.J. Morgan, *The Official History of Colonial Development*, vol. 5 (London, 1980), pp. 27–55.
14. There is an interesting correspondence between them at the height of the Buganda crisis in 1954 in PP 514/5.

15. Perham to Cohen, 7 Jan. 1955, PP 29/3.
16. Gorell-Barnes to Perham, 27 March 1958, PP 29/3.
17. Perham to Macleod, 13 Nov. 1961, PP 29/3.
18. Perham to Lennox-Boyd, 1 Dec. 1958, PP 457/1 f.14.
19. Lennox-Boyd to Perham, 24 April 1959, PP 29/3.
20. Lennox-Boyd to Perham, 24 Feb., 9 March 1967, PP 520/12.
21. Perham to Harold Wilson, 16 March, and R.J. Dawe to Perham, 12 April 1967, PP 520/12.
22. See Chapter 14 below.
23. M. Lee and M. Petter, *The Colonial Office, War, and Development Policy* (London, 1982); Margery Perham, *Colonial Sequence 1930–1949* (London, 1967), pp. 225 sqq..
24. Dawe was among those who visited Lugard at Abinger, and apparently met and talked to Margery at length there. Private Diary, 27 Nov., 5 Dec. 1938, Jan. 1939, PP 33/4.

Margery Perham and Broadcasting: a personal reminiscence

Prudence Smith

Margery Perham's broadcasting career spanned a period of forty-three years. There have been a number of people, therefore, who shared with her the often curiously intense relationship that the pressures of broadcasting bring about. A proper study of Margery as a broadcaster would canvass opinions and memories from producers in the various services to which she contributed – including Schools, General Overseas, African, Caribbean, Home Talks. All that I myself have been able to do is to spend a few hours in the BBC archives and in the Perham archive at Rhodes House, in order if possible to round out, or test out, my own memories of her and my own opinion of her qualities formed over a number of years as a BBC talks producer. From this some points seemed to emerge which I believe have a bearing on the interpretation of aspects of her career as they were presented at the conference.

My main purpose is to comment on Margery Perham's historical importance in the field of broadcasting and forming public opinion. But first, a personal word: in common with very many others in various professions, I feel that she helped me and enlightened me, and I valued her friendship very highly; her qualities of mind and spirit made working with her an excitement. She was almost always cheerful and even-tempered, no matter how late the hour or short the time. (It is true that when reading a script she often *sounded* rather melancholy and despairing, irrespective of the situation under discussion; it was something to do with certain cadences in her voice, and we worked quite hard on those cadences). Despite her incredibly busy life, her dealings were always calm, reasonable and patient, and with this went what I – and others – recall as her essential 'humility'. In my capacity as producer and editor, I always found her glad of criticism and direction, of cutting and rearrangement; while retaining her own judgement, she was ready to adopt a perfectly open and workmanlike approach towards improving her use of the medium. Her occasional letters of reproach to the BBC Bookings Manager (about expenses for instance) are short, courteous and reasonable.

The span of forty-three years covers about one hundred and ten separate broadcasts; so far as I can tell only two of these are not about Africa. Taken together with the fact that talks about places and politics are most usually invited by the BBC when something has gone wrong, it will be seen that we have in this archive an extraordinary conspectus of what one might call – and Margery Perham did call – the colonial reckoning: her accounts of and reflections upon most of the alarums and excursions in Africa from questions of 'native policy' in the dying empire to her championship of newly independent nations, especially when they found themselves in difficulty. Through all these talks, and also in the many background pieces she did for schools and sixth forms, there runs the plea for sensitive understanding of the issues and the peoples involved, and for a withholding of political and moral judgement until that effort had been made.

To judge from the correspondence files in the BBC, Margery Perham was not in the beginning very keen on this work, or confident of her ability to do it well. The first letter I could find, of November 1932, is a reply to the redoubtable Mary Adams who had invited her to give a Schools talk on the centenary of the abolition of slavery. She agreed to do it, but she wrote of her fear that 'it will be very difficult to be "popular" and yet correct enough'. She was staying and working with Lord Lugard at the time, and clearly supposed that this new medium was a trifle beneath a scholar's notice, yet was characteristically concerned not to give offence.

She changed her mind about the medium, fortunately, and began, from about 1938, to undertake quite frequent commissions and to take trouble to understand the medium and improve her use of it. In December 1938 Evelyn Gibbs of the BBC sent her the results of some listener research on a schools broadcast. The listeners had praised the content in the most fulsome way, but some had been critical of the delivery – 'too excited ... spoke too quickly ... swallowed the ends of her sentences'. Margery Perham wrote to thank Evelyn for the comments: 'most interesting, though except for [those] about enunciation, not very helpful'.

Up to 1949, when I was recruited to broadcasting at the inception of the Third Programme, she had done only two or three programmes for the general Home audience; the rest had all been for Schools, or Empire Transmission, or the African or North American services. But after the war and after Indian independence the whole African picture changed, public opinion and expectation changed, and the BBC was prepared to devote greatly increased resources and air-time to African issues. My own BBC career began with frequent travels throughout most of the continent with a recording machine, interviewing almost anyone willing to answer my questions. On my return I edited these interviews into composite programmes, or as talks and discussions. At the same time, I had also to provide for the broadcasting of analysis, comment and opinion on the events thrown up by the accelerating rush towards independence in nearly every African territory; and I set my face against using the 'stage army' of speakers who had appeared frequently before and to some extent during the war. They were mostly ex-colonial administrators – men who had retired, generally with fairly fixed opinions, in the 1940s or even 1930s. Similarly out of touch were some of the radicals and revolutionaries on the political scene.

In this context Margery Perham was for me, and I believe for the British public, that rare and precious thing, a cautious, respectable radical. As is recorded elsewhere in these articles, she was constantly revising the time-scale for the end of colonialism. Even she, despite her travels and her wide contacts in Africa, was always being surprised by events; and to all the conflicts and catastrophes as well as to the triumphs she gave passionate and thoughtful attention. I commissioned and produced many speakers during the 1950s and 1960s, but the talks which I remember most clearly – on Kenya and Mau Mau, on Ghana's independence, on Central African Federation – are hers; and particularly I recall (although I was not in the BBC at the time) the superb talk she gave on the Nigerian crisis following the murder, in January 1966, of Sir Abubakar Tafawa Balewa. She had become so convinced of her role in sustaining an informed public opinion that she had written directly to the Controller of the Third Programme to ask if she could be given, urgently, a space to comment on the implications of that event. For me this talk and one which she gave in September 1968 – again on the Third Programme – reporting on her visit to the war in Nigeria, and also her radio appeal to Colonel Ojukwu while in Nigeria, represent the apogee of her broadcasting.

Her Reith Lectures, delivered in 1961, in a rather different way have a claim to that. Certainly they represent the most considerable and sustained effort that she made in the medium. I had planned them with her, and had helped to secure her selection, but had to retire into domestic life before she gave the lectures. She wrote to me afterwards saying: 'I enjoyed enormously giving those. They came just at the right moment when I was ready to think over all I had been working upon, and generalize about it at what was, probably, the right historical moment.' She felt, with reason, that she still had a real place in the formation of public opinion.

But I think myself, as a broadcaster, that her finest pieces were those on the Nigerian civil war, where the agony shows through. Almost all broadcasting, because it relies upon the human voice, is a more personal medium than print, and good practitioners use it in a personal way; that is, they try to speak and sound like whole people, not just brains. Margery Perham became very good at this; she came a long way from her fears of 1932 that in speaking 'popularly' she might not be 'correct' enough.

In conclusion I would like to draw attention to another type of broadcast which she gave which could be of especial use to a biographer. This is the personal interview. I suspect that such broadcasts were the mainspring of her autobiographical works. Certainly they are very revealing and will repay study, although being transcribed from unscripted speech and consequently full of errors and distortions, most of them make difficult reading. All the same, I have deposited some of these scripts in the Rhodes House archive. They are full of surprises. For example:

> *Interviewer*: 'Miss Perham ... is there beneath the don a creative writer struggling to get out?'
> *Margery Perham*: 'Yes. ... I feel it would have been much better if I'd never attempted to be a serious student, but had gone on with imaginative writing. ... I'd have got more fun out of it myself and I think it's a more important thing to do. Anybody can write ... these sort of dull, conscientious books about any subject in the world ... but to do imaginative work would have been wonderful.'

In evaluating those remarks, one would have to bear in mind that Margery Perham had perfect manners, and that her interlocutor was – Elspeth Huxley. Nevertheless it is a pointer, among many others (her love of poetry, for example) to the strength of her feelings for beauty, love, friendship and the tears of things. These, once she allowed them to, glow through most of her later broadcasts even while she is describing, analysing and reflecting upon the complexities of African situations .

The pattern sketched here of Margery Perham's influence as a force in British thinking on African problems is rather different from what has been suggested elsewhere in these articles. It may be that in direct dealings with those in power – whether colonial governors in Africa or politicians and senior civil servants in London – her authority diminished fairly rapidly from the mid-1950s. But in the world of broadcasting, the 1950s and 1960s were precisely the period when the task of adjusting public consciousness and public debate to the end of empire was at its most urgent; and in this important political field her influence was supreme.

The Nigerian Civil War

Martin Dent[1]

Margery Perham had in the course of her career covered an immense span of writing upon the affairs of colonial Africa, of its nationalist leaders and of its decolonization. She had, in a special sense, been the enlightened conscience of British colonial rule. But with the coming of independence to so many countries, including Nigeria in 1960, she may have felt that her role had ended, for she was, at this time, sixty-six years' old. She was not so much at home with the politics of independent African states and saw their acute dilemmas through the spectacles of British colonial history. She was respected in much of Africa, as well as in Britain, as a distinguished historian and commentator of the colonial period, but somehow lacked the empathy and driving interest to concern herself with attempts to advise on the problems of post-colonial African states. She wrote, for instance, with sadness of the abrupt end of British rule in the Sudan, but failed to play any part in attempting to halt the civil war between the South and the North of the Sudan, which followed so tragically after independence.

She had spoken with understanding of African nationalism in her Reith Lectures, but perhaps she felt that the new world of youth and radical ideas, which shaped so much of independent Africa, was not her world. In this sense, she lacked the sympathetic vision of more left-wing commentators, such as Thomas Hodgkin. Some time in the late 1960s she remarked to me with emphasis and a desire for a well-earned rest, that the time had come for her to behave like Prospero:

> I'll break my staff
> bury it certain fathoms in the earth,
> and, deeper than did ever plummet sound,
> I'll drown my book.

From this rest she was pushed back into action by the tragedy of the Nigerian Civil War and the need to do what she could to shorten it and to ensure an outcome of true reconciliation between the combatants. She had broadcast on Nigeria's independence celebrations in October 1960, emphasizing again and again the need for the preservation of unity, and had looked to the Ibo people as, in a special sense, the cement of that unity. She saw the role of Dr Azikiwe as that of the future governor-general as the focus of Nigerian unity and that of the Federal prime minister, Alhaji Abubakar Tafawa Balewa, as a most precious possession of Nigeria. She sketched the history of each Region and of the creation of the Nigerian entity by Lord Lugard, as governor-general, laying much emphasis on the peculiar characteristics of each of the three major tribes, the Hausa/Fulani in the North, the Yoruba in the West, and the Ibo in the East, but curiously enough, making no mention of the minority tribes, who were, at the moment of the crisis before and during the civil war, to save the unity of Nigeria.[2] Perhaps she failed to see that the ferment of Nigerian politics could make it possible in due course for tribal attitudes and stereotypes to be at least in part replaced by a new sense of Nigerian unity.

There is no record in her files of her comments upon the sad affairs of the First Republic until its overthrow in January 1966, with the assassination of Abubakar Tafawa Balewa, the Federal prime minister, and of the Northern and Western premiers, the Sardauna of Sokoto and Chief Akintola, in a military coup launched by officers, predominantly of Ibo origin, and accompanied by the murder of four Northern, two Yoruba and one Ibo senior officers. She then approached the BBC Third Programme with great urgency to be allowed to speak to condemn the 'political murders'. A speaker, previously booked, kindly offered to defer his talk and so she was able to broadcast to express her shock and outrage. She correctly forecast that these murders would be followed not by the creation of a peaceful, political order, but by more violence. She acknowledged that there had been electoral corruption and that Abubakar Tafawa Balewa had become a lonely figure, but did not regard the political corruption of the First Republic as sufficient justification for the violence of its overthrow for, 'as Walpole discovered, corruption may be that degree of patronage that keeps a still immature party and parliament working smoothly'. This view may have been correct while the scale of corruption was still relatively small under the First Republic, though in succeeding regimes it was to escalate alarmingly. She spoke of the Ibo people as giving one 'a sense of riotous thrust and vigour: the crowds of market women, uninhibited, shouting, clutching' and 'taking jobs, any jobs, doing them well, hanging together and becoming anything but popular in the west and the north'.[3] She ignored, I think, the subtlety of the love/hate relation that characterized so much of Nigeria; the antagonism against Ibo immigrants in North and West was indeed present, but so, as post-civil war reconciliation was to show, was the ability to live together in amity at local level.

She received a number of letters from different sources, including Nigerian students in Britain. A Northerner wrote to express his thanks for the 'noble and kind sentiments you expressed in your tribute to the late Sir Abubakar Tafawa Balewa and his colleagues'.[4] An Ibo wrote condemning her for being so one-sided and having an 'apparent dislike of Ibos'; he asked how the corrupt and Northern dominated regime of the First Republic could have been ended without military violence, and accused her of intellectual dishonesty, and of getting Nigerians, and Africans generally, 'well stuffed up with the ideals of Britain. ... this process fails every day in Africa but few people try to find out "WHY" '.[5] A British officer who had served with General Ironsi (who, after the coup, emerged as the Supreme Commander and Head of the Federal Military Government), gave a most unflattering view of his honesty and military devotion, describing him as 'in the pockets of the Federal politicians at Lagos', and always determined to use his military career as a means to achieve political power.[6]

The exact opposite view was put in two letters from Hugh Elliot, an old friend and at this time a Permanent Secretary (Ministry of Agriculture), in the East. In April 1966, he wrote that the army were doing very well and that Nigeria was a most hopeful place. Few people, he said, regretted the death of the Sardauna. There was 'ample evidence that Ironsi did not seek the position he now holds' and that 'it was a voluntary handover...by the rest of the Federal cabinet, who were scared stiff'. The military, he said, really wanted to hand back power, and discipline in the civil service was much better. However, there was a danger of 'too much control by young economists/planners, who have supreme confidence in their blue-prints and in their superior intelligence and who are also secularists', alienating both the Catholic Church and the Muslims.[7]

Whether this was true in April is not clear, but by May the burning hostility in the North against the government of Ironsi boiled over in civilian riots and attacks against Ibos. One cause was the abolition of a federal form of government in Decree Number 34 of May. Hugh Elliott, writing again in June, supported the unification, for 'the Regions were pulling apart disastrously'.[8] He failed to see that while it was possible to create more states and make the federal system more centre-leaning, it was not possible to abolish federalism altogether and create a unitary state, for too many jobs in the state civil service were at stake, and distrust of the Federal government, which was seen as Ibo-dominated, was at this time too prevalent. This was exacerbated by the fact that those who had murdered fellow officers in the January coup had not been tried. Even in June, Elliot argued that the North was not against the government, but in July came the successful military coup and the murder of over two hundred Ibo soldiers, including General Ironsi himself.

There is in the Perham archive an excellent statement on the Nigerian troubles issued by the Church Missionary Society, quoting the Archbishop of West Africa:

> There has been surprisingly little condemnation among Christians of the murders committed in January, May and July. Are we sure that we truly condemn them *all*, and, while deprecating revenge, desire to punish the murderers? ... A sincere and unanimous demand from all Churches that any government ... should regard murder as the sin and crime it is, and should relentlessly punish those who break the law and commandment, would have an effect.[9]

Alas, each group tended to condemn the murders perpetrated by others and to ignore those committed by its own people. In any case, successful violence seemed to create its own spurious legitimacy, and the Federal government clearly lacked the power to punish the many murderers who had killed Ibos in May, July and August 1966. Margery Perham found the situation agonizing and bewildering, with her friends in different parts of Nigeria moving towards war with one another. A terrible outbreak of murder of innocent Ibo civilians took place in the North and a smaller outbreak of murder of Northerners in the East (where there were far fewer to attack). She attended a seminar at St Antony's College, Oxford, which I was addressing, on the coup and the crisis in Nigeria, and asked many questions but had no clearer idea than the rest of us of what ought to be done.

When the civil war started in July 1967 her sympathies moved towards the Biafrans, for the Ibos, among whom she had many friends, were suffering the most. She wrote to *The Times*, making a plea for there to be a ceasefire, asking for a 'mediated conclusion',[10] and for the British supply of arms to Nigeria to be stopped.[11] She earnestly wished unity to be maintained, but thought that there should be negotiation with the Biafran authorities, in which their legitimate fears would be recognized, and the safety of Ibos in all parts of the country guaranteed, rather than the conquest of Biafra by the Federal government. When the Nigerian Students' Action Committee invited her to address a large Nigerian student meeting which was held at Church House on 2 March 1968, in support of the position of the Federal government, she replied courteously, expressing her wish that Nigeria might remain one, but stating that because of the atrocities committed against the Ibos in 1966 she could not attend. I was invited as a speaker and did attend, and reported to her in a letter that

> I was present at the 'teach in' at Church House, Westminster, when

your letter was read out in full. I must admit that the students running the teach-in were good in the way that they read out the full text slowly, said that they did not agree with the conclusion but that they must give credit to the sincerity of your desire (stated in the first paragraph) that Nigeria should, if possible, be kept one. In this sense, they are more ready to accept and consider contrary views than are the 'Biafrans', who seem to want 100% support or nothing.

I sympathize with your compassion for the Ibos, but I am myself sure that if two political communities and not one emerge from this war, the bitterness will be perpetuated, and for the next two or three generations we shall see a series of wars between Nigeria and Biafra, with inevitable involvement of big powers as the patrons of either side.

On the other hand, I am hopeful of the African ability to make effective reconciliation once there is a ceasefire with 'one Nigeria' maintained. There is, of course, a nice balance of forces between those who want reconciliation with the Ibos and those who want subjugation, but from a lot of evidence which comes to me, I believe that those who want reconciliation will triumph. I believe that it is our job to encourage them, rather than to give false hopes to the Ibos to continue a resistance that will, I believe, ultimately be useless.[12]

I sent her also a copy of my address to the student gathering, asking for an 'operation fatted calf' after the end of hostilities in order to welcome back the Ibos now in secession into the new Nigeria. I took for granted the statement of the Federal government that the war would be over by April 1969, and suggested that Easter 1969 would be symbolically a more satisfactory date, since the circumstance of having to kill one's brothers 'is a kind of death, and from this death the New Nigeria must rise again'. Margery Perham marked in the margin this passage and a number of others. I spoke of the great change in attitudes that had occurred, and that it would

be possible for you [Nigerians] to amaze the world by the rapidity with which, once the ceasefire has occurred with one Nigeria maintained, you reconcile the conflicts and heal the scars of war. I see already indications of this, both in the generosity of the aims proclaimed by Gowon and the Federal government, and in the reception given to Mr Asika [the Federal Administrator of the East Central State, and an Ibo] throughout the North. I was in the North in 1966 as well as in 1967, the change in attitude to the Ibos was most noticeable. A year ago a reception of honour and great public welcome like that given to Asika would have been impossible. The North has, in a sense, a bad conscience about the events of 1966, and this is a sign of the way things are moving. People realize that all sections bear a share of blame for the tragedy of Nigeria, but that it is the Ibos who have suffered the most.[13]

In August 1968, Dame Margery received a letter from Chief Anthony Enahoro, the Federal Commissioner for Information, through the Nigerian High Commission, inviting her to come to see for herself whether or not the Federal Government was sincere in its professed intention to protect the Ibo people and to welcome them back into Nigeria. He assured her that she would be free to go where she liked, and that although 'we do not agree with the views you have expressed on the civil war, we continue to view you with respect and affection for your work as a historian of Nigeria.'[14]

Margery Perham quickly accepted the offer, and the government's hospitality, though requesting that she stay in a hotel rather than official accommodation, so that she could retain her independence of view.[15] It was agreed that her visit would be under the auspices of the Nigerian Institute of International Affairs.

She flew out at the end of August 1968 for an eleven-day visit during the course of which she travelled widely to see things for herself.[16] She saw many Ibo people living peacefully and unmolested in Lagos and elsewhere. She went to Enugu and saw the peaceful existence of Ibos in former Biafran areas occupied by the First Division, and administered by E. O. Asika, the Administrator of East Central State, an Ibo political scientist formerly at Ibadan University. She saw many people on the Federal side and cross-questioned them. She flew to Port Harcourt and met the 'Black Scorpion' Colonel Adekunle, who blamed her for British attitudes to the war. With an eloquence perhaps unexpected in one who had a reputation as a rough soldier, he told her that they were fighting not only for the unity of Nigeria but for the territorial integrity of all African states.[17] She met Colonel Hassan Katsina, the former governor of the North, and was impressed by his generous attitudes to those now in rebellion. Philip Asiodu, an Ibo from the Mid West (as it then was), and a brilliant Oxford scholar, wrote to invite her to dinner at his house in Ikoyi, Lagos, with a number of graduates from Oxford and other universities who wanted to renew their acquaintance with her and pay tribute to a revered academic. She went and much enjoyed this family occasion, while the honour obviously given to Asiodu as a respected Federal Permanent Secretary convinced her that Ibos were not regarded as second-class citizens.[18]

Finally, Margery Perham went to see Yakubu Gowon, the Head of the Federal Military Government, and had a three-hour conversation with him. There is no record of exactly what was discussed, but there is no doubt that Gowon's sincerity and obvious goodwill to all Nigerians, including the Ibos, shone through the discussion and convinced her that the Federal government would pursue a generous policy to those in secession once the war ended with one Nigeria maintained. Gowon, in a later letter to Dame Margery, spoke humorously and modestly of the discussion saying that he hoped that his 'three hours' lecture' did not bore her and that he might have earned a 'poor Ph.D. Honoris Causa – Oxon (Dodan Barracks) – personally from you'.[19] From a correspondent of *Newsweek* who went to see Gowon after Dame Margery, I gathered that she told him that Gowon had given her an accurate history of past events, as well as a promise for the future. My own experience, from a long interview with Gowon at this time, was that he was very keen to set the record straight as to events in 1966 and 1967, so that he and the Federal government should stand well with history.

She also came to visit me at the house of the late Chief (then Mr) Tarka with whom I was staying in Lagos. It was noteworthy that the moment that breakfast was finished, she firmly insisted that all those sitting round the table should put away their plates and cups and enter a seminar discussion with her on past events, and on the prospects for return to civilian rule after the end of the civil war! As always, she took copious notes and recorded the essentials in her diary.

Before she left Lagos Margery Perham made what was possibly the most important broadcast of her whole career. In a short address she solemnly asked Ojukwu to surrender, since 'Biafra is being surrounded by Federal troops, and it cannot be long before you and your people will have to face defeat.' She made it clear that she was in no sense an agent of Federal government but was acting independently according to her conscience as a Christian, with a long connection with Nigeria.

> From what I have seen and heard, not only in Lagos but in visits to other parts, the East and the North, I do not believe that your people would be in danger of massacre or revenge. You must know, even if your people do not, that an immense effort is now being made to prepare the way back for your people into life in Nigeria. I therefore beg you not to take upon yourself the terrible responsibility of refusing to surrender and of fighting to the end.[20]

She used also the argument that even if the Federal government had wished to maltreat the Biafrans, which she did not believe to be the case, they could not do so in the full glare of the world's press and public opinion. This was an argument that had been made to me a year before by Chief Awolowo in an interview, and which I had included in the address to the Nigerian Students' Action Committee meeting at Church House, of which I sent her a copy. It argued that evidence pointed to the collapse of the resistance of Biafra as an organized entity within some three months, and that therefore we must first 'do anything that we can to shorten the agony of war, and to ease the return of those now in rebellion to the Nigerian Federation again, and second to ensure that the Nigeria for which soldiers have given their lives is well built and worthy of their sacrifice'.[21]

This prospect of imminent Biafran collapse was entirely reasonable at this time and it was partially upon this basis, as well as upon the inherent desirability of establishing one Nigeria, that Margery Perham made her appeal, and this was, in my view, a weakness in her text. For in September and October a flood of arms came in unexpectedly from France via Gabon and Fernando Po by air and caused a needless prolongation of the agony. It was not enough to save Biafra from defeat but sufficed to cause tens of thousands of deaths in a year's unnecessary fighting. This was the cost of de Gaulle's interference and the machinations of M. Foccart, the *éminence grise* of President de Gaulle's African policy. They preferred the dissolution of the Nigerian Federation to the continuance of a united Anglophone state which would be predominant in West Africa.

When Dame Margery returned to England she wrote a long article in *The Times* ending with the forceful conclusion 'Nigeria needs the Ibos; even more the Ibos need Nigeria.'[22] During the following weeks she received a spate of letters, many from Ibos which 'scorched the page'. From I.S. Kogbara, however, the Biafran representative in Britain, she received a remarkably courteous letter asking why she had made the appeal for surrender from Lagos and not from London.[23] Faced with this barrage of criticism and with the evidence of continuing Biafran resistance fortified with French arms, Dame Margery came to doubt her conviction that Biafran surrender was the only possible way of ending the war. She reverted to her earlier views and wrote to *The Times*, and an open letter to Gowon, suggesting that there should be a ceasefire and arbitration, since the Federal troops operating at the end of long lines of communication would not be able to win a military victory.[24] This unfortunate reversal sprang, I think, from the false premise of basing the appeal for Biafran surrender and return to Nigeria partly on the military position on the ground, and not wholly on the inherent merits of the case itself. The 'arbitrament of battle' is always an uncertain one, and it is not the best judgement of truth.

The change of view by Margery Perham provoked a vitriolic attack in the *New Nigerian* (a Federal Nigerian newspaper published in the North) asking why she had written to Gowon to ask him to halt the Federal troops when they were 'poised for another bout'. It suggested that this might be due to failure of her mental powers owing to senility.[26] In fact, of course, Margery was influenced by feelings of emotion and sympathy and by a liberal reluctance to contemplate the prolonged use of force. Nonetheless this revised view was a wrong one and, if followed, would undoubtedly have resulted in failure to establish Nigerian unity and the waste of all the efforts made by the Federal army.

She had included in an earlier letter to Gowon, however, a very wise appeal to him to make a formal statement promising reconciliation to those in secession,[27] and this he had promised to do and had done in a number of statements asking for an end 'without victor and without vanquished' and for the 'binding up of the nation's wounds'.[28] The Lincoln parallel showed that one could not re-establish the unity of the Federation by any other way than continuing the war until victory, and that after victory there could be a generous reconciliation.[29] Nigeria, in fact, was to achieve a reconciliation far more generous than that of the United States after the Civil War. One of the corner-stones of the 'reconciliation, reconstruction and rehabilitation' was Gowon's insistence that those Biafrans who had previously been in the service of the Federal government should be restored to their positions. On the very day that Biafra surrendered, Gowon asked his Supreme Military Council to implement this policy. When some members raised objections he threatened to resign and won his point, subject only to the setting up of a commission under General Adebayo to review the cases of Biafrans who had previously been in the Federal Armed Forces, to determine who could be re-admitted to the Federal Armed Forces and who would be retired on pension or dismissed.[30]

Gowon paid no attention to Margery Perham's January 1969 appeal for a ceasefire. He had already sent her a most courteous letter congratulating her on her September 1968 appeal to the Biafrans to surrender. He said that it had had some effect and that Biafrans were now a divided camp but that Ojukwu had a mad determination to continue. He thanked Dame Margery for her care for Nigeria and all Nigerians, especially the Ibos, and assured her again that he would never allow them to be treated 'as second-class citizens'. He ended with the charming greeting 'Cheerio Dame!'[31]

In 1973, three years after the civil war had ended and when a triumphant reconciliation had been attained in Nigeria, Margery Perham received a letter from a distinguished Ibo, Albert Osakwe, which must have gladdened her heart. He thanked her for her broadcast, said that it had helped to establish the Federal determination to adopt a generous policy to the Ibos, and that already in 1968, at the time that the broadcast was made, people like him in Biafra had come to know that the mass killing of Ibos had ended, and that Ibos in the Federal areas were being well treated, as Dame Margery had said in her broadcast.[32]

Her broadcast from Lagos in 1968 had been the last important intervention of Margery Perham in African affairs and it was a most courageous and creative farewell.

NOTES

1. This is a personal view of Margery Perham's involvement in the Nigerian Civil War, based on memory, private records, and a brief look at some of the files labelled 'Biafra' in the Perham Papers.
2. The notes for her broadcast are in the Perham Papers (hereafter PP), Rhodes House Library, Box 347/file 8.
3. Broadcast of 22 Jan. 1966 entitled 'Personal View: Dame Margery Perham'; the transcript and article published in the *Listener*, 27 Jan. 1966, are in PP 347/14.
4. S.K. Dabo to Perham, 22 Jan. 1966, PP 347/14.
5. A.B. Chidolue to Perham, 22 Jan. 1966, PP 347/14.
6. A. Stacpoole to Perham, 22 Jan. 1966, PP 347/14.
7. Elliot to Perham, 24 Apr. 1966, PP 347/14.
8. Elliot to Perham, 19 June 1966, PP 347/14.
9. From a call to prayer and repentance, reprinted in a CMS press release to Church papers entitled 'Against background of recent violence, Nigerian Christians call for repentance and a stronger Christian witness', copy sent to Perham by CMS information officer, Miss H.M. Burness, 23 Sept. 1966, after seeing Perham's letter to *The Times*, 8 Sept. 1966.
10. *The Times*, 4 Aug. 1967.
11. *The Times*, 19 Aug. 1967.
12. Dent to Perham, 26 March 1968, PP 412/5.
13. Précis of address to Nigerian Students' Action Committee by M.J. Dent, 2 March 1968 (duplicated), enclosed in Dent to Perham, 26 March 1968, PP 412/5.
14. Enahoro to Perham, 23 Aug. 1968, PP 415/1.
15. Perham to Enahoro, 26 Aug. 1968, PP 415/1.
16. The programme put out by the Nigerian Institute of International Affairs is in PP 415/1.
17. *Daily Times* (Nigeria), 6 Sept. 1968, cutting in PP 415/1.
18. Her diary notes on the visit are in 415/2; notes on interviews with Adekunle, Asika, Asiodu and others are in PP 415/3.
19. Gowon to Perham, 28 Oct. 1968, PP 416/1.
20. Manuscript and typescript drafts, and the transcript of the broadcast of 7 Sept. 1968, are in PP 415/5; *Colonial Sequence 1949–1969*, p. 337.
21. Dent, Address to Nigerian students, 2 March 1968, PP 412/5.
22. 'The Nigerian War', *The Times*, 12 Sept. 1968, *Colonial Sequence 1949–1969*, p. 342.
23. Kogbara to Perham, 11 Sept. 1968, PP 413/2.
24. 30 Oct. 1968.
25. Perham to Gowon, 27 Jan. 1969, published in the *Spectator*, 31 Jan. 1969, PP 416/1.
26. *New Nigerian*, 5 Feb. 1969, cutting in PP 413/2.
27. Perham to Gowon, 12 Sept. 1968, PP 416/1.
28. John D. Clarke, *Yakubu Gowon: faith in a united Nigeria* (London, 1987), p. 137.

29. I had, over the previous two years, sought to bring this parallel to Gowon's attention by giving him a copy of the life of Lincoln with the great and generous speeches underlined.
30. Evidence from one of the Military Governors who was present at the meeting of the Supreme Military Council, related to the author seven years after the event.
31. Gowon to Perham, 28 Oct. 1968, PP 416/1.
32. Osakwe to Perham, 17 March 1973, PP 413/3.

Margery Perham and her Archive

Patricia Pugh

With the exception of the papers of Cecil Rhodes himself, no manuscript collection in Rhodes House Library can more properly be said to have come home than the papers of Dame Margery Perham. When she was a young lecturer at St Hugh's College, Oxford, the Rhodes Trust had sponsored her study of colonial administration by means of a travelling fellowship and later, by contributing towards the endowment of her university post, enabled her to communicate its results. Much of her teaching was done in Rhodes House and all her books are on the library shelves. She was pre-eminent among those who in the 1960s launched the Colonial Records Project whereby colonial administrators were persuaded to donate their papers and memoirs to the Library. The Perham Papers now constitute one of the largest and most important personal collections in Rhodes House, and its value is enhanced by the way in which it relates to so many other colonial and academic records, particularly those deposited in Oxford.

A considerable proportion of the archive was transferred from Margery Perham's house in Oxford after her death in 1982. But ever since 1960, when the second volume of her life of Lord Lugard[1] was published, she had been depositing in Rhodes House material for which she no longer had any use. In that way the Library acquired the first section of Lord Lugard's papers, arranged and listed by her assistant, Isabel Roberts (née Ferguson). Those seventy volumes have been used by scholars for nearly three decades. With the final accession to the Perham archive came more of Lugard's papers and some of Joseph Oldham's, which had been left in her custody for as long as she might need them for her work on Kenya. Thus one hundred and sixty-four boxes of Lugard's papers were added to his original bound volumes and listed in an enlarged, revised guide. Oldham's eleven boxes were separately calendared.[2] Arranging, listing and indexing these three collections entailed five years' work.

An archivist's approach to a manuscript collection is very different from that of the historian or political scientist. The archivist has to deal with the whole collection, to discover the way in which it accumulated and developed and to reconstitute its significant structure. Care must be taken to avoid emphasizing the importance of one aspect or section for fear of obscuring another. Because fields of research change with the years, material that may seem of little interest today can be of unforeseen value to academics of a later generation. Small collections with simple, obvious forms can often be preserved and listed just as they are received: the problems presented by large collections are complicated and subtle.

The Perham archive presented the irresistible challenge to achieve both physical and intellectual control over a great mass of papers with sensitivity, so that the nature of the collection was not destroyed in the interest of efficiency. Though personal papers tend to multiply beyond reason and become disordered through frequent use, there is always an underlying structure, a dendrous growth, which makes the whole meaningful. Consequently, while pruning is essential, the archivist cannot hack and slash but, learning all the time, must allow the shape of the material to reveal itself and restore it. Infinite care must be taken not to destroy contiguities that have evidential value – those small, internal arrangements that are independent of, or may even run contrary to, the main structure, but which reveal the way in which the owner of the papers was involved with or thinking about a certain issue at a particular time. If the catalogue reveals how the papers relate to each other, how and why they were amassed and retained, and the way in which the donor used them, the reader's historical understanding deepens. Clues to this supplementary but very important information emerge during listing. As relationships, reasons, purposes, aims and uses are uncovered, so too are the original owner's thoughts, observations, emotions and beliefs. An entire person is thereby conjured up, more fully revealed than ever in life. In that lies the magic of a personal archive.

The Perham archive is not merely an accumulation of materials used in research and teaching, it is a wonderfully intimate collection of papers. Within it can be found relics of Margery Perham's life at an earlier age than any of those consulting her papers could possibly have known her. Readers of her second novel, *Josie Vine*,[3] speculate on how far it can be judged autobiographical. Some of their questions can now be answered because she treasured the notebooks containing the verses, songs and plays that she and her youngest, favourite brother, Edgar, wrote and performed for family entertainment, the diaries recording family holidays and Edgar's life at school, and an account by Wilfrid, the brother nearest in age to them, of the games of fantasy they played (3, 4, 279/1–3).[4] Margery and Edgar continued to develop their fantasy adventures and their private language in school holidays until the time he went up to Oxford. A map of one imaginary country in which these adventures were set still exists. Family photographs reveal Margery at the age of three or four, demurely bonneted but with formidable determination evident in every contour of her face, her brothers playing with pistols in rough country, the whole family sitting in the dining room in Harrogate, and her scruffy, adored dog, Nobby (747/1–7). There are also photographs of Margery taking part in school events. To fill a documentary gap, the present headmistress of St Anne's School, Abbots Bromley, very kindly sent photocopies of extracts from its magazine referring to her career there and copies of some of her poems (5/2, 33/1).

Play-writing continued while Margery was an undergraduate at St Hugh's College, Oxford, reading history and divinity. Possibly the example of her sister Ethel, who had gone to Africa intending to be a missionary, induced her to study divinity for a year. Margery produced and, of course, acted in the plays which were performed in aid of various wartime charities. Some scripts survive, together with notes taken at lectures and some of the essays written then (5/3, 60–75, 277–82). A fragmentary, introspective diary was written during the First World War, some of it in an attempt to come to terms with Edgar's death as a soldier in France in 1916 (33/3). Unfortunately, there is nothing in the material relating to this period of her life which gives any insight into her attitude towards her studies or her contemporaries at St Hugh's, though some friendships forged then lasted for many decades.

In 1917 Margery qualified for a first class honours degree in history, for which St Hugh's College issued its own certificate (2/2) – it was not until 1920 that women were admitted as full members of Oxford University and were formally awarded degrees. Accordingly she was persuaded by her tutors and her conscience, though against her real inclination, to go to Sheffield University as a lecturer in history, becoming the only woman on the faculty. The post was intended as a temporary one, to ease the pressure in the university as young men returning from the war resumed their studies, but within a year her appointment was confirmed as permanent. One can see from the texts of the lectures she gave there that an immense amount of work went into their preparation. At that time she obviously read her lectures; later in life she spoke from notes only. Later lectures were no less carefully prepared, though some material tended to stray from one course to another (226/1, 227/1–2). Files of letters reveal that she had a group of friends and admirers in Sheffield – young men who shared her love of riding or walking on the Yorkshire moors, who rode motor-bikes as she did and whose indoor recreation was amateur dramatics. After acting in two or three university society productions, she crowned her dramatic career by writing, directing and playing the lead in 'Aethelburga', a play about King Edwin's consort who, with her chaplain St Paulinus, brought Christianity to Northumbria (281/1–3).

One reason for choosing that subject was her undoubted need to examine her own spiritual life at this time. When Margery had a problem she always wrote something in the process of solving it – a play, a novel, or a letter to *The Times*. As far as one can tell, her early faith, despite bouts of schoolgirl piety and her brief study of divinity, had never developed beyond the formal Anglicanism encouraged by her parents and her school. After her brother's death it failed her. With her personal world thus shattered she turned instead to a belief in political measures as a means of setting the world to rights. Therefore in her vacations, under the Army Education Scheme, she lectured to soldiers in France and in camps on Salisbury Plain, tracing the causes of the Great War and expounding the prospects for a post-war settlement (5/4). Not until 1943 did her faith revive. In those harrowing days of the Second World War, with members of her family again in dire peril, Margery was given a new insight into the life of Christ and his teaching while listening in Holy Week to Dorothy Sayers' radio play, *The Man Born to be King*.[5] As her faith was rekindled, she set about rebuilding her spiritual life as an active Christian, ultimately becoming president of the Universities Mission to Central Africa at the time when it merged in 1965 with the Society for the Propagation of the Gospel (15/1–8).

Lecturing in Sheffield had brought neither contentment nor satisfaction. Her life became full of great activity and pressure in both work and play, the pressure increased by her feeling that teaching was not her real vocation. Moreover, the undergraduates who had returned from the fighting were a constant reminder of her brother who had not. As a result, her health suffered and in 1921 she was granted a year's sick leave which she spent, not in Switzerland or the Lake District as her mother wished, but in getting as near as she could to fulfilling her childhood ambition to be a big game hunter in Africa by accompanying her sister Ethel, her brother-in-law Harry Rayne and their children to Somaliland (352/3). Ethel's photograph album shows Margery as part of that family, living in a military-administrative setting (751/2). She rode, sailed and played tennis with the young men and took a passionate interest in their work, whenever possible she shared their way of life, shooting game and even going on patrol with them. While there she recorded her impressions in a form of diary, she observed and took notes on the Somalis and wild life, played with the pet leopard cub, exulted that she and Ethel were the first white women to live in that particular part of Africa and took pride in the dangers they encountered and overcame (34/1–4). Life in Somaliland could not last forever, but it was good training for her later travels. Yet even in Africa she continued her study of British history, taking notes and reviewing her own preconceptions.

For two years Margery returned to Sheffield University, where she introduced a new subject into the syllabus: colonial history. Although she tried to settle down she still longed for Somaliland and so her novel *Major Dane's Garden* became her 'recollection in tranquillity' of what she had seen, felt and thought while in Africa.[6] When she was invited by St Hugh's College in 1924 to return as a tutor – a little later a fellow – in Modern History and Modern Greats (Philosophy, Politics and Economics), she hoped what she called her 'black periods' would be dispelled. Those were times when she doubted her own ability and worth, could see no point in what she was doing and dreaded the future. Unfortunately they persisted for many years, though she concealed this well from all but one or two intimate friends and her fragmentary diary (34/6). In photographs of this period she appears either as a rather flamboyant figure in evening dress or as a serious young don (748/3). In her second novel, *Josie Vine*, published in 1927, she appears to be working out some of the difficulties she faced in her own personality. When she tried to write a third novel, merely in order to comply with the terms of her publisher's contract, she failed (17/1). The manuscript of 'Leslie Lemaitre' remains with similar fragments among her papers, but she knew it was unconvincing, possibly because it did not draw on any deep personal reserves (284/1–6), and she eventually abandoned the attempt.

In these years her work began to find its true, academic direction, although not until the next decade did she publish her first book on colonial administration.[7] As her note-books and lecture texts show, in 1926 Margery began giving courses of lectures on British imperialism and the people who shaped it in the nineteenth century (78–9, 227/5–12, 288/1–5). In the process she embarked on some original research into early British native policy in a region which she could expect to be well-documented – colonial America. This led her to investigate the life of Sir William Johnson who, in the mid-eighteenth century, settled 150 miles north of New York and established amicable relations with the Six Nations along the banks of the Mohawk River. There were two reasons for developing this interest. In 1926 a Tropical Administrative Services Course funded by the government was set up in Oxford; the first probationers arrived in Michaelmas Term. Reginald Coupland, as Beit Professor of Colonial History, was responsible for the section of the course on British Rule in Tropical Africa and Margery, guided by him, equipped herself to teach the historical background to the principles of British native administration. In 1928 she therefore delivered two separate courses of lectures on 'British Policy towards Native Races'. The other reason was that the Permanent Mandates Commission of the League of Nations had been in operation long enough to be worth studying and Margery, motivated by an established interest in the League itself, her professional responsibility as a tutor in politics for keeping up to date with major developments, and her predilection for watching people at work, had gone to Geneva to observe a session of the Mandates Commission in 1927. That in itself had been stimulating, but in addition she had a wonderful time socially as her working notes and diary fragments reveal (34/6).

A narrative of the next phase of Margery's life has been preserved in the four published diaries describing her journeys on the Travelling Fellowship awarded by the Rhodes Trustees in 1929, so that she might extend her original research into native administrative policy by direct observation. It was for her the great adventure. The journey started in the Pacific, and from there she travelled to South, Central and East Africa in 1929–1930; in 1931–2 she visited West Africa. They produced some fascinating records, which fall into three main groups. First, there are the materials which went into the composition of the four published diaries.[8] She arranged for typed duplicates of her letters home to be sent to a select number of people who could then pass on news of her to other friends. The originals were saved for her further use on her return. They present a more or less consecutive account of where she had been, whom she had met, what she had done and seen on the way. Since she had always been an insatiable reader of books by African explorers, at the back of her mind there was undoubtedly an idea of publishing some account of her travels. In fact, in 1933 she discussed producing an edited version of the diaries with a member of the Oxford University Press[9] and, some time between then and the outbreak of war when the idea was shelved, made a first attempt to prepare them for publication (18/1). Consequently, we have in the archive not only some original diary letters but also edited manuscript and typescript versions, with her own photographs inserted in the text itself (35–44, 46–48).

Next, there are note-books full of facts gathered on the journeys (78–86, 88, 91, 93–101, 106–14). When, after retiring from university teaching, she returned to editing the diaries for eventual publication, additional information was gleaned from her note-books to elucidate some points.[10] They hold the notes taken when studying reports in district commissioners' offices and while watching them hear cases in local courts. In them are also accounts of what she had learned from conversations, written late at night after she and her hosts, whether young assistant district officers or the governor himself, had sat for hours after dinner talking shop. Many discussions continued by letter for years and can be traced both through the correspondence about her different journeys and through files of later correspondence on particular territories or colonial problems.[11] Because her own letters were usually hand-written her side of the discussion is missing from her own papers.[12] When on home leave these correspondents often visited her in Oxford, keeping her in touch with events and opinions in their area, and correcting a too academic view of colonial administration. She kept a record of such visits in her note-books devoted to particular territories or to the files of material on specific administrative topics such as education or health.[13]

There are also the official documents collected as primary sources for subsequent study. Members of secretariats and district officers weighed her down with reports while she was visiting them, and when they could they sent duplicates of official papers to Oxford to help her in her teaching and research. Later her repeated visits to the Sudan produced an enormous sequence of material on administration and local political development that is not, as far as I know, matched elsewhere; certainly the Sudan Archive at Durham University does not duplicate it (536/97). Many of these records first collected by Margery Perham have inevitably lost, individually, the unique value they then possessed as research materials. On the other hand they have acquired a collective historical value which can be appreciated when they are all viewed in conjunction, and when their contents are compared with what was then presented in the press, in history books and in political commentaries. This peculiar value is increased by the fact that so many of these documents were collected by one unusually privileged person and used by her as a primary source, added to the fact that she was acquainted with many of their creators or could approach them through those she had met on her travels whenever she needed further elucidation on particular subjects. Her influence also extended through her writing and teaching and mounting reputation. Within the now restored territorial and subject arrangement of a large part of this archive, next to the official documents are preserved the views of historians, politicians and journalists, with many of whom she was also acquainted and able to discuss their statements and personal views. Any user of these papers is likely to regret that there are fewer letters commenting on specific topics than he could wish; such deficiencies must be attributed to Margery's preference for, and opportunities for, face-to-face discussion. Despite this, the Perham archive presents an unmatchable purview of contemporary thought on the administration of empire in the half-century following her round-the-world journey as a Rhodes Fellow.

In the early 1930s, having relinquished her fellowship at St Hugh's College, Margery was nominally unemployed. In one way she was not sorry; as she admitted to Dorothy Brackett, the secretary of the International Institute of African Languages and Culture, she dreaded returning to the life of a tutor in Oxford (8/2). Though St Hugh's awarded her a non-stipendiary research fellowship, her future was precarious, and so she set about making good use of her time by analysing and communicating what she had learned. She now turned to serious journalism and accepted invitations to lecture and give broadcasts. From her earlier struggles with the impact of words in her novels and plays, all three modes of communication inherited colour, a touch of drama and the memorable, finely-tuned sentence. Conscious of the need to know more of African societies, in 1931 she studied anthropology briefly under Bronislaw Malinowski at the London School of Economics (8/1–2, 10/1, 105).

Thus, in the Perham archive the way in which her thought was developing and being augmented by her experience is represented by several parallel series of material. These are the sections covering her note-books, lectures, writings, broadcast talks and the unpublished travel diaries, all of which are enriched by the letters she received. For almost any date a survey across the different sections and sub-sections of the archive can produce not only the text of whatever Margery Perham was writing at that time, whether it was published or not, but also a record of the amount of personal experience and research that went into its preparation. It is revealing that she did not feel any need to keep a regular, narrative diary when in England. Pocket diaries – often filled in by her assistants – noting dates of lectures and engagements sufficed (32/ Items 1–43). The solitary exception is a collection of verse fragments and meditations written at irregular intervals between 1932 and 1951 (33/4).

One series of material, closely related to the more academic writing, was her journalistic output, which began with two articles in April 1930 on 'White Rule in Samoa'.[14] Similar articles expressed her increasingly authoritative views on Africa. From some of them emerged the book produced jointly with Lionel Curtis in 1935, *The Protectorates of South Africa*.[15] This book, her later collaboration with Elspeth Huxley, *Race and Politics in Kenya*,[16] which had a similar origin, and the more contrived, unfinished 1957–9 text of 'Dear Mr Mboya' (343/1–2), all demonstrate how much Margery enjoyed an informed, often hard-hitting, though always civil, dialogue on defined African problems which occasionally revealed a quite disarming humility. The purpose of all three works was to 'clear the minds' of the protagonists and the readers on political principles, issues and methods, and through understanding to establish a basis of agreement on the right way to act.

Throughout her life Margery encouraged others to write and communicate their knowledge and experience as she did. The year after the book on the Protectorates was published she, as editor and with the help of

Audrey Richards and others, brought out a very different work, *Ten Africans*, which reproduced the stories, more or less in their own words, of ten black Africans in varying stages of westernization.[17] While she was actually travelling she had encouraged her African servants to write down their own impressions of the journeys, and these journals are also preserved in the collection (45/1–4).

In 1937, eight years after first meeting Lord Lugard, who had become her mentor and a family friend, she published *Native Administration in Nigeria*; this established her reputation. In the first part of the book she dealt at some length with his occupation of Northern Nigeria, his establishment of indirect rule and the amalgamation of the North with Southern Nigeria. Lugard, I believe, saw in Margery the daughter he and Flora might have had. He certainly did all he could in the 1930s to encourage her and supplied her with blue books and maps for her studies and journeys (761–5). The official publications have been removed, but the maps remain in the archive. As chairman of the International Institute of Languages and Cultures he persuaded Joseph Oldham, its administrative director, to obtain bursaries for her to take the short course in anthropology and to extend her study of native administration to the Sudan and East Africa (8/1–2). Lugard also encouraged learned bodies with colonial interests to invite her to read papers. 'A Restatement of Indirect Rule', delivered to the Royal African Society in 1933, opened the way to the award of the Society's silver medal in 1939.[18] Lord Lothian, as secretary of the Rhodes Trust, was most probably responsible for first interesting Geoffrey Dawson, the editor of *The Times*, in the articles she offered to that paper. Together with Lugard he ensured that she was included as an adviser to the project which resulted in Lord Hailey's *An African Survey* (1938).[19] Lugard seems to have influenced her appointment to the Colonial Office Advisory Committee on Education in the Colonies, but he failed to persuade Malcolm MacDonald to appoint her as Hailey's (and indirectly his own) successor on the Permanent Mandates Commission.[20]

Lugard exerted a considerable influence on what Margery chose to hoard. While writing and revising the *Dual Mandate in British Tropical Africa* he amassed a great collection of cuttings from *Hansard*, from other journals and from newspapers as source material, meticulously noting on each the page or pages of his book where he used that particular fact.[21] On her frequent visits to Abinger to discuss imperial problems with him, those files of printed material were in constant use. Margery collected similar cuttings and ephemera in vast numbers, filing them according to their subject and the relevant territory. Now that the continuously-used papers have been restored to their original working order they provide a comprehensive, historical survey of the information and ideas that were making a daily impact on her. Some of her early statements are more readily understood in the general climate of opinion presented by these files of cuttings. Because they proved so useful in her daily work she instituted a parallel cuttings and pamphlets collection for the library of the Oxford Institute of Colonial Studies of which she was director from 1945 to 1948. Both collections contain some ephemera virtually impossible to track down elsewhere and the latter, modified to meet modern requirements, is still being used and systematically augmented.

Writing the life of Lord Lugard meant that from 1945 to 1960 Margery was collecting a great mass of material which has certain unique characteristics. It reveals much about the way in which she worked on it throughout those fifteen years, and faced up to the pressure exerted upon her not only to hurry to complete the biography but also to produce the kind of commemoration of his brother that Major Edward Lugard considered it his sacred duty to supervise and assist. During the writing many of Lord Lugard's papers became interlaced with her own. This presented a considerable problem when severing the two collections. The criterion adopted was to restore to the Lugard collection those papers which were still in the state in which Lord Lugard himself handled them, while keeping in the Perham archive anything Lugard had specifically given to Margery at any time and all data for the biography sent to her by Major Lugard or by his brother's friends and colleagues. Material received from Major Lugard consisted not only of frequent letters and his answers to the questionnaires Margery sent him, but also edited transcripts made of Lord Lugard's personal correspondence, before the letters themselves were burned according to his expressed wish, and some of the actual letters with sections either excised or obscured by patches of paper stuck over the words or by use of a blue pencil. Since Lord Lugard could never have seen the letters in such a state they have been judged Perham research material rather than Lugard archive and have been retained in her papers as a distinct group within the Writings Section (293–319).

Commitment to the Lugard biography, undertaken gladly as an act of devotion and respect, though in the later years it became a burden, prevented Margery from completing many of the books she planned to write. Pre-eminent among these projects were an intended book on native administration in the Sudan and a political history of Kenya in the late 1920s and early 1930s, the period of the Hilton Young Report and the Joint Parliamentary Commission on Closer Union in East Africa. A great deal of preparatory research was done by Margery and her assistants, as the Abortive Projects sub-division of the Writings Section and the Sudan sub-section illustrate (329–43, 540–2); had there been a book on the Sudanese administration it might well have completed a trio, with those on Nigeria and Ethiopia.[22] Some of the deficiencies in *Lugard: the Years of Authority* can be blamed on the ever-present plan to write separately and more generally about those years when Lugard, though retired, was in London taking an active part in the controversy over Closer Union in East Africa. Editing his East African diaries and the Nigerian one with the help of Mary Bull, and supervising and prefacing the fifth, posthumous, edition of *The Dual Mandate*, which he had been constantly revising for twenty-two years, were all offshoots from the biography.[23] They distracted her from producing the more personal major publications that were always at the back of her mind in the 1950s and 1960s.

Another major distraction from writing was her responsibility for supervising the research for and editing three Nuffield College series of publications on Colonial Legislatures, the Economics of a Tropical Dependency, and Colonial and Comparative Studies. The last series did indeed provide three books on the Sudan, by Mekki Abbas, Kenneth Henderson and Arthur Gaitskell.[24] Margery provided introductions to these and, during their making, guidance, criticism, source material and an unfailing interest. Nevertheless, she continued to prepare for writing her own books; the material collected is principally in the abortive projects section (329–43). In these years and after her retirement she relied on research assistants to scan the files in the Public Record Office, the columns of *Hansard* and the contents of private collections in Rhodes House and elsewhere. The avid delving into original material, vital to her early work, was missing in later years.

In the 1960s Margery's work took a different line. In 1961 she was invited by the BBC to deliver the Reith Lectures and preparation for these demanded a reconsideration of twentieth-century colonial history, much re-reading of old notes compiled for other purposes, a re-examination of her life's work, and reassessment of her own and others' assumptions and conclusions in the light of decolonization. Her papers were in constant use and often disarranged during this exercise. Four books emerged: first came *The Colonial Reckoning*, an expanded version of the Reith Lectures; next *African Outline* – also an assessment of what had happened; then the two volumes of *Colonial Sequence*, an anthology of pieces written for journals and newspapers, including letters to *The Times*, which provides a chronological record both of colonial issues from 1930 to 1960 and of the way in which Margery's colonial philosophy developed in response. The equally revealing printed material which Margery considered and rejected when compiling this anthology is also still in the archive (322/1–4).

A quite distinct, though again parallel, series of records derives from Margery's radio broadcasts (346–54). The first was in 1933 when she contributed to a series of centenary lectures on the abolition of slavery. There remain the scripts of the other speakers, Sir John Harris, Lady Simon, Professor Coupland, and Viscount Cecil of Chelwood, but no record of what she herself said. From that time she kept records of nearly all her broadcast talks – letters, scripts as broadcast and reports in the *Listener*. On the BBC Schools, West Africa and West Indies Services, and in interviews relayed to audiences in the United States she explained the meaning of the empire and the intentions of British colonial policy, providing the historical background and speaking from personal experience.

The high spot of her broadcasting career was undoubtedly the Reith Lectures in 1961. They imposed a great strain on her. Her many notes indicate several tentative approaches before her subject attained its final form (222–3). Related letters and papers reveal her making last-minute revisions, even on the train up to London on the day of a recording (349–50). Three succeeding series of broadcasts, *Thinking Aloud about Africa, The Time of My Life* and *Travelling on Trust*, were more overtly based on her own life and exploits, were a more enjoyable experience for her and, as fan letters illustrate, they were a delight to many listeners (351–3). In the archive are recordings of the last two series (770/4–9). In view of the interest aroused by her talks the next logical step was to complete the long-shelved editing of the travel diaries, two of which were published by 1976.

Margery Perham's role as a catalyst as well as a communicator is represented by the texts and notes of lectures, her teaching notes and material on the Colonial Service and colonial studies (770/4–9). From 1935, as lecturer and then Reader in Colonial Administration at Oxford University, she taught the historical background to colonial administration to both undergraduates and the young graduates taking the reconstructed Colonial Service course. Just as in some of her broadcast talks she had drawn upon her own knowledge of colonial peoples and conditions to explain to them the underlying reasons for Westminster's decisions and Whitehall's actions, so for her lectures she used what she had learned in her travels from district officers and from former pupils' letters to make her part of their curriculum academically stimulating and also relevant to the cadets' practical needs.

Accordingly, during the war, when the Colonial Secretary asked a committee of the vice-chancellors and registrars of Oxford, Cambridge and London Universities to help redesign the Colonial Service courses to meet post-war needs, Margery was called upon to brief the Oxford representatives. She seized this opportunity to press, successfully, for the refresher courses that many of her friends in the service had told her would help them to feel less cut off from the changes in thought at home on colonial development, and to contribute their own experience. They became known as the Devonshire B Courses. This is one of the many instances in which the Perham Papers link up with other archives. The memoranda she prepared and correspondence about them, together with her subsequent comments on the courses during the first decade can be found in the University archives and the records of the Colonial Office,[26] while the notes and correspondence upon which she based her arguments are dispersed throughout her own papers. Similarly the story of the way she directed research at the Oxford Institute of Colonial Studies and Nuffield College into colonial legislatures and colonial economic structures in the immediate post-war period, lies partly in the Writings and Colonial Studies Sections of her collection, partly in the archives of the University and of Nuffield College, which was responsible for publication of the results, and partly in the files of the Colonial Office, which encouraged and supported the work by grants issued under the provision for research made in the Colonial Development and Welfare Act.[27]

Margery's relationships with political figures in Britain and in Africa are also illustrated in the archive. As her published and unpublished travel diaries and her correspondence show, their number was legion and some of them, governors and African leaders alike, became personal friends.[28] The trust engendered by such friendships enabled Margery to offer advice and criticism, and even to play an occasional active part in African politics. One example of this was her involvement in 1950 in the reconciliation of Seretse Khama with his uncle Tshekedi after his marriage with an English girl had caused anxiety over the succession to the chieftainship of the Bamangwato of Bechuanaland. In her life of Tshekedi Khama, Mary Benson has described how a small group of people – David Astor, Michael Scott, Margery Perham and herself – who were concerned about the tribe's future and knew the two men, contrived a private meeting between them, away from pressure from media and officials, in David Astor's country house near Oxford. There the Khamas resolved their differences and agreed upon a common front to be presented to the Secretary of State for Commonwealth Affairs. To supplement the records of the Africa Bureau, Margery lent Mary Benson her own rather more extensive files of letters and supporting documents. Naturally, the archives reveal far more of each member's actions, reactions and opinions than could possibly be included in the Benson biography.[29] Margery's long-standing respect for Tshekedi impelled her to do battle on his behalf with Patrick Gordon-Walker, making notes on the case she would put and afterwards noting his argument. The archive also shows the extent to which she took control of the campaign to get the Commonwealth Relations Office to listen to the Khamas rather than to the district commissioners and those who feared reactions in South Africa. She briefed and organized Michael Scott, sent densely argued letters to *The Times* and overruled David Astor's reluctance to accompany her on her confrontation with the Secretary of State. It is clear that throughout she thought the Colonial Office would have handled this affair far better than the Commonwealth Relations Office.

The journey to Nigeria in 1968, undertaken in an attempt to reconcile the two sides in the Civil War, was her last direct incursion into African political affairs. The Biafran sub-section of the archive contains the deluge of propaganda that provoked her initial stand supporting Biafra, notes on her interviews with General Gowon in Nigeria, others elucidating the process of her conversion to the Federal Government's position, the broadcast appeal to Colonel Ojukwu to end the fighting, the vituperation invoked by her public recantation, together with her subsequent reflections on the Nigerian Civil War (413, 415/6). In all this she had kept to her principles in dealing with African affairs: 'Do the right thing as intelligently as possible with all precautions and take the risk.'[30]

Though some officials and district officers might quail at Margery's approach, certain Secretaries of State for the Colonies consulted and confided in her. Sadly there are few letters of any import from them in her papers. Many years ago she confessed that she had burned virtually all her letters from Creech Jones soon after his death, regretting it immediately. His widow, Violet Creech Jones, knowing this, returned all her personal, manuscript letters to him before depositing his papers in Rhodes House, but they do not adequately compensate for what is lost.[31] Letters from other ministers commenting on contemporary political problems may have been judged by her equally sensitive and destroyed in like manner; if so there is no documentary proof in her collection. Letters from her found in other private collections or in the Public Record Office may indicate their former existence. However, conversations with ministers were recorded in her note-books whenever they contained matter relevant to her work (214). In fact, there are many small gems in those note-books, but to find them one needs to scan the pocket diaries for dates of meetings, dig deep and, in the end, be blessed with a considerable amount of luck.

Luck and lateral thinking when using the personal index to the catalogue are also needed when seeking information about the many committees and organizations, official and unofficial, on which Margery Perham served. Most important to her was her educational work with the

Colonial Office, and especially the twenty-six years on the Inter-University Council for Higher Education in the Colonies. She was also a long-standing member of the Colonial Social Science Research Council, and she was a member of or adviser to such unofficial bodies as the Fabian Colonial Bureau, Oxfam, the Africa Bureau, the Africa Protectorates Trust, the Capricorn Society, the Universities Mission to Central Africa. It is perhaps disappointing to find that these files contain only the circulated minutes and reports, although sometimes these are annotated by Margery, or contain her notes on odd scraps of paper. Her views may appear in letters dealing primarily with other subjects and so are filed elsewhere; while to other members of committees whom she met frequently, such as Douglas Veale, Norman Chester or Christopher Cox, she would speak on the telephone or send handwritten letters, which must be sought in their papers.[32]

That Margery's distinctive handwriting appears in a great many collections in Rhodes House Library is no mere coincidence. In the early 1960s, when she was hoping to settle down to some long-postponed writing in her retirement, she did as much travelling in Africa as she could squeeze in between her other commitments. During these tours she was disturbed by the amount of official and private papers which would probably be destroyed or even just left to rot as colonies gained their independence and the British administrators went home. Her first concern was to press her friends among the senior officials in Africa to make legal and practical provision for conservation of official records after independence. She also set in hand a project for the photographic copying *in situ* of official records in danger of disintegration. Together with colleagues in Oxford she formed a committee to consider means of offering sanctuary within the university to private papers that their owners anticipated they would find difficulty in preserving themselves and therefore might destroy before they left their posts. From this action emerged the search and retrieval operation directed by Jack Tawney, but of which Margery was the chairman, known as the Oxford Colonial Records Project.[33] Most of the manuscript collections donated to the project are deposited in Rhodes House Library and in constant use.[34] Some, however, have been more appropriately housed in other repositories, such as the Middle East Centre of St Antony's College, Oxford, the Sudan Archive in Durham and the South-East Asian Archive in Cambridge. So many donors of material were known personally to Margery that often one side of a correspondence can be found in her papers and the other in an entirely different collection lying just a few feet away in the stack of Rhodes House Library, the value of both collections being thereby enhanced.[35] Even in collections given to the Library entirely independently of the

Project, such as the papers of the Africa Bureau or the United Society for the Propagation of the Gospel (SPG), the same phenomenon occurs because she was a founding committee member of the former and president of the Universities Mission to Central Africa in 1963–64 when it amalgamated with the SPG.

The Perham archive, the Oldham Papers and the additional Lugard material added nearly 850 boxes of papers, maps and photographs to the holdings of original material in Rhodes House. In addition, the Library has been able to fill many lacunae in its printed works with unannotated pamphlets and official publications found among the Lugard and the Perham Papers. Because her books were catalogued in 1978 at the behest of the University of Cape Town, for completeness a separate card index has now been compiled of these other printed papers.[36] There is, indeed, far more in Margery Perham's gift to Rhodes House Library and to scholarship than can be described here. Though designated personal papers, the three collections shed light on a great many issues in colonial history, both political and administrative. Traces of most people involved with the formulation of British colonial policy from the Conference of Berlin onwards can be found in them. They offer a purview of ideas, theories and opinions on colonial rule throughout the succeeding century, as well as a unique record of a celebrated commentator on British administration in Africa.

NOTES

1. Margery Perham, *Lugard: the Years of Adventure, 1858–1898*, and *Lugard: the Years of Authority, 1898–1945* (London, 1956 and 1960).
2. Lugard Papers, MSS Brit. Emp. s. 30–99; Lugard Papers, Box 1–161; Papers of Joseph Houldsworth Oldham, MSS Afr. s.1829, Rhodes House Library, Oxford.
3. M.F. Perham, *Josie Vine* (London, 1927).
4. References to box and file numbers in the Perham Papers are placed in brackets in the text.
5. Private Diary, 12 Nov. 1942, PP 33/4.
6. M.F. Perham, *Major Dane's Garden* (London, 1925; New York, 1926).
7. Margery Perham, *Native Administration in Nigeria* (London, 1937, reprinted 1962).
8. Margery Perham, *African Apprenticeship: an autobiographical journey* (London, 1974); *East African Journey* (London, 1976); *West African Passage*, ed. A.H.M. Kirk-Greene (London, 1983); *Pacific Prelude*, ed. A.H.M. Kirk-Greene (London, 1988).
9. W.D. Hogarth to Perham, 1933, PP 18/1.
10. Margery Perham wrote a stern warning to herself to make sure nothing was added while editing which she could not have known at the time. PP 36/3.
11. For example, the several batches of correspondence with Sir Donald Cameron, Sir Philip Mitchell and many others traceable by means of the personal index in the catalogue.

12. Some of these letters can be found in the papers of the recipients, e.g. Sir James Robertson and Sir Gawain Bell in the Sudan Archive, University of Durham.
13. For a description of the structure and internal arrangement of the territorial sections and sub-sections see the table of contents and the introduction to boxes 355–664 in the catalogue. See also the note-books, PP 80–221.
14. Reprinted in Margery Perham, *Colonial Sequence 1930–1949* (London, 1967), p.4.
15. Lionel Curtis and Margery Perham, *The Protectorates of South Africa* (London, 1935).
16. Elspeth Huxley and Margery Perham, *Race and Politics in Kenya*, with a foreword by Lord Lugard (London, 1944, revised edition, 1956).
17. Margery Perham (ed.), *Ten Africans* (London, 1936).
18. Margery Perham, 'A Restatement of Indirect Rule', *Africa*, July 1934.
19. Lugard Papers 149/2; Oldham Papers, MSS Afr. s.1829, Box 1.
20. Lugard Papers 119/6.
21. Lugard Papers 26–7, 37–48.
22. Margery Perham, *The Government of Ethiopia* (London, 1948, 2nd edition with Christopher Clapham, 1968).
23. Margery Perham (ed.), *The Diaries of Lord Lugard, Vols 1–3 East Africa* (London, 1959); *Vol. 4 Nigeria*, with Mary Bull (London, 1963); Frederick Lugard, *The Dual Mandate in Tropical Africa*, 5th edition (London, 1965, first published in 1922).
24. Mekki Abbas, *The Sudan Question: the dispute over the Anglo-Egyptian Condominium, 1884–1951* (London, 1952); K.D.D. Henderson, *The Making of the Modern Sudan* (London, 1953); A. Gaitskell, *Gezira: a story of development in the Sudan* (London, 1959).
25. Margery Perham, *The Colonial Reckoning* (London, 1963); *African Outline* (London, 1966); *Colonial Sequence 1930–49* and *Colonial Sequence 1949–69* (London, 1967 and 1970).
26. Oxford University Archive, Col. 1–4 *passim*; Public Record Office, CO 900, 901.
27. Perham Papers 291, 254–6; Oxford University Archive, Col. 1–4 and 6/1; Nuffield College Minutes, 1942–50.
28. Correspondence with, for example, Sir Philip Mitchell, Sir Andrew Cohen, Tom Mboya, and General Yakubu Gowon, can be traced through the index to the catalogue.
29. PP 379; Africa Bureau Papers, Rhodes House Library, MSS Afr. s. 1681, 225–6.
30. Africa Bureau Papers, MSS Afr. s. 1681, 226/4 f 32.
31. Personal communications from Margery Perham and Violet Creech Jones. PP 23/1–2.
32. Papers of Sir Norman Chester, Nuffield College, Oxford; Papers of Sir Christopher Cox, now in the Public Record Office; PP 25–9, 706–46.
33. PP 258–62; see also Patricia Pugh, 'The Oxford Colonial Records Project and the Oxford Development Records Project', *Journal of the Society of Archivists*, Vol.6, No.2, Oxford 1978; and 'John Joseph Tawney', obituary, *ibid.*, Vol.7, No.1, April 1982.
34. Annual Reports of the Oxford Colonial Records Project, Rhodes House Library, for lists of the accessions 1963–72.
35. Papers of e.g., Sir Ralph Furse, MSS Brit. Emp. s. 415, 9/1–2, 10/1; Albert Thomas Matson, MSS Afr. s. 1792, 1/4, 1/6, Rhodes House Library.
36. PP 21/9 Item 1 contains the catalogue; the card index can be consulted in Rhodes House Library.

Chronology of Margery Perham's Life

1895	Born 6 September, at Bury, Lancashire, the youngest of seven children; family soon moved to Harrogate.
1909–14	Educated at St Anne's School, Abbot's Bromley, Staffordshire.
1914–17	Read Modern History at St Hugh's College, Oxford.
1917–24	Lecturer in History at Sheffield University.
1921–2	Visited her sister Ethel and brother-in-law, Harry Rayne, a District Commissioner in Somaliland, while on sick leave.
1924–30	Fellow and Tutor in Modern History at St Hugh's College, Oxford.
1928–63	Lectured, when in Oxford, to Colonial Service cadets.
1929–30	Travelled across America and the Pacific to Southern and Eastern Africa, having been awarded a Rhodes Trust Travelling Fellowship.
1931–2	Visited Nigeria and the Cameroons.
1935–9	Research Lecturer in Colonial Administration, Oxford University.
1936–8	Two visits to East Africa and the Sudan.
1937 & 38	Vice-chairman of Oxford Summer Conferences on Colonial Administration.
1939–63	Official Fellow of Nuffield College, Oxford.
1939–48	Reader in Colonial Administration, Oxford University.
1939–45	Member of the Colonial Office Advisory Committee on Education in the Colonies.
1941–7	Director of Nuffield College Colonial Studies Project.
1943	Member of the Asquith Committee on Higher Education in the Colonies.
1944	Member of the Irvine Commission on Higher Education in the West Indies, visited the West Indies and the USA.
1945–8	Director of the Institute of Colonial Studies, Oxford University.
1946–66	Member of the Executive Committee of the Inter-Universty Council for Higher Education in the Colonies (Overseas); member of the Council until 1971.
1947–63	Attended and spoke at the Colonial Office (Cambridge) Summer Schools on African Administration.
1948–63	Fellow in Imperial Government, Nuffield College.

1948   Awarded CBE. Visited Uganda and the Sudan, advised on the training of Sudanese administrative officers.

1949–63 Made short visits to Africa most years.

1949   Member of the Colonial Office Committee of Enquiry into Constitutional Development in the Smaller Colonial Territories.

1949–61 Member of the Standing Committee of the Colonial Social Science Research Council.

1961   Delivered BBC Reith Lectures on 'The End of Britain's African Empire'.

1963   Retired from teaching in Oxford University.
        Elected first President of the African Studies Association of the United Kingdom.

1963–4 President of the Universities Mission to Central Africa.

1963–72 Chairman of the Oxford University Colonial Records Project.

1965   Created Dame Commander of the Most Distinguished Order of St Michael and St George (DCMG).

1968   Travelled to Nigeria to investigate the Nigerian Civil War.

1982   Died 19 February, at Burcot, Oxfordshire.

Bibliography of Books by Margery Perham

This list contains only the major books which Margery Perham wrote, edited and contributed to. A full bibliography, including letters and articles in newspapers and journals, and broadcasts, is given in Patricia Pugh, *Catalogue of the Papers of Dame Margery Perham* (Bodleian Library, Oxford, 1989). Nearly 150 of Margery Perham's articles and letters are printed in the two volumes of *Colonial Sequence* (1967 and 1970).

Books

1925   *Major Dane's Garden*. Hutchinsons, London; Houghton Mifflin, Boston and New York, 1926; Rex Collings, 1970; New York Africana Publications, 1971.

1927   *Josie Vine*. Hutchinsons, London.

1935   *The Protectorates of South Africa*, with Lionel Curtis. Oxford University Press, London.

1936   *Ten Africans*, ed. Fabers, London.

1937   *Native Administration in Nigeria*. Oxford University Press, London; reprinted 1962.

1941   *Africans and British Rule*. Oxford University Press, London.

1942   *African Discovery: an anthology of exploration*, ed. with J. Simmons. Fabers, London; reprinted 1943, 1945, 1946, 1949; 2nd ed. 1957, 1963; Penguin, 1948.

1944   *Race and Politics in Kenya*, with Elspeth Huxley. Fabers, London; revised ed. 1956.

1948   *The Government of Ethiopia*, Fabers, London; 2nd ed. 1968.

1956   *Lugard: the Years of Adventure, 1858–1898*. Collins, London.

1959   *The Diaries of Lord Lugard*, vols. 1·3, East Africa, ed. Fabers, London.

1960   *Lugard: the Years of Authority 1898–1945*. Collins, London.

1962   *The Colonial Reckoning*: an expanded version of the Reith Lectures, 1961. Collins, London.

1963   *The Diaries of Lord Lugard*, vol. 4, West Africa, ed. with Mary Bull. Fabers, London.

1966   *African Outline*. Oxford University Press, London.

1967   *Colonial Sequence, 1930–1949*. Methuen, London.

1970   *Colonial Sequence, 1949–1969*. Methuen, London.

1974   *African Apprenticeship: an autobiographical journey in South Africa, 1929*. Fabers, London.

1976   *East African Journey, 1929–30*. Fabers, London.

1983   *West African Passage: a journey through Nigeria, Chad, and the Cameroons, 1931–1932*, published posthumously, edited by A.H.M.

Kirk-Greene. Peter Owen, London.

1988   *Pacific Prelude: travels in Samoa and Australasia, 1929*, published post-humously, edited by A. H. M. Kirk-Greene. Peter Owen, London.
Nuffield College series of publications

Margery Perham supervised the research, edited and wrote prefaces for these works, which were published by Fabers, London.

Studies in Colonial Legislatures:

1946   *The Development of the Legislative Council*, by Martin Wight.
1947   *The Gold Coast Legislative Council*, by Martin Wight.
1948   *The Northern Rhodesian Legislative Council*, by J. W. Davidson.
1950   *The Nigerian Legislative Council*, by Joan Wheare.
1951   *The Legislatures of Ceylon*, by S. Namasivayam.
1952   *The Legislative Council of Trinidad and Tobago*, by H. Craig.

Economics of a Tropical Dependency:

1946   *The Native Economies of Nigeria*, by Daryll Forde and Richenda Scott.
1948   *Mining, Commerce and Finance in Nigeria*, by P. A. Bower, A. J. Brown, C. Leubuscher, J. Mars and Sir Alan Pim.

Colonial and Comparative Studies:

1951   *The Metropolitan Organization of British Colonial Trade: four regional studies*, by Kathleen Stahl.
1952   *The Sudan Question: the dispute over the Anglo-Egyptian Condominium, 1884–1951*, by Mekki Abbas.
1953   *The Making of the Modern Sudan: the life and letters of Sir Douglas Newbold*, by K. D. D. Henderson.
1954   *Britain and the United States in the Caribbean: a comparative study in methods of development*, by Mary Proudfoot.
1959   *Gezira: a story of development in the Sudan*, by A. Gaitskell.

Introductions, forewords or prefaces to other works

1947   *Path to Nigerian Freedom*, by Obafemi Awolowo. Fabers, London.
1952   *East African Future:* a Report to the Fabian Colonial Bureau.
1956   *The Kenya Question: an African answer*, by Tom Mboya. Fabian Colonial Bureau pamphlet, Tract No. 302.
1961   *Tshekedi Khama*, by S. M. Gabatswame. Cape Town.
1963   *Yesterday's Rulers*, by Robert Heussler. Oxford University Press, London.
1963   *Mau Mau Detainee*, by J. M. Kariuki. Oxford University Press, London.
1965   *Principles of Native Administration in Nigeria*, by A. H. M. Kirk-Greene. Oxford University Press, London.
1965   *The Dual Mandate in British Tropical Africa*, by Sir Frederick Lugard, 5th edition (first published 1922). Frank Cass, London.
1965   *The History of East Africa, Vol. II*, edited by Vincent Harlow and E. M. Chilver, assisted by Alison Smith. Oxford University Press, London.
1974   'Lord Lugard': entry in the 15th edition of *Encyclopaedia Britannica*.

Notes on Contributors

Roland Oliver is Emeritus Professor of African History in the University of London and President of the British Institute in Eastern Africa. He has written widely on African history, including *The Missionary Factor in East Africa* (1952), *Sir Harry Johnston and the Scramble for Africa* (1957) and, most recently, *The African Experience* (1991). He delivered the opening address of Margery Perham's memorial service.

Cherry Gertzel is Senior Lecturer in Politics and Head of Department at the Flinders University of South Australia. She was a graduate student at Nuffield College, Oxford, and has taught at the universities of Makerere, Dar es Salaam, and Zambia. Among her publications are *Government and Politics in Kenya* (co-editor, 1969), and *The Politics of Independent Kenya 1963–68* (1970).

Deborah Lavin is Principal of Trevelyan College in the University of Durham, and lectures in the Department of History. She has taught at the University of Witwatersrand, Johannesburg, and at the Queen's University, Belfast. She has written on South African history, has recently completed a life of Lionel Curtis, and has edited two volumes on the Condominium in the Sudan, *The Making of the Sudanese State* and *Transforming the Old Order in the Sudan (1991)*.

Anthony Kirk-Greene is Lecturer in the Modern History of Africa and a Fellow of St Antony's College, Oxford. He was a member of the Colonial Administrative Service from 1950–1966, serving in Northern Nigeria. He edited Margery Perham's two posthumously published travel diaries, *West African Passage* (1983) and *Pacific Prelude* (1988), and contributed the chapter 'Margery Perham and Colonial Administration: a direct influence on indirect rule' in A.F. Madden and D.K. Fieldhouse (eds.), *Oxford and the Idea of the Commonwealth* (1982). He is currently working on a history of colonial administrators in Africa.

Andrew Porter is a Professor of History and Head of Department at King's College, London. His recent work includes *Money, Finance and Empire 1790–1985*, (edited with Robert Holland, 1985), *British Imperial Policy and Decolonization 1938–64* (edited with A.J. Stockwell, 2 vols., 1987, 1989) and 'Scottish Missions and Education in Nineteenth Century

India' in *Theory and Practice in the History of European Expansion Overseas: essays in honour of R.E. Robinson*, which he edited with Robert Holland (1988). His current research lies in the field of missionary history and British expansion.

Michael Twaddle is Lecturer in Commonwealth Studies in the University of London and has written extensively on East Africa. His recent publications include *Uganda Now: between decay and development* (1988) and *Changing Uganda: the dilemmas of structural adjustment and revolutionary change* (1991) both with H.B. Hansen. He is currently working on a study of Asians in East Africa.

Edward Ullendorff is Emeritus Professor of Semitic Languages and of Ethiopian Studies in the University of London. Having served in the British administrations in Eritrea and Palestine from 1942–48, he was Research Officer and Librarian at the Institute of Colonial Studies in Oxford in 1948–49. He subsequently held senior posts at St Andrews, Manchester and the London School of Oriental and African Studies, and made a number of research visits to Ethiopia. His publications include *The Ethiopians* (3rd ed. 1973), and he translated and annotated the autobiograhy of the Emperor Haile Selassie, *My Life and Ethiopia's Progress* (1976).

Mary Bull was research assistant to Margery Perham at Nuffield College, Oxford, and assistant editor of *The Diaries of Lord Lugard* (1959, 1963). She has carried out research and editing work at the Institute of Commonwealth Studies, London, and on the Oxford Colonial Records Project at Queen Elizabeth House. She wrote on 'Indirect Rule in Northern Nigeria, 1906–1911' in *Essays in Imperial Government presented to Margery Perham*, ed. Kenneth Robinson and Frederick Madden (1963).

William Roger Louis is Kerr Professor of English History and Culture at the University of Texas, Austin, and a Fellow of St. Antony's College, Oxford. In 1960–62 he studied under Margery Perham and A.J.P. Taylor at Oxford. His books include *Imperialism at Bay* (1977) and *The British Empire in the Middle East* (1984). With Prosser Gifford he has edited *The Transfer of Power in Africa* (1982), and *Decolonization and African Independence* (1988).

Alison Smith was Research Officer at the Institute of Commonwealth Studies, London, and subsequently at the Institute of Commonwealth

Studies, Queen Elizabeth House, Oxford. She contributed, as author and editor, to the three volume Oxford *History of East Africa* (1965–76), on which she worked with Margery Perham, and to *Britain and Germany in Africa*, ed. Wm.R. Louis and Prosser Gifford (1967). She took part in the reactivation in the 1980s of the Oxford Colonial Records Project, and is currently a member of the Centre for Cross-Cultural Research on Women at Queen Elizabeth House, Oxford.

Kenneth Robinson worked in the Colonial Office from 1936 to 1948, when he became a Fellow of Nuffield College and Reader in Commonwealth Government at Oxford, in succession to Margery Perham. He was subsequently Director of the Institute of Commonwealth Studies and Professor of Commonwealth Affairs, London, and Vice-Chancellor of the University of Hong Kong. His publications include *Essays in Imperial Government presented to Margery Perham* (edited with A.F. Madden, 1963), and *The Dilemmas of Trusteeship* (1965).

Prudence Smith joined the BBC as a talks producer as a young Oxford graduate in 1949. With domestic intervals, and four years in publishing, she worked mainly in educational broadcasting for twenty-seven years. Since retirement she has worked in distance teaching projects in several developing countries.

Martin Dent is a Fellow of Keele University (Department of Politics). He was a District Officer in Northern Nigeria from 1952–61, and studied under Professor Kirkwood at St Antony's College, Oxford, before his appointment to Keele. He has made frequent research visits to Nigeria, and has contributed to a number of books on Nigeria, including *Improving Nigeria's Draft Constitution* (1977), and 'Corrective Government: military rule in perspective', in *Soldiers and Oil*, ed. K.S. Panter-Brick (1977).

Patricia Pugh is an archivist and historian who has recently completed the cataloguing of the Margery Perham papers at Rhodes House Library, Oxford. Between 1964 and 1968 she was chief archivist to the Oxford Colonial Records Project. Her other archival work, chiefly at Rhodes House Library and at Nuffield College, includes cataloguing the papers of the Africa Bureau, Thomas Fowell Buxton and the Fabian Society. At Nuffield College she wrote the history of the Fabian Society, *Educate, Agitate, Organize* (1984), and she is currently completing a study of Arthur Creech Jones's colonial policy.

Index